Mathematics
Almost Everywhere

In Memory of Solomon Marcus

Other Related Titles from World Scientific

Randomness and Complexity, From Leibniz to Chaitin
edited by Cristian S. Calude
ISBN: 978-981-277-082-0

The Human Face of Computing
edited by Cristian S. Calude
ISBN: 978-1-78326-643-2

Information and Complexity
edited by Mark Burgin, Cristian S. Calude
ISBN: 978-981-3109-02-5

Mathematics
Almost Everywhere

IN MEMORY OF SOLOMON MARCUS

Editors

Alexandra Bellow
Northwestern University, USA

Cristian S Calude
University of Auckland, New Zealand

Tudor Zamfirescu
Technical University of Dortmund, Germany

"Simion Stoilow" Mathematical Institute of the
Roumanian Academy, Roumania

 **World Scientific**

NEW JERSEY · LONDON · SINGAPORE · BEIJING · SHANGHAI · HONG KONG · TAIPEI · CHENNAI · TOKYO

Published by

World Scientific Publishing Co. Pte. Ltd.
5 Toh Tuck Link, Singapore 596224
USA office: 27 Warren Street, Suite 401-402, Hackensack, NJ 07601
UK office: 57 Shelton Street, Covent Garden, London WC2H 9HE

Library of Congress Cataloging-in-Publication Data
Names: Bellow, A. (Alexandra), 1935– editor.
Title: Mathematics almost everywhere : in memory of Solomon Marcus /
    edited by Alexandra Bellow (Northwestern University, USA) [and three others].
Description: New Jersey : World Scientific, 2018. | Includes bibliographical references and index.
Identifiers: LCCN 2018011303 | ISBN 9789813237308 (hardcover : alk. paper)
Subjects: LCSH: Marcus, Solomon. | Mathematicians--Romania. |
    Mathematical linguistics. | Mathematical analysis. | Festschriften.
Classification: LCC QA29.M3565 M38 2018 | DDC 510.92 [B] --dc23
LC record available at https://lccn.loc.gov/2018011303

British Library Cataloguing-in-Publication Data
A catalogue record for this book is available from the British Library.

For any available supplementary material, please visit
http://www.worldscientific.com/worldscibooks/10.1142/10912#t=suppl

Printed in Singapore

In Memory of Solomon Marcus (1925–2016)

Preface

The renowned Roumanian mathematician, theoretical computer scientist and interdisciplinary researcher, one of the initiators of mathematical linguistics and mathematical poetics, passed away in Bucharest on March 17, 2016. "Solomon Marcus' Heritage" Memorial Symposium was organised as part of the DCFS2016 Conference on 5 July 2016, http://www.csit.upei.ca/dcfs2016/index.php?page=23.

Solomon Marcus was born on March 1, 1925 in the city of Bacău, Roumania, the youngest of the eight children of Sima and Alter Marcus.

In 1944 he graduated from Ferdinand I High School in Bacău — a school whose alumni include well-known Roumanian personalities, like the poet G. Bacovia, the neurosurgeon C. N. Arseni and the actor T. Caragiu.

In school, Marcus had to repeat one year, an excessively harsh and a posteriori ironical punishment, which gave satisfaction to an openly anti-semitic teacher. Nevertheless, Marcus was classified first at "Baccalaureate" (the Roumanian high-school graduation exam) in Moldavia county! That punishment, officially given because he failed to fully recite a poem, is ironic, because literature, especially poetry and theatre, have been his lasting passions; till the very end of his life he was able to recite many poems, in Roumanian, French and German.

His exposure to non-Euclidean geometries in 1944 stimulated his life-long interest for mathematics. He completed his studies in mathematics at the University of Bucharest: BSc in 1949, PhD in 1956 (with the Thesis *Monotone Functions of Two Variables* under the supervision of M. Nicolescu) and State Doctor in Sciences in 1968.

Marcus started his academic career at the University of Bucharest — an institution he was affiliated with for more than 70 years — as an assistant professor in 1953, a lecturer in 1955; he continued as professor in 1966 and emeritus professor from 1991.

Marcus has important contributions to pure mathematics. In the first ten years of his research career he published almost 100 papers in mathematical analysis, set theory, measure and integration theory and topology, including the joint paper with P. Erdős, Sur la décomposition de l'espace Euclidien en ensembles homogènes, *Acta Mathematica Academiae Scientiarum Hungaricae* vol. 8, nr. 3–4 (1957), 443–452.

From 1964 on he published many papers and books in theoretical computer science, linguistics, poetics and theory of literature, semiotics, cultural anthropology, biology, history and philosophy of science, and education. In these fields he published more than 45 books in Roumanian, English, French, German, Italian, Spanish, Russian, Greek, Hungarian, Czech, Serbo-Croatian, and more than 300 research articles. His book *Grammars and Finite Automata*, Ed. Academiei, Bucharest, 1964 (in Roumanian) is arguably the first monograph devoted to regular languages. He authored three pioneering books in mathematical linguistics and poetics: *Introduction mathématique à la linguistique structurelle*, Dunod, Paris, 1967, *Algebraic Linguistics; Analytical Models*, Academic Press, New York, 1967, and *Mathematische Poetik*, Ed. Academiei, 1973. The book by S. Marcus, *Words and Languages Everywhere*, Polimetrica, Milano, 2007, includes a collection of his papers in language theories.

Writing was a passion for Marcus. We have to add to the above impressive list more than a hundred hand-written (mostly mathematical) notebooks and hundreds of articles and interviews, scattered in various magazines and newspapers, on a variety of topics, from science, art and education to teaching, philosophy and sport.

He is cited by more than a thousand authors, including mathematicians, computer scientists, linguists, literary researchers, semioticians, anthropologists and philosophers. Complementary information can be found on his websites at the `http://www.imar.ro/~smarcus/` at the Institute of Mathematics of the Roumanian Academy and the `http://fmi.unibuc.ro/ro/marcus_solomon/` at the University of Bucharest. His papers, even those written in Roumanian, continue to be a source of inspiration for many authors. An example is the PhD Thesis by L. J. A. Kempthorne, *Relations Between Modern Mathematics and Poetry: Czesław Miłosz; Zbigniew Herbert; Ion Barbu/Dan Barbilian*, Victoria University of Wellington, 2015, `http://researcharchive.vuw.ac.nz/xmlui/handle/10063/4274`, which cites 16 papers by Marcus, three in Roumanian.

Marcus crossed many frontiers, geographical and transdisciplinary, and acquired not only erudition, but also encyclopaedic knowledge. As a public intellectual he saved gifted scientists and scholars from marginalisation. With equal ease, in his impeccable French, he magisterially debated the great French virologist Luc Montagnier a few years ago, on the stage of the *Ateneul Român*.

Marcus features in the books *People and Ideas in Theoretical Computer Science*, Springer, Singapore, 1998 and *The Human Face of Computing*, Imperial College Press, London, 2015 (edited by C. Calude). The 1,500–page book dedicated to his 85th birthday, *Meetings with Solomon Marcus*, Spandugino House, Bucharest, 2010 (edited by L. Spandonide and G. Păun) includes his autobiography and articles by several hundred people. His 90th birthday celebrations at the University of Bucharest and Roumanian Academy have been national academic events in 2015.

Marcus was elected a member of the Roumanian Academy in 2001; he received many prizes including the *Royal Decoration of Nihil Sine Deo* (2011) and the *Star of Roumania* in the rank of officer, awarded by the Roumanian President (2015).

He was never bored, he never felt the need of a proper vacation: in his last telephone conversation with one of us, when he was in hospital, his strongest desire was to continue to work. Unfortunately, he left behind many unfinished projects.

In his long career he inspired, stimulated, encouraged and advised many students, undergraduate and graduate, in Roumania and abroad, to do research; his 16 PhD students form just a part of this group.

Marcus, personal memories

It may be of interest to let the editors speak in their individual voices about their own encounters with Solomon Marcus, their personal memories.

Alexandra Bellow:
I jumped ship in my adolescence, I chose mathematics over medicine — the family tradition (my parents were both physicians). My first year as a student at the University of Bucharest, the Mathematics Department (1953–54), was formative, decisive; I came under the spell of mathematical analysis. The analysis course was taught by C. T. Ionescu Tulcea in an abstract, axiomatic manner, the revolutionary new Bourbaki-style; rigour and elegance were sine qua non. The analysis seminar was led by the young assistant professor Solomon Marcus; with his inquisitive mind, his irrepressible intellectual curiosity, he searched the literature and presented us with a

wide and colourful array of examples, problems, theorems. Solomon Marcus became my life-long friend, my mentor, my protector. The last few times I saw him again, in Roumania, he was in his eighties, but he seemed ageless to me.

C. Calude, A. Bellow, S. Marcus, N. Dinculeanu at the
Sixth Congress of Romanian Mathematicians, Bucharest 2007

Cristian Calude:
I was extremely privileged to be Professor Marcus' undergraduate student (real analysis in 1972–3 and mathematical linguistics in 1974–5) and graduate student (PhD, 1976), collaborator and friend. He was for me an inspiration and a role model. Nobody else had more influence on my scientific career than him. In the last 24 years we have been separated by more than 18,000 Km, but this distance didn't alter our close relationship and collaboration.

Tudor Zamfirescu:
Among my teachers I had the privilege to have Gheorghe Vrănceanu, Nicolae Dinculeanu and Solomon Marcus, great mathematicians and professors.

To Vrănceanu I had a very close relationship, as between friends, despite the huge age difference, but mathematically I could not develop any affinity to his kind of differential geometry. Dinculeanu's black board was perfect, like a book, very much like my father's, who taught at the Polytechnic School. Most students liked Dinculeanu's teaching of analysis most. Marcus' teaching was like a theatre play. For me this was the most appealing way of teaching, and he was the only professor who, briefly repeating parts of the previous lecture, enabled me to understand everything on the spot. His teaching strongly influenced my later research work. It was a huge honour for me that Marcus spoke (in Mulhouse, 2014) about my deeds on the occasion of my 70th birthday.

S. Marcus and T. Zamfirescu, Mulhouse 2014

Short presentation of the papers

The contributions are grouped into four parts.

The first part includes papers in "Logic, Complexity and Algebra". The paper *On Bases of Many-Valued Truth Functions* by Arto Salomaa presents some important and beautiful results about the composition theory of truth functions in n-valued logic, $n \geq 2$, and the resulting classes of functions. Ludwig Staiger's paper *Quasi-periods of Infinite Words* gives a characterisation of the set of infinite strings having a certain word as quasi-period. This makes possible to calculate the maximal subword complexity of quasi-periodic infinite strings having a given quasi-period. The paper *Early*

Romanian Contributions to Algebra and Polynomials by Doru Ştefăanescu presents earlier contributions of Romanian mathematicians to algebra and the analytic theory of polynomials. The paper *Distributed Compression through the Lens of Algorithmic Information Theory: A Primer* by Marius Zimand deals with distributed compression, i.e. the task of compressing correlated data by several parties, each one possessing one piece of data and acting separately. In this context the author discusses an analogue of the classical Slepian-Wolf theorem in the framework of Algorithmic Information Theory.

The second part includes papers in "Integrals, Operators, AF Algebras, Proof Mining and Monotone Nonexpansive Mappings". In their chapter *Monotonically Controlled Integrals* Thomas Ball and David Preiss study the (MC_α) derivative and the indefinite (MC_α) integral. The (MC) integral (monotonically controlled integral) had been introduced by Bendová and Malý. An exciting relationship with other notions of integral is revealed: Lebesgue integrable functions need not be (MC_α) integrable, for $0 < \alpha < 1$; for $1 \leq \alpha \leq 2$, the (MC_α) integral coincides with the Denjoy-Perron integral; there is a function that is (MC_α) integrable for every $\alpha > 2$ which is not Denjoy-Khintchine integrable. George Dincă's fine survey *Fine Properties of Duality Mappings* starts with several governing ideas of G. H. Hardy. After some definitions, it presents the theorem of Beurling-Livingston, recalls Klee's result about the duality between strict convexity and smoothness, proves that the duality mapping satisfies the hypotheses of Minty-Browder's theorem and gives examples of duality mappings on some smooth function spaces. Gâteaux and Fréchet differentiability of norms are investigated. Also, connections to partial differential equations and the relationship with the reflexivity of Banach spaces are pointed out. Petryshyn's characterisation of strictly convex Banach spaces in terms of duality mappings ends this substantial chapter. Aldo Lazar's contribution *Primitive Ideal Spaces of Postliminal AF Algebras* provides a characterisation of these primitive ideal spaces, given without proof by Bratteli and Elliott. The article *An Application of Proof Mining to the Proximal Point Algorithm in CAT(0) Spaces* by Laurenţiu Leuştean and Andrei Sipoş, which is part of the program of proof mining, aims to apply methods of mathematical logic to extract quantitative information out of ordinary mathematical proofs, which may not be necessarily constructive. In this context paper presents a computation of uniform rates of metastability for the proximal point algorithm in the context of CAT(0) spaces. In *Generic Well-posedness of the Fixed*

Point Problem for Monotone Nonexpansive Mappings, the authors Simeon Reich and Alexander J. Zaslavski show by using the Baire category approach, the generic well-posedness of the fixed point problem for monotone nonexpansive mappings — a class of nonlinear mappings which is the subject of a rapidly growing area of research.

The third part is devoted to "Linguistics, Computer Science and Physics". Mark Burgin's paper *Analytical Linguistics and Formal Grammars* presents Marcus' foundational contributions to two directions in mathematical linguistics. Gheorghe Păun's paper *A Contagious Creativity* gives an overview of Marcus' contributions to theoretical computer science including an almost complete list of references. The article *Entanglement through Path Identification* by Karl Svozil shows that entanglement — one of the most important quantum physics effects — in multipartite systems can be achieved by the coherent superposition of product states, generated through a universal unitary transformation, followed by spontaneous parametric down-conversions and path identification.

The last part includes two personal recollections of Marcus. "Much of the early part of [my] — Andrew Bruckner's — career was influenced by Solomon Marcus, both through his work and through correspondence." Bruckner's paper *Memories about Solomon Marcus* reminiscences about their long and productive interaction. Monica Marcus' *Memories With and About My Uncle* is a touching evocation of "the uncle" Solomon Marcus.

Acknowledgements

We express our gratitude to Professors David Preiss and Karl Svozil for invaluable editorial help. We thank Spandugino Publishing House for granting permission to publish the articles by Andrew Bruckner and Gheorghe Păun. The cooperation with World Scientific staff, particularly, with D. Rajesh Babu, Alisha Nguyen and Tan Rok Ting, was efficient and pleasant — we thank them all.

Alexandra Bellow, Cristian S. Calude, Tudor Zamfirescu
Chicago, Auckland, Bucharest
March 2018

Contents

Integrals, Operators, AF Algebras, Proof Mining and Monotone Nonexpansive Mappings   67

PART 1
Logic, Complexity and Algebra

Chapter 1

On Bases of Many-Valued Truth Functions

Arto Salomaa

Turku Centre for Computer Science

University of Turku, Quantum 392, 20014 Turun yliopisto, Finland

asalomaa@utu.fi

Abstract. Truth functions in n-valued logic, $n \geq 2$, can be viewed as functions from a Cartesian power of a finite set (the set of truth values) consisting of n elements into the set itself. This partly expository paper will deal with some important and formally beautiful results about the composition theory of truth functions and the resulting classes of functions. Striking differences between the cases $n = 2$ and $n \geq 3$ are obtained.

1.1 Preliminaries

Consider functions $f(x_1, \ldots, x_k)$ of finitely many variables, ranging over a fixed finite set S with $n \geq 2$ elements, and whose values are in S, that is, functions whose domain is the Cartesian power S^k and whose range is included in S. The class of such functions is denoted by $\mathcal{F}_S$, $\mathcal{F}_n$, or simply $\mathcal{F}$ if n is understood.

When we speak of functions in this paper, we always mean functions in $\mathcal{F}_S$, and n refers to the cardinality $card(S)$ of $S = \{1, \ldots, n\}$.

There are n^n functions of one variable, whereas the total number of functions of k variables is n^{n^k}. Although these numbers are finite, in the classes considered below the number k of variables is unbounded. A specific function can always be defined by listing the function values for different combinations of the argument values.

This set-up occurs in many diverse situations, [3]. The interpretation we have in mind in this paper is *many-valued logic*. The set S consists

3

of n *truth values*, and the functions are *truth functions*. However, the material in this paper is independent of any interpretation and semantic considerations concerning the "meaning" of the truth values are irrelevant. Axiomatization of many-valued logics, [6,8,13], lies outside the scope of the paper.

For any subclass $\mathcal{H}$ of functions, we consider *compositions* of functions in $\mathcal{H}$. For instance, starting with a binary function $f(x,y)$, we obtain among others the following functions:

$$f_1(x) = f(x,x), \quad f_2(x,y,z) = f(x, f(y,z)), \quad f_3(x,y) = f(y, f(x,y)).$$

We omit here the formal definition of compositions. Compositions must be expressed in terms of function symbols, and variables coming from a denumerably infinite supply. Elements of S may not appear in compositions.

If a function is expressed as a composition of some functions, we say that the latter functions *generate* the former function.

Definition 1.1. The *closure* $CL(\mathcal{H})$ of a class $\mathcal{H}$ of functions consists of all functions generated by functions in $\mathcal{H}$. A class of functions $\mathcal{H}$ is *closed* if $CL(\mathcal{H}) = \mathcal{H}$. A subclass $\mathcal{H}_1$ of a class $\mathcal{H}$ of functions is said to be *complete in $\mathcal{H}$* if

$$CL(\mathcal{H}_1) = \mathcal{H}.$$

Classes complete in $\mathcal{F}_n$ are termed, briefly, *complete*. A complete subclass of $\mathcal{H}$ is a *basis* of $\mathcal{H}$ if no proper subclass of it is complete in $\mathcal{H}$.

It is well-known that, for any n, there are singleton complete classes. Functions in such singleton classes are called *Sheffer functions*, [6,7,9,10, 16]. A general fact concerning the cardinality of the class of all bases was presented in [14].

If a class of functions is finitely generated, it always has a basis. However, it will be seen below that a class can have a basis without being finitely generated. One of the central problems is whether or not a given class of functions is finitely generated.

Functional constructions involving $\mathcal{F}_2$ are very limited in comparison with constructions involving $\mathcal{F}_n$, $n \geq 3$. Indeed, a complete classification of closed subclasses of $\mathcal{F}_2$ was given by Post in [5]. There are only denumerably many such subclasses, and each of them is finitely generated. Each class $\mathcal{F}_n$, $n \geq 3$, possesses, in addition to finitely generated subclasses, a continuum of closed subclasses, none of which is finitely generated.

Definition 1.2. A closed subclass $\mathcal{H}'$ of a class $\mathcal{H}$ of functions is termed *precomplete* in $\mathcal{H}$ if it is not complete in $\mathcal{H}$ but

$$CL(\mathcal{H}' \cup \{g\}) = \mathcal{H}, \text{ for every } g \in (\mathcal{H} - \mathcal{H}').$$

Classes precomplete in $\mathcal{F}_n$ are termed, briefly, *precomplete*.

Precomplete classes constitute a central auxiliary notion in the study of completeness. In 2- and 3-valued logic (that is, in $\mathcal{F}_2$ and $\mathcal{F}_3$) there are 5 and 18 precomplete classes, respectively, [5, 17]. All of these precomplete classes are finitely generated, [1, 5]. The 5 precomplete classes of $\mathcal{F}_2$ are:

- Class of functions f satisfying $f(1, \ldots, 1) = 1$.
- Class of functions f satisfying $f(2, \ldots, 2) = 2$.
- Monotonous functions.
- Linear functions, that is, functions representable by a linear polynomial modulo 2.
- Self-dual functions, that is, functions f satisfying

$$f x_1, \ldots, x_k) = P(f(P(x_1), \ldots, P(x_k))),$$

where P is the transposition of 1 and 2.

In the definitions above the basic set S is finite, and closure refers to composition of functions. Most of the notions and many of the results discussed in this paper carry over to a much more general set-up. This is due to the fact that closure under composition satisfies the axioms of the general topological closure operation.

Indeed, let the basic set S be arbitrary and CL a general closure operation for subsets of S, satisfying the following four conditions.

(1) $X \subseteq CL(X)$, for all $X \subseteq S$.
(2) $CL(CL(X)) = CL(X)$, for all $X \subseteq S$.
(3) $X \subseteq Y$ implies $CL(X) \subseteq CL(Y)$, for all $X, Y \subseteq S$.
(4) $CL(\emptyset) = \emptyset$.

Then the notions of closed, complete and precomplete sets, as well as sets having a basis, carry over without changes. So do most of the results concerning these notions.

1.2   Independent classes. The depth of a class.
The construction of Yanov and Muchnik

We now introduce the notion of an *independent class* of functions. It can be used to construct a continuum of closed subclasses of $\mathcal{F}_n$, $n \geq 3$, each of which has no basis and possesses some further properties. This is a striking contrast with $\mathcal{F}_2$.

Definition 1.3. An infinite class of functions

$$\mathcal{G} = \{g_i | i \geq 1\}$$

is *independent* if

$$g_j \notin CL\{g_i | i \geq 1,\ i \neq j\}, \text{ for all } j \geq 1.$$

The next Lemma is an immediate consequence of Definition 1.3.

Lemma 1.1. *If $\mathcal{G}$ is an independent class of functions, then $CL(\mathcal{G})$ is not finitely generated but possesses a basis.*

We will present below using the result in [18], see also [15], a general method of constructing independent subclasses of $\mathcal{F}_n$, $n \geq 3$. To get an initial idea of such constructions we begin with a simple example. Assume for the moment that the basic set S is the set of natural numbers. Then one obtains an independent class of one-variable functions as follows.

For an arbitrary subset X of natural numbers ≥ 3, we define the function $f_X(y)$ mapping S into S by

- $f_X(y) = y$ if $y \in X$.
- $f_X(y) = y + 1$ if $y \notin X$.

The class $\mathcal{X}$ of such functions is independent because an arbitrary function $f \in \mathcal{X}$ satisfies the condition $f(1) = 2$, whereas an arbitrary composition g of the functions in $\mathcal{X}$ satisfies $g(1) > 2$. This shows that none of the functions in the class $\mathcal{X}$ is generated by other functions in the class. There is a continuum of subsets X and, hence, also a continuum of functions in the class $\mathcal{X}$.

One can obtain independent classes also in our initial setup, where $card(S) \geq 3$ is finite. Then the construction is more involved, and the functions have more than one variable. Results concerning independent classes are closely related to results concerning the *depth* of a class. The depth of a closed class indicates how "far" the class is from $\mathcal{F}_n$. The notion of depth can be defined with respect to an arbitrary closed class. We define it here only with respect to $\mathcal{F}_n$.

Definition 1.4. The *depth* of a closed class $\mathcal{H}$ is defined inductively as follows. The depth of $\mathcal{F}_n$ equals 0. The depth of $\mathcal{H} \neq \mathcal{F}_n$ equals $d > 0$ if, for all elements $f \in \mathcal{F}_n - \mathcal{H}$, the depth of $CL(\mathcal{H} \cup \{f\})$ is less than or equal to $d - 1$ and, for some $f_0 \in \mathcal{F}_n - \mathcal{H}$, the depth of $CL(\mathcal{H} \cup \{f\})$ equals $d - 1$. A closed class $\mathcal{H}$ is of *infinite depth* if, for all natural numbers t, there are functions $f_1, \ldots, f_t$ such that

$$f_1 \notin \mathcal{H}, \quad f_i \notin CL(\mathcal{H} \cup \{f_1, \ldots, f_{i-1}\}),$$

for all i, $2 \leq i \leq t$. A closed class $\mathcal{H}$ is of *strongly infinite depth* if there is an infinite sequence of functions $f_1, f_2, \ldots$ such that the above conditions hold for all values of i.

Thus, every precomplete class is of depth 1. Every class of strongly infinite depth is of infinite depth. The converse does not hold true. Observe that the existence of an arbitrarily long sequence of elements satisfying a certain condition does not imply the existence of an infinite sequence satisfying the same condition.

By a well-known result of Post, [5], every subclass of $\mathcal{P}_2$ has a basis. It can be seen from *Post's lattice*, [5], that the truth functions corresponding to conjunction, disjunction and implication generate each a singleton class of infinite depth. The depths of the singleton classes generated by the truth functions of negation and equivalence are, respectively, 5 and 2.

The following result, [11, 15], gives an appropriate tool for the comparison between infinite depth and strongly infinite depth. These matters will be further clarified in Section 3.

Theorem 1.1. *For each $n \geq 2$, the class $\mathcal{F}_n$ contains a class not finitely generated exactly in case $\mathcal{F}_n$ contains a class of strongly infinite depth. More specifically, if a class $\mathcal{H}$ with a basis is included in a class not finitely generated, then $\mathcal{H}$ is of strongly infinite depth. Conversely, every class of strongly infinite depth is a subclass of some class not finitely generated.*

The construction presented by Yanov and Mucnik, [18], was the first to exhibit closed classes without a basis. At the same time we get a class of independent functions.

Assume that $n \geq 3$. Define an infinite sequence of functions

$$f_k(x_1, x_2, \ldots, x_k), \quad k = 2, 3, \ldots$$

as follows. Each of the functions f_k assumes only values 1 and 2. The function f_k assumes the value 2 exactly in case

(1) all variables assume the value 3, or else
(2) exactly one variable assumes the value 2 and all the other variables assume the value 3.

The sequence of functions f_k is referred to as the *YM-sequence*.

Lemma 1.2. *The YM-sequence constitutes a class of independent functions.*

Proof. We show that, for each $k \geq 2$,

$$f_k \notin CL\left(\bigcup_{i \neq k} f_i\right).$$

Assume the contrary: some function $f_k(x_1, x_2, \ldots, x_k)$ can be expressed as a composition of some other functions in the YM-sequence. We distinguish two cases, depending on the form of the composition.

(i) There are at least two inner functions in the composition, that is, the composition is of the form $g_1(X, g_2(\ldots), g_3(\ldots))$. Here the $g's$ are functions in the YM-sequence and X may contain other function expressions or independent variables, if any. The order of the items may be different. We now assign the value 3 for each variable. Then f_k assumes the value 2, whereas the composition assumes the value 1.

(ii) There is only one inner function in the composition. This means that the composition looks like $g_1(X, g_2(\ldots))$, where X consists of $t \geq 1$ independent variables. Now we assign the value 2 to a specific variable x_j in X and the value 3 to all other variables in the composition. Again f_k assumes the value 2, whereas the composition assumes the value 1.

Thus, a contradiction arises in both cases, and the Lemma follows. $\square$

By Lemma 1.2, the class $CL(\bigcup_i^{\infty} g_i)$ is not finitely generated but still has a basis. The following corollary shows the most significant difference between $\mathcal{F}_2$ and $\mathcal{F}_3$.

Corollary 1.1. *For $n \geq 3$, the class $\mathcal{F}_n$ contains closed subclasses that are not finitely generated.*

The YM-sequence can be immediately generalized as follows. Assume that $n \geq 3$ and a, b, c are three distinct elements in the set $\{1, 2, \ldots, n\}$. For $k = 2, 3, \ldots$, define the function f_k^{abc} as follows:

- $f_k^{abc}(c, c, \ldots, c) = b$,
- If exactly one of the variables x_i assumes the value b and the other variables assume the value c, then $f_k^{abc}(x_1, x_2, \ldots, x_k) = b$,
- $f_k^{abc}(x_1, x_2, \ldots, x_k) = a$ in all other cases.

Denote by $\mathcal{G}^{abc}$ the subclass of $\mathcal{P}_n$, consisting of functions $f_2^{abc}, f_3^{abc}, \ldots$. Then the class $\mathcal{G}^{abc}$ consists of independent functions. The proof follows the proof of Lemma 1.2.

The construction of Yanov and Mucnik can be used to prove results stronger than Lemma 1.2, as will be seen in the next section. If one only wants to construct closed classes that are not finitely generated, the following construction is perhaps the simplest.

Let $n = 4$ and $S = \{0, 1, 2, 3\}$. (For arithmetical reasons, we in this particular example begin the basic set with 0.) Let $\mathcal{L}$ consist of the linear functions

$$f_1 = 0, \quad f_k(x_1, \ldots, x_k) = 2x_1 + \ldots + 2x_k \ (mod \ 4),$$

for $k = 2, 3, \ldots$. Then $\mathcal{L}$ is closed and is not finitely generated because also the class of functions $\{f_i | i \leq k\}$ is closed, for any k. Identifying two variables in f_k produces the function f_{k-2}. In general, any proper composition of functions in the set $\{f_i | i \leq k\}$ gives a function f_i with $i < k$. The class $\mathcal{L}$ has no basis.

We have shown that a class not finitely generated can have a basis but does not necessarily have one.

1.3 Precomplete classes. Depth revisited

Lemma 1.2 yields almost directly results stronger than Corollary 1.1. Denote by $\mathcal{G}$ the class of functions in the YM-sequence. (The following considerations hold also for the generalization of the YM-sequence, described above.)

Let $\mathcal{G}_1$ be an infinite subclass of $\mathcal{G}$ such that also the difference $\mathcal{G} - \mathcal{G}_1$ is infinite. We get the following result.

Theorem 1.2. *The class $\mathcal{G}_1$ is not finitely generated. Consequently, there is a continuum of closed subclasses of $\mathcal{F}_n$, $n \geq 3$, none of which are finitely generated.*

Proof. Clearly, also the class $\mathcal{G}_1$ is independent. By Lemma 1.1, $\mathcal{G}_1$ is not finitely generated. The second sentence of the theorem follows because there are non-denumerably many different choices for $\mathcal{G}_1$. $\square$

Theorem 1.2 provides a striking contrast to the structure of $\mathcal{F}_2$. Post's lattice, [5], shows that there are only denumerably many closed subclasses of $\mathcal{F}_2$.

It is very interesting that there are only denumerably many closed classes of *linear* functions in $\mathcal{F}_n$, $n \geq 2$, see [2]. Linear functions have in general many interesting exceptional properties. We plan to return to this topic in another contribution.

One can take a further step in applying the construction of Yanov and Mucnik. Consider the class $\mathcal{G}$ in Theorem 1.2. Let $\mathcal{G}_1$ be an infinite subclass of $\mathcal{G}$ such that also the difference $\mathcal{G} - \mathcal{G}_1$ is infinite. The elements of the difference $\mathcal{G} - \mathcal{G}_1$ constitute a sequence showing that $\mathcal{G}_1$ is of strongly infinite depth. Since there are non-denumerably many different choices for $\mathcal{G}_1$, we get the following strengthening of Theorem 1.2.

Corollary 1.2. *For each $n \geq 3$. The class $\mathcal{F}_n$ contains a continuum of subclasses, each of which is of strongly infinite depth and is not finitely generated.*

Corollary 1.2 shows that, for $n \geq 3$, there is a one-to-one correspondence between all subclasses of $\mathcal{F}_n$ and subclasses of $\mathcal{F}_n$ of strongly infinite depth. The class $\mathcal{F}_2$ possesses no subclasses of strongly infinite depth but possesses subclasses of infinite depth. (This is one way of showing that not every class of infinite depth is of strongly infinite depth.) Every subclass of $\mathcal{F}_2$ has a basis.

The following Theorem, [11,12,15,17] summarizes some basic facts concerning precompleteness.

Theorem 1.3. *If $\mathcal{H}$ is a closed finitely generated class, then an arbitrary closed class $\mathcal{H}' \neq \mathcal{H}$ can be extended to a class precomplete in $\mathcal{H}$. The number of classes precomplete in a closed finitely generated class $\mathcal{H}$ is finite.*

Corollary 1.3. *For $n \geq 2$, every closed class properly contained in $\mathcal{F}_n$ can be extended to a precomplete class. The number of precomplete classes is finite.*

Although the numbers of precomplete classes in $\mathcal{F}_2$ and $\mathcal{F}_3$ are known to be 5 and 18, respectively, all known upper bounds in the case of a general

n are huge. It is not known whether every precomplete class has a basis, although this is a known fact for $n = 2, 3$.

We now introduce a strengthening of the notion of precompleteness. In the stronger notion it is required that precompleteness extends to certain natural subclasses of the class considered. For simplicity, we consider only closed subclasses of $\mathcal{F}_n$.

By the *k-restriction $RE_k(\mathcal{H})$*, where $k = 1, 2, \ldots$, of a class $\mathcal{H}$ we mean the class of all functions in $\mathcal{H}$ having at most k variables.

Definition 1.5. A subclass $\mathcal{H}$ of $\mathcal{F}_n$ is *strongly precomplete* if $CL(RE_k(\mathcal{H}))$ is precomplete in $CL(RE_k(\mathcal{F}_n))$, for all $k \geq 1$.

Clearly, every strongly precomplete class is precomplete. Moreover, it is generated by functions in it with 2 variables. All strongly precomplete classes can be listed, [12, 15]. It turns out that there are very few of them.

Theorem 1.4. *There are no strongly precomplete classes in $\mathcal{F}_n$ for $n \geq 4$. In $\mathcal{F}_3$ (resp. $\mathcal{F}_2$) linear (resp. monotonous) functions constitutes the only strongly precomplete class.*

1.4   On the primality of $card(S)$

In many cases one obtains stronger results if the number of elements of S is prime. This is well-known in the construction of Sheffer functions, [9, 10, 16]. In this final section we will present along these lines a not very well-known fact concerning $CL(X)$, where the outcome depends on the primality of $card(S)$. The result is also significant for the synchronization of finite automata, [4, 17].

Problem $P(n)$. Let $card(S) = n$ be fixed. Consider the functions $c, f \in \mathcal{F}_n$, where c is a circular permutation of S and f assumes at most $n - 1$ values. Does it follow that $CL(c, f)$ contains a constant function?

Consider first small values on n. The answer to $P(2)$ is trivially affirmative because f must be a constant. Also for $P(3)$ the answer is affirmative. This follows immediately if f is a constant. Otherwise, f assumes some value a twice, and a different value b once, where a results from b by one or two applications of the circular permutation c. Consequently, $fc^i f$ is a constant, for one of the values $i = 0, 1, 2$.

For $n = 4$ the situation is different. Consider the circular permutation $c = (1234)$ and the function f assuming the *value sequence* $1, 1, 3, 3$ for the argument values $1, 2, 3, 4$, respectively. Then $CL(c, f)$ contains only powers of c and functions g with the value sequence $i, i, i + 2, i + 2$, for some $i = 1, 2, 3, 4$. (The addition is carried out modulo 4.) Indeed, the application of c or f to such a function g produces a function of the same form. Consequently, there is no constant in $CL(c, f)$.

The argument for $n = 4$ can be readily extended to the case, where n is composite. Write n in the form $n = pr$, where p is the smallest prime factor of n and $r > 1$. We choose the circular permutation $c = (12 \ldots n)$. The function f assumes r different values. The value 1 is assigned to the argument values $1, 2, \ldots, p$. The value $p + 1$ is assigned to the argument values $p + 1, \ldots, 2p$, and so forth. Finally, the value $(r - 1)p + 1$ is assigned to the argument values $(r - 1)p + 1, \ldots, rp$.

Consider now the set $CL(c, f)$. We claim that it consists of the powers of the permutation c, as well as of the functions g_i, $1 \leq i \leq n$, possessing the value sequence

$$(i, \ldots, i)(p + i, \ldots, p + i), \ldots, ((r - 1)p + i, \ldots, (r - 1)p + i),$$

where the length of each block in parentheses is p. (Observe that $g_1 = f$ and that addition is carried out modulo n.) Indeed, it can be immediately verified that the composition of c with any of the functions g_i, $1 \leq i \leq r$, is again one of the functions g_j. This holds true for both compositions cg_i and $g_i c$. Similarly, for each i, $1 \leq i \leq r$, the compositions fg_i and fg_i are among the functions g_j.

We have shown that $CL(c, f)$ contains only permutations and functions assuming $r > 1$ values. Consequently, if n is a composite number, the answer to our Problem $P(n)$ is "no".

As an example, assume that $n = 15$. The functions c and f are defined as above. Hence, the value sequence of f is 1, 1, 1, 4, 4, 4, 7, 7, 7, 10, 10, 10, 13, 13, 13. The set $CL(c, f)$ consists of powers of c and of the functions g_i, $1 \leq i \leq 15$. The dependencies are shown in the table below. Addition is carried out modulo 15. Compositions are read from right to left. The table indicates also the pattern of compositions in the case of a general composite n.

i	cg_i	g_ic	fg_i	g_if
1	g_2	g_1	g_1	g_1
2	g_3	g_1	g_1	g_2
3	g_4	g_4	g_1	g_3
4	g_5	g_4	g_4	g_4
5	g_6	g_4	g_4	g_5
6	g_7	g_7	g_4	g_6
7	g_8	g_7	g_7	g_7
8	g_9	g_7	g_7	g_8
9	g_{10}	g_{10}	g_7	g_9
10	g_{11}	g_{10}	g_{10}	g_{10}
11	g_{12}	g_{10}	g_{10}	g_{11}
12	g_{13}	g_{13}	g_{10}	g_{12}
13	g_{14}	g_{13}	g_{13}	g_{13}
14	g_{15}	g_{13}	g_{13}	g_{14}
15	g_1	g_1	g_{13}	g_{15}

We get quite different results if n is prime. Consider again a circular permutation c and a function f assuming $t < n$ values. Does it follow, independently of the choice of c and f that $CL(c, f)$ contains a constant function? The following Lemma is of basic importance.

Lemma 1.3. *Assume that c is a circular permutation of S, and f is a function assuming $t < n$ different values $a_1, \ldots, a_t$. Let S_i, $1 \leq i \leq t$, be the maximal subset of S such that $f(S_i) = a_i$. Assume, further, that the sets S_i, $1 \leq i \leq t$ are not all of the same cardinality. Then $CL(c, f)$ contains a function h assuming only $t_1 < t$ values.*

Proof. We may assume, by a renumbering, that $c = (12 \ldots n)$. Then, for any i, j, $1 \leq i \leq j \leq n$, we have $c^{j-i}(i) = j$. We number the sets S_i in such a way that $a_1 < a_2 < \ldots a_t$. Observe that in general the sets S_i do not consist of consecutive numbers. Let $S_q = U$ be a set (among the sets S_i) of maximal cardinality, $card(U) = u$. By the assumption, $tu > n$.

We will now show that there is a power α of c such that c^α maps two of the numbers a_i to the set U. This implies that the function $h = fc^\alpha f \in CL(f, c)$ assumes less than t values.

Consider the sets

$$U_i = c^{a_i - a_1}(U), \quad 1 \leq i \leq t.$$

They cannot be pairwise disjoint because they are all of cardinality u and $tu > n$. (Clearly, $U_1 = U$.) Let U_r and U_s, $r < s$, have a common element. This implies that also the sets U and $c^{a_s - a_r}(U)$ have a common element. (Indeed, this follows by subtracting $a_r - a_1$ from the exponents $a_r - a_1$ and $a_s - a_1$ of c.)

We have now reached the following conclusion. There is an element $b \in U$ such that the element $b' = c^{a_s - a_r}(b) \in U$. Since c is circular, we can find an exponent α such that $c^{\alpha}(a_r) = b$. On the other hand,

$$c^{\alpha}(a_s) = c^{\alpha}(c^{a_s - a_r}(a_r)) = c^{a_s - a_r}(c^{\alpha}(a_r)) = c^{a_s - a_r}(b) = b'.$$

Consequently, c^{α} maps two of the numbers a_i into U. $\square$

If n is a prime number, then the assumption concerning the cardinalities of the sets S_i is always satisfied. Hence, by a repeated application of Lemma 1.3, we obtain the next result. (Observe that once we have generated a constant, all constants are obtained by using the circular permutation.)

Lemma 1.4. *Assume that n is prime, c is a circular permutation of S, and f is a function assuming less than n values. Then $CL(c, f)$ contains all constants.*

Lemma 1.3 cannot be used to reach the conclusion of Lemma 1.4 for composite values of n. Although we can reduce the number t once, the sets corresponding to the S_i sets may be of the same cardinality at one of the following stages.

Summarising we get the following final result. The result shows clearly the importance of the primality of n.

Theorem 1.5. *If n is prime, then a circular permutation c of S and a function f assuming less that n values always generate all constants. If n is composite, this conclusion holds for some c and f only.*

Dedication. The paper is written to the memory of *Academician Solomon Marcus*. I am indebted to this great scientist in many ways. Professor Marcus embodied a true *renaissance* spirit. *Nihil humanum a me alienum puto.* Although I had met him sometimes earlier, I got to really know Professor Marcus during his annual visits to Turku beginning 1990. I had the privilege of long discussions with him, mostly about mathematics and computer science but also about literature, art, music and even sports.

Indeed, his annual visits to Turku took place at the time of the French Open tennis tournament which he followed keenly. Professor Marcus always had original ideas. He presented interesting new openings. His lectures were always about a fresh topic. Recently we discussed much about education in mathematics and computer science. His visit to Turku for spring 2016 was already being planned when the sad tidings arrived. I will miss Professor Marcus deeply. The present paper can be viewed as a reminiscence of our discussions concerning *Gr. C. Moisil.*

References

[1] V.M. Gnidenko, On the orders of precomplete classes in three-valued logic. *Problemy Kibernetiki* 8 (1962) 341–346 (in Russian).

[2] D. Lau, Über die Anzahl von abgeschlossenen Mengen linearer Funktionen der n-wertigen Logik. *Elektr. Informationsverarb. Kybern.* 14 (1978) 561–563.

[3] D. Lau, *Function Algebras on Finite Sets. Basic Course on Many-Valued Logic and Clone Theory.* Springer-Verlag (2006).

[4] A. Mateescu and A. Salomaa, Many-valued truth functions, Cerny's conjecture and road coloring. *EATCS Bulletin* 68 (1999) 134–150.

[5] E.L. Post, The two-valued iterative systems of mathematical logic. *Princeton Annals of Math. Studies* 5 (1941).

[6] J. B. Rosser and A. R. Turquette, *Many-Valued Logics.* North-Holland, Amsterdam (1952).

[7] A. Salomaa, A theorem concerning the composition of functions of several variables ranging over a finite set. *J. Symb. Logic* 25 (1960) 203–208.

[8] A. Salomaa, On many-valued systems of logic. *J. Philosophical Soc. Finland* 22 (1959) 115–159.

[9] A. Salomaa, On the composition of functions of several variables ranging over a finite set. *Ann. Univ. Turkuensis* Ser. AI, 41 (1960).

[10] A. Salomaa, On basic groups for the set of functions over a finite domain. *Ann. Acad. Scient. Fennicae* Ser. AI, 338 (1963).

[11] A. Salomaa, On the heights of closed sets of operations in finite algebras. *Ann. Acad. Scient. Fennicae* Ser. AI 363 (1965).

[12] A. Salomaa, On some algebraic notions in the theory of truth functions. *Acta Philos. Fennica* 18 (1965) 193–202.

[13] A. Salomaa, On axiomatizations of general many-valued propositional calculi. In G. Păun, G. Rozenberg and A. Salomaa (eds.) *Discrete Mathematics and Computer Science*, Editura Academiei Române, Bucuresti, (2014) 259–270.

[14] A. Salomaa, From infinite to finite by identifying variables in many-valued logic. Submitted for publication (2016).

[15] A. Salomaa, Depth of closed classes of truth functions in many-valued logic. In S. Konstantinidis, N. Moreira, R. Reis and J. Shallit (eds.) *The Role*

of *Theory in Computer Science. Essays Dedicated to Janusz Brzozowski*, World Scientific, to appear (2017).

[16] R.S. Stanković and J.T. Astola (eds.) *On the Contributions of Arto Salomaa to Multiple-Valued Logic*, TICSP series 50 (2009). The papers [7–12] are reprinted in this volume.

[17] S.V. Yablonskij, Functional constructions in k-valued logic. *Publ. Matem. Inst. V.A. Steklov* 51 (1958) 5–142 (in Russian).

[18] Ju.I. Yanov and A.A. Muchnik, On the existence of k-valued closed classes not having a finite basis. *Doklady Acad. Nauk SSSR* 127 (1959) 44–46 (in Russian).

Chapter 2

Quasiperiods of Infinite Words

Ludwig Staiger

Martin-Luther-Universität

Institut für Informatik, Von-Seckendorff-Platz 1 06120 Halle, Germany

ludwig.staiger@informatik.uni-halle.de

Abstract. A quasiperiod of a finite or infinite string is a word whose occurrences cover every part of the string. An infinite string is referred to as quasiperiodic if it has a quasiperiod.

We present a characterisation of the set of infinite strings having a certain word q as quasiperiod via a finite language P_q consisting of prefixes of the quasiperiod q. It turns out its star root is a suffix code having a bounded delay of decipherability.

This allows us to calculate the maximal subword (or factor) complexity of quasiperiodic infinite strings having quasiperiod q and further to derive that maximally complex quasiperiodic infinite strings have quasiperiods aba or $aabaa$.

2.1 Introduction

Around 2000 Solomon Marcus presented some tutorials dealing with language-theoretic properties of infinite words [12–14]. One topic of interest was their *subword complexity* (or *factor complexity* [8]). Besides the asymptotic behaviour of the factor complexity, also known as their topological entropy [8, Section 4.2.2] Marcus was also interested in the behaviour of the complexity function $f(\xi, n)$ assigning to a natural number $n \in \mathbb{N}$ the number of subwords of the infinite word (ω-word) ξ.

In his tutorial [14] Solomon Marcus provided some initial facts on quasiperiodic infinite words. Here he was also concerned with recurrences in ω-words and their influence to subword complexity. A well-known fact established by Grillenberger is that the asymptotic subword complexity (or topological entropy) of an almost periodic (or uniformly recurrent) ω-word can be arbitrarily close (but not equal) to the maximal subword complexity (see [8, Theorem 4.4.4]).

In [14] Marcus posed several questions on the complexity of quasiperiodic infinite words. The papers [10, 11] studied in more detail quasiperiodic infinite words generated by morphisms and their relation to Sturmian words. Their results concern mainly infinite words of low complexity. This fits into the line pursued in the tutorial [3] or the book [1] where also mainly infinite words of low (polynomial) complexity were considered. Some results on high (exponential) subword complexity were derived in [24] or concerning the relation between subword and Kolmogorov complexities in [23, Section 5].

The investigations of the present paper are related to Question 2 in Marcus' tutorial [14] and to the question posed in [10] of finding the maximally possible complexity functions for those words. Here (and in the above cited papers) we consider the (subword) complexity function $f(\xi, n)$.

As a final result we deduce that the maximally possible complexity functions for quasiperiodic infinite words ξ are bounded from above by a function of the form $f(\xi, n) \leq c \cdot t_P^n, n \geq n_\xi$, where n_ξ is a number depending on ξ and t_P is the smallest Pisot-Vijayaraghavan number, that is, the unique real root t_P of the cubic polynomial $x^3 - x - 1$, which is $t_P \approx 1.324718$. We show also that this bound is tight, that is, there are ω-words ξ having $f(\xi, n) \approx c \cdot t_P^n$. Moreover, we estimate the quasiperiods for which this bound can be achieved.

The paper is organised as follows. After introducing some notation we derive in Section 2.3 a characterisation of quasiperiodic words and ω-words having a certain quasiperiod q. Moreover, we use the finite basis sets P_q and its dual R_q ($\mathcal{L}(q)$ and $\mathcal{R}(q)$ in [16]) from which the sets of quasiperiodic words or ω-words having quasiperiod q can be constructed. In Section 2.4 it is then proved that the star root of P_q is a suffix code having a bounded delay of decipherability and, dually, the star root of R_q is a prefix code.

This much prerequisites allow us, in Section 2.5, to estimate the number of subwords of the language Q_q of all quasiperiodic words having quasiperiod q. It turns out that $c_{q,1} \cdot \lambda_q^n \leq f(Q_q, n) \leq c_{q,2} \cdot \lambda_q^n$ where $f(Q_q, n)$ is the number of subwords of length n of words in Q_q and $1 \leq \lambda_q \leq t_P$ depends on q. We construct, for every quasiperiod q, a quasiperiodic ω-word ξ_q with quasiperiod q whose subword complexity $f(\xi_q, n)$ is maximal.

Finally, we estimate the quasiperiods q for which the subword complexity of Q_q is maximal.

Some of the results of this paper were presented at the conference "Workshop on Descriptional Complexity of Formal Systems 2010" [17].

2.2 Notation

In this section we introduce the notation used throughout the paper. By $\mathbb{N} = \{0, 1, 2, \ldots\}$ we denote the set of natural numbers. Let X be an alphabet of cardinality $|X| = r \geq 2$. By X^* we denote the set of finite words on X, including the *empty word* e, and X^ω is the set of infinite strings (ω-words) over X. Subsets of X^* will be referred to as *languages* and subsets of X^ω as ω-*languages*.

For $w \in X^*$ and $\eta \in X^* \cup X^\omega$ let $w \cdot \eta$ be their *concatenation*. This concatenation product extends in an obvious way to subsets $L \subseteq X^*$ and $B \subseteq X^* \cup X^\omega$. For a language L let $L^* := \bigcup_{i \in \mathbb{N}} L^i$, and by $L^\omega := \{w_1 \cdots w_i \cdots : w_i \in L \setminus \{e\}\}$ we denote the set of infinite strings formed by concatenating words in L. Furthermore $|w|$ is the *length* of the word $w \in X^*$ and $\mathbf{pref}(B)$ is the set of all finite prefixes of strings in $B \subseteq X^* \cup X^\omega$. We shall abbreviate $w \in \mathbf{pref}(\eta)$ ($\eta \in X^* \cup X^\omega$) by $w \sqsubseteq \eta$.

We denote by $B/w := \{\eta : w \cdot \eta \in B\}$ the *left derivative* of the set $B \subseteq X^* \cup X^\omega$. As usual, a language $L \subseteq X^*$ is *regular* provided it is accepted by a finite automaton. An equivalent condition is that its set of left derivatives $\{L/w : w \in X^*\}$ is finite.

The sets of infixes of B or η are $\mathbf{infix}(B) := \bigcup_{w \in X^*} \mathbf{pref}(B/w)$ and $\mathbf{infix}(\eta) := \bigcup_{w \in X^*} \mathbf{pref}(\{\eta\}/w)$, respectively. In the sequel we assume the reader to be familiar with basic facts of language theory.

A word $w \in X^* \setminus \{e\}$ is called *primitive* if $w = v^n$ implies $n = 1$, that is, w is not the power of a shorter word. The following facts are known (e.g. [4, 20])

Claim 2.1. Every word $w \in X^* \setminus \{e\}$ has a unique representation $w = v^n$ where v is primitive.

Claim 2.2. If $w \cdot v = v \cdot w$, $w, v \in X^*$ the w, v are powers of a common (primitive) word.

As usual a language $L \subseteq X^*$ is called a *code* provided $w_1 \cdots w_l = v_1 \cdots v_k$ for $w_1, \ldots, w_l, v_1, \ldots, v_k \in L$ implies $l = k$ and $w_i = v_i$. A code L is said to be a *prefix code* (*suffix code*) provided no codeword is a prefix (suffix) of another codeword.

2.3 Quasiperiodicity

2.3.1 *General properties*

A finite or infinite word $\eta \in X^* \cup X^\omega$ is referred to as *quasiperiodic* with quasiperiod $q \in X^* \setminus \{e\}$ provided for every $j < |\eta| \in \mathbb{N} \cup \{\infty\}$ there is a prefix $u_j \sqsubseteq \eta$ of length $j - |q| < |u_j| \le j$ such that $u_j \cdot q \sqsubseteq \eta$, that is, for every $w \sqsubseteq \eta$ the relation $u_{|w|} \sqsubset w \sqsubseteq u_{|w|} \cdot q$ is valid. Informally, η has quasiperiod q if every position of η occurs within some occurrence of q in η [2, 16].

Let for $q \in X^* \setminus \{e\}$, Q_q be the set of quasiperiodic words with quasiperiod q. Then $\{q\}^* \subseteq Q_q = Q_q^*$ and $Q_q \setminus \{e\} \subseteq X^* \cdot q \cap q \cdot X^*$. In order to describe the set of quasiperiodic strings having a certain quasiperiod $q \in X^* \setminus \{e\}$ the following definition is helpful.

Definition 2.1. A family $\left(w_i\right)_{i=1}^{\ell}$, $\ell \in \mathbb{N} \cup \{\infty\}$, of words $w_i \in X^* \cdot q$ is referred to as a *q-chain* provided $w_1 = q$, $w_i \sqsubset w_{i+1}$ and $|w_{i+1}| - |w_i| \le |q|$.

It holds the following.

Lemma 2.1.

(1) $w \in Q_q \setminus \{e\}$ if and only if there is a q-chain $\left(w_i\right)_{i=1}^{\ell}$ such that $w_\ell = w$.

(2) An ω-word $\xi \in X^\omega$ is quasiperiodic with quasiperiod q if and only if there is a q-chain $\left(w_i\right)_{i=1}^{\infty}$ such that $w_i \sqsubset \xi$.

Proof. It suffices to show how a family $\left(u_j\right)_{j=0}^{|\eta|-1}$ can be converted to a q-chain $\left(w_i\right)_{i=1}^{\ell}$ and vice versa.

Consider $\eta \in X^* \cup X^\omega$ and let $\left(u_j\right)_{j=0}^{|\eta|-1}$ be a family such that $u_j \cdot q \sqsubseteq \eta$ and $j - |q| < |u_j| \le j$ for $j < |\eta|$.

Define $w_1 := q$ and $w_{i+1} := u_{|w_i|} \cdot q$ as long as $|w_i| < |\eta|$. Then $w_i \sqsubseteq \eta$ and $|w_i| < |w_{i+1}| = |u_{|w_i|} \cdot q| \le |w_i| + |q|$. Thus $\left(w_i\right)_{i=1}^{\ell}$ is a q-chain with $w_i \sqsubseteq \eta$.

Conversely, let $\left(w_i\right)_{i=1}^{\ell}$ be a q-chain such that $w_i \sqsubseteq \eta$ and set

$$u_j := \max_{\sqsubseteq}\{w' : \exists i (w' \cdot q = w_i \wedge |w'| \le j)\}, \text{ for } j < |\eta|.$$

By definition, $u_j \cdot q \sqsubseteq \eta$ and $|u_j| \le j$. Assume $|u_j| \le j - |q|$ and $u_j \cdot q = w_i$. Then $|w_i| \le j < |\eta|$. Consequently, in the q-chain there is a successor w_{i+1}, $|w_{i+1}| \le |w_i| + |q| \le j + |q|$. Let $w_{i+1} = w'' \cdot q$. Then $u_j \sqsubset w''$ and $|w''| \le j$ which contradicts the maximality of u_j. $\square$

Lemma 2.1 yields the following consequences.

Corollary 2.1. *Let $u \in \mathbf{pref}(Q_q)$. Then there are words $w, w' \in Q_q$ such that $w \sqsubseteq u \sqsubseteq w'$ and $|u| - |w|, |w'| - |u| \leq |q|$.*

Corollary 2.2. *Let $\xi \in X^\omega$. Then the following are equivalent.*

(1) ξ is quasiperiodic with quasiperiod q.
(2) $\mathbf{pref}(\xi) \cap Q_q$ is infinite.
(3) $\mathbf{pref}(\xi) \subseteq \mathbf{pref}(Q_q)$.

2.3.2 Finite generators for quasiperiodic words

In this part we introduce finite languages P_q and R_q which generate the set of quasiperiodic words as well as the set of quasiperiodic ω-words having quasiperiod q.

We set

$$P_q := \{v : e \sqsubset v \sqsubseteq q \sqsubset v \cdot q\}. \tag{2.1}$$

Then we have the following properties.

Proposition 2.1.

$$Q_q = P_q^* \cdot q \cup \{e\} \subseteq P_q^*, \tag{2.2}$$

$$\mathbf{pref}(Q_q) = \mathbf{pref}(P_q^*) = P_q^* \cdot \mathbf{pref}(q). \tag{2.3}$$

Proof. In order to prove $Q_q \subseteq P_q^* \cdot q \cup \{e\}$ we show that $w_i \in P_q^* \cdot q$ for every q-chain $(w_i)_{i=1}^\ell$. This is certainly true for $w_1 = q$. Now proceed by induction on i. Let $w_i = w_i' \cdot q \in P_q^* \cdot q$ and $w_{i+1} = w_{i+1}' \cdot q$. Then $w_i' \cdot v_i = w_{i+1}'$. Now from $w_i \sqsubset w_{i+1}$ we obtain $e \sqsubset v_i \sqsubseteq q \sqsubset v_i \cdot q$, that is, $v_i \in P_q$.

Conversely, let $v_i \in P_q$ and consider $v_1 \cdots v_\ell \cdot q$. Since $q \sqsubseteq v_i \cdot q$ the family $(v_1 \cdots v_j \cdot q)_{j=0}^\ell$ is a q-chain. This shows $P_q^* \cdot q \cup \{e\} \subseteq Q_q$.

Eq. (2.3) is an immediate consequence of Eq. (2.2). □

Proposition 2.1 implies the following characterisation of ω-words having quasiperiod q.

$$\{\xi : \xi \in X^\omega \wedge \xi \text{ has quasiperiod } q\} = P_q^\omega \tag{2.4}$$

Proof. Since P_q is finite, $P_q^\omega = \{\xi : \xi \in X^\omega \wedge \mathbf{pref}(\xi) \subseteq \mathbf{pref}(P_q^*)\}$. □

A dual generator of Q_q is obtained by the right-to-left duality of reading words using the suffix relation $\leq_s$ instead of the prefix relation $\sqsubseteq$.

$$R_q := \{v : e <_s v \leq_s q <_s v \cdot q\} . \tag{2.5}$$

Analogously to Proposition 2.1 we obtain

Proposition 2.2.
$$Q_q = q \cdot R_q^* \cup \{e\} \subseteq R_q^* , \tag{2.6}$$
$$\mathbf{pref}(Q_q) = \mathbf{pref}(q) \cup q \cdot \mathbf{pref}(R_q^*) . \tag{2.7}$$

The proof is similar to the proof of Proposition 2.1 using the reversed version of q-chain. A slight difference appears with an analogy to Eq. (2.4).

$$\{\xi : \xi \in X^\omega \wedge \xi \text{ has quasiperiod } q\} = q \cdot R_q^\omega . \tag{2.8}$$

An alternative derivation of the languages P_q and R_q can be found in [16, Definition 2]. Here the borders, that is, prefixes which are simultaneously suffixes of the quasiperiod q, are used:

$$P_q = \{v : \exists w(w \sqsubset q \wedge w <_s q \wedge q = v \cdot w)\}, \text{ and}$$
$$R_q = \{v : \exists w(w \sqsubset q \wedge w <_s q \wedge q = w \cdot v)\} .$$

In the subsequent sections we focus on the investigation of P_q due to the left-to-right direction of ω-words.

2.3.3 *Combinatorial properties of P_q*

We investigate basic properties of P_q using simple facts from combinatorics on words (see [4, 20]).

Proposition 2.3. $v \in P_q$ if and only if $|v| \leq |q|$ and there is a prefix $\bar{v} \sqsubset v$ such that $q = v^k \cdot \bar{v}$ for $k = \lfloor |q|/|v| \rfloor$.

Proof. Sufficiency is clear. Let now $v \in P_q$. Then $v \sqsubseteq q \sqsubset v \cdot q$. This implies $v^l \sqsubseteq q \sqsubset v^l \cdot q$ as long as $l \leq k$ and, finally, $q \sqsubset v^{k+1}$. $\square$

Corollary 2.3. $v \in P_q$ if and only if $|v| \leq |q|$ and there is a $k' \in \mathbb{N}$ such that $q \sqsubseteq v^{k'}$.

Now set $q_0 := \min_\sqsubseteq P_q$. Then in view of Proposition 2.3 and Corollary 2.3 we have the following.

$$q = q_0^k \cdot \bar{q} \text{ for } k = \lfloor |q|/|q_0| \rfloor \text{ and some } \bar{q} \sqsubset q_0 . \tag{2.9}$$

Corollary 2.4. *The word q_0 is primitive.*

Proof. Assume $q_0 = q_1^l$ for some $l > 1$. Then $\bar{q} = q_1^j \cdot \bar{q}_1$ where $\bar{q}_1 \sqsubseteq q_1$, and, consequently, $q \sqsubseteq q_1^{k \cdot l + j + 1}$ contradicting the fact that q_0 is the shortest word in P_q. $\qquad\square$

Proposition 2.4. *Let* $q \in X^*, q \neq e$, $q_0 = \min_{\sqsubseteq} P_q$, $q = q_0^k \cdot \bar{q}$ *and* $v \in P_q^* \setminus \{e\}$.

    (1) If $w \sqsubseteq q$ *then* $v \cdot w \sqsubseteq q$ *or* $q \sqsubseteq v \cdot w$.
    (2) If $w \cdot v \sqsubseteq q$ *then* $w \in \{q_0\}^*$.
    (3) If $|v| \leq |q| - |q_0|$ *then* $v = q_0^m$ *for some* $m \in \mathbb{N}$.

Proof. The first assertion follows from $q \sqsubseteq v \cdot q$ and $v \cdot w \sqsubseteq v \cdot q$ by induction.

Since $q_0 \sqsubseteq v$, it suffices to prove the second assertion for q_0. First one observes that, $w \sqsubseteq q$ and $|w| \leq |q| - |q_0|$. Thus $w \sqsubseteq q_0^{k-1} \cdot \bar{q}$. Therefore, we have $w \cdot q_0 \sqsubseteq q$ and $q_0 \cdot w \sqsubseteq q$ which implies $w \cdot q_0 = q_0 \cdot w$ and, according to Claim 2.2, w and q_0 are powers of a common word. The assertion follows because q_0 is primitive.

The third assertion follows from the second one as $v \cdot q_0 \sqsubseteq q$ for $v \in P_q^*$ with $|v| \leq |q| - |q_0|$. $\qquad\square$

Next we investigate the relation between a quasiperiod $q = q_0^k \cdot \bar{q}$ where $q_0 = \min_{\sqsubseteq} P_q$ and $\bar{q} \sqsubseteq q_0$ and its *shortening* $q' := q_0 \cdot \bar{q}$. Since $q \in Q_{q'}$, we have $Q_{q'} \supseteq Q_q$.

We continue with a relation between P_q and $P_{q'}$. It is obvious that $q_0^i \in P_q$ for every $i = 1, \ldots, k$. Then Proposition 2.4.(3) shows that[1]

$$\{q_0^i : i = 1, \ldots, k\} \subseteq P_q$$
$$\subseteq \{q_0^i : i = 1, \ldots, k-1\} \cup \{v' : v' \sqsubseteq q \wedge |v'| > |q| - |q_0|\}. \qquad (2.10)$$

Lemma 2.2. *Let* $q \in X^*, q \neq e$, $q_0 = \min_{\sqsubseteq} P_q$, $q = q_0^k \cdot \bar{q}$ *and* $q' = q_0 \cdot \bar{q}$ *the shortening of* q. *Then*

$$P_q = \{q_0^i : i = 1, \ldots, k-1\} \cup \{q_0^{k-1} \cdot v : v \in P_{q'}\}.$$

Proof. Let $v \in P_{q'}$, that is, $v \sqsubseteq q_0 \bar{q} \sqsubseteq v \cdot q_0 \bar{q}$. Then $q_0^{k-1} \cdot v \sqsubseteq q_0^k \cdot \bar{q} \sqsubseteq q_0^{k-1} \cdot v \cdot q_0 \bar{q} \sqsubseteq q_0^{k-1} \cdot v \cdot q_0^k \cdot \bar{q}$, that is, $q_0^{k-1} \cdot v \in P_q$.

Conversely, let $v' \in P_q$ and $v' \notin \{q_0^i : i = 1, \ldots, k-1\}$. Then, according to Proposition 2.4.(3) there is a unique $v \neq e$ such that $v' = q_0^{k-1} \cdot v$. Now $v' = q_0^{k-1} \cdot v \sqsubseteq q = q_0^k \cdot \bar{q} \sqsubseteq v' \cdot q = q_0^{k-1} \cdot v \cdot q_0^k \cdot \bar{q}$ implies $v \sqsubseteq q_0 \cdot \bar{q} \sqsubseteq v \cdot q_0^k \cdot \bar{q}$. Since $|v| \leq |q_0 \cdot \bar{q}|$ and $q_0 \cdot \bar{q} \sqsubseteq q_0^k \cdot \bar{q}$, we have $v \sqsubseteq q_0 \cdot \bar{q} \sqsubseteq v \cdot q_0 \cdot \bar{q}$. $\qquad\square$

---

[1] Observe that $q_0^k \sqsubseteq q$ and $|q_0^k| > |q| - |q_0|$.

As a particular result we obtain from Lemma 2.2 and Eq. (2.10) that $P_{q_0\bar{q}} \subseteq \{v : \bar{q} \sqsubset v \sqsubseteq q_0\bar{q}\}$. This result can be generalised as follows.

Lemma 2.3. *If q is primitive, $\bar{q} \sqsubset q$ and $v \in P_{q\bar{q}}$ then $\bar{q} \sqsubset v$.*

Proof. Assume $v \sqsubseteq \bar{q}$ and $v \in P_{q\bar{q}}$. Then $v \sqsubseteq q\bar{q} \sqsubset vq\bar{q}$ implies $vq \sqsubseteq q\bar{q}$. On the other hand $qv \sqsubseteq q\bar{q}$. Thus $qv = vq$, and $|v| < |q|$ contradicts the fact that q is primitive. $\square$

2.3.4   *Primitivity and Superprimitivity*

In this section we consider the inclusion relations between the languages $P_q, q \neq e$. These languages are generators for the set of quasiperiodic words Q_q in the sense of Eq. (2.2). As we can see from Lemma 2.2 and Eq. (2.2) the language P_q is not always the smallest one which generates Q_q. In order to obtain the smallest one we consider the star root of languages. Define now the *star-root* of a language $L \subseteq X^*$ as usual as the smallest language L' satisfying $(L')^* = L^*$:

$$\sqrt[*]{L} := L \setminus (L^2 \cdot L^* \cup \{e\}).$$

From Lemma 2.2 we obtain immediately the following result.

Lemma 2.4. *Let $q \in X^*, q \neq e$ and $q_0 = \min_{\sqsubseteq} P_q$. Then $P_q = \sqrt[*]{P_q}$ if and only if $|q_0| > |q|/2$.*

Proof. It is obvious that $q_0 \in \sqrt[*]{P_q}$ and $q_0^m \neq \sqrt[*]{P_q}$ if $m \geq 2$. It suffices to show that $v \in P_q \setminus \{q_0\}^*$ belongs to $\sqrt[*]{P_q}$. To this end observe that in view of Proposition 2.4 (3), for $v' \in P_q$, the product $v \cdot v'$ is longer than q. Thus $v \in \sqrt[*]{P_q}$. $\square$

Cast into the language of borders, it holds $\sqrt[*]{P_q} = P_q$ if and only if the longest proper border of q has length $< |q|/2$.

Corollary 2.5.

$$\sqrt[*]{P_q} = \left(P_q \setminus \{q_0\}^*\right) \cup \{q_0\}.$$

Analogously to the primitivity of words in [2, 16] a word was referred to as *superprimitive* if it is not covered by a shorter one. This leads to the following definition.

Definition 2.2 (superprimitive). A non-empty word $q \in X^* \setminus \{e\}$ is *superprimitive* if and only in Q_q is maximal w.r.t. "$\subseteq$" in the family $\{Q_q : q \in X^* \setminus \{e\}\}$.

The next proposition relates Lemma 2.4 to superprimitivity.

Proposition 2.5. *If $q \in X^* \setminus \{e\}$ is superprimitive then $|\min_{\sqsubseteq} P_q| > |q|/2$, and if $|\min_{\sqsubseteq} P_q| > |q|/2$ then q is primitive.*

Proof. If $q_0 = \min_{\sqsubseteq} P_q$ and $|q_0| \leq |q|/2$ then $q = q_0^k \cdot \bar{q}$ for some $\bar{q} \sqsubseteq q_0$. Thus $q \in Q_{q_0\bar{q}}$ and $q_0\bar{q} \notin Q_q$.

As $q = q_1^m$ with $m > 1$ implies $|q_0| \leq |q_1| \leq |q|/2$, the other assertion follows. □

The converse of Proposition 2.5 is not valid.

Example 2.1. Let $q = abaabaababaab$. Then $P_q = \{abaabaabab, q\}$, and $|\min_{\sqsubseteq} P_q| = 8 > 13/2$ but $abaabaababaab \in Q_{abaab}$ is not superprimitive.

The word $q = ababa$ is primitive but $q_0 = ab$ has $|q_0| \leq |q|/2$. □

Lemma 2.5. *Let q_ℓ be the longest word in $P_q \setminus \{q\}$. Then $P_{q_\ell} \supseteq P_q \setminus \{q\}$. Moreover, if $q = q_0^k$ for $q_0 = \min_{\sqsubseteq} P_q$ and some $k \geq 2$ then $P_{q_\ell}^* \supseteq P_q^*$.*

Proof. Let $v \in P_q \setminus \{q\}$. Then $e \sqsubset v \sqsubset q \sqsubset v \cdot q$. Since $0 < |v| \leq |q_\ell|$ and $q_\ell \sqsubset q$, we obtain the required relation $v \sqsubset q_\ell \sqsubset v \cdot q_\ell$.

If $q = q_0^k$ then $P_{q_\ell} \supseteq P_q \setminus \{q_0^k\}$ and $q_0 \in P_{q_\ell}$. □

In Lemma 2.5 equality as well as proper inclusion are possible.

Example 2.2. Let $q = abaaba$. Then $P_q = \{aba, abaab, q\}$ and $P_{abaab} = \{aba, abaab\} = P_q \setminus \{q\}$. □

Example 2.3. Let $q = abaaabaa$. Then $P_{q^2} = \{abaa, abaaaba, q\}$ and $P_{abaaaba} = \{abaa, abaaab, abaaaba\} \supset P_q \setminus \{q\}$. □

In contrast to the fact that the word $q_0 = \min_{\sqsubseteq} P_q$ is always primitive, it need not satisfy $|\min_{\sqsubseteq} P_{q_0}| > |q_0|/2$ let alone be superprimitive.

Example 2.4. $q = aabaaabaaaa$ has $P_q = \{aabaaabaa, q\}$, that is $q_0 = aabaaabaa$ which, in turn has $P_{q_0} = \{aaba, aabaaaba, q_0\}$ with $|aaba| = 4 < |q_0|/2$. □

2.4 P_q and R_q as Codes

In this section we investigate in more detail the properties of the star root of P_q. It turns out that $\sqrt[*]{P_q}$ is a suffix code which, additionally, has a bounded delay of decipherability. This delay is closely related to the largest power of q_0 being a prefix of q.

According to [4, 6, 9, 22] a subset $C \subseteq X^*$ is a code of a *delay of decipherability* $m \in \mathbb{N}$ if and only if for all $v, v', w_1, \ldots, w_m \in C$ and $u \in C^*$ the relation $v \cdot w_1 \cdots w_m \sqsubseteq v' \cdot u$ implies $v = v'$. Observe that $C \subseteq X^* \setminus \{e\}$ is a prefix code if and only if C has delay 0.

First we show that $\sqrt[*]{P_q}$ is a suffix code. This generalises Proposition 7 of [16].

Proposition 2.6. $\sqrt[*]{P_q}$ *is a suffix code.*

Proof. Assume $u = w \cdot v$ for some $u, v \in \sqrt[*]{P_q}$, $u \neq v$. Then $u \sqsubseteq q$ and Proposition 2.4 (2) proves $w \in \{q_0\}^* \setminus \{e\}$. Consequently, $|v| \leq |q| - |q_0|$. Now Proposition 2.4 (3) implies $v \in \{q_0\}^*$ and hence $u \in \{q_0\}^*$. Since $u, v \in P_q$, we obtain $u = v = q_0$ contradicting $u \neq v$. $\qquad\square$

Using the duality of P_q and R_q one shows in an analogous manner that R_q is a prefix code.

We conclude this part by investigating the delay of decipherability of $\sqrt[*]{P_q}$. We prove that the delay depends on the relation between the quasiperiod q and the minimal w.r.t. $\sqsubseteq$ word $q_0 \in P_q$.

Theorem 2.1. *Let* $q \in X^* \setminus \{e\}$, $q_0 = \min_{\sqsubseteq} P_q$, $q_0^m \sqsubset q \sqsubseteq q_0^{m+1}$ *and* $|\sqrt[*]{P_q}| > 1$. *Then* $\sqrt[*]{P_q}$ *is a code having a delay of decipherability of* m *or* $m + 1$.

Proof. We have $q_0, q \in \sqrt[*]{P_q}$ if $q \sqsubset q_0^{m+1}$ or, as $|\sqrt[*]{P_q}| > 1$, in view of Proposition 2.4 (3) we have $q_0, q' \in \sqrt[*]{P_q}$ where $q_0^m \sqsubseteq q' \sqsubset q_0^{m+1}$. In both cases, $q_0 \cdot q_0^{m-1} \sqsubset q'$ for $q_0 \in \sqrt[*]{P_q}$ and some $q' \in \sqrt[*]{P_q}$ implies that the delay of decipherability is at least m.

Next we show that it cannot exceed $m+1$. Assume $v \cdot w_1 \cdots w_{m+1} \sqsubseteq v' \cdot u$ for $v, v', w_1, \ldots, w_{m+1} \in \sqrt[*]{P_q}$ and $u \in P_q^*$. From Proposition 2.4 (1) we obtain $u \sqsubseteq q$ or $q \sqsubseteq u$ and, since $|w_i| \geq |q_0|$, also $q \sqsubseteq w_1 \cdots w_{m+1}$. Moreover, $v_1, v_2 \in P_q$ implies $|v_1| + |q| \geq |v_2| + |q_0|$.

If $v \sqsubset v'$, in view of the inequality $|v| + |q| \geq |v'| + |q_0|$ our assumption yields $v' \cdot q_0 \sqsubseteq v \cdot q$. Therefore, $w \cdot q_0 \sqsubseteq q$ for the word $w \neq e$ with $v \cdot w = v'$ and, according to Proposition 2.4 (2) $w \in \{q_0\}^*$. This contradicts the fact that $\sqrt[*]{P_q}$ is a suffix code.

If $v' \sqsubset v$, then $|u| > |w_1 \cdots w_{m+1}| \geq |q|$, and via $|v'| + |q| \geq |v| + |q_0|$ we obtain $v \cdot q_0 \sqsubseteq v' \cdot q$ from our assumption. This yields the same contradiction as in the case when $v \sqsubset v'$. $\qquad\square$

Thus, if $q_0^m \sqsubset q \sqsubseteq q_0^{m+1}$ and $| \sqrt[*]{P_q}| > 1$ the code $\sqrt[*]{P_q}$ may have a minimum delay of decipherability of m or $m + 1$. We provide examples showing that both cases are possible.

Example 2.5. Let $q := aabaaaaba$. Then $q_0 = aabaa$, $m = 1$ and $\sqrt[*]{P_q} = P_q = \{ q_0, aabaaaab, q \}$ which is a code having a delay of decipherability 2.
    Indeed $aabaaaabaa = q_0 \cdot q_0 \sqsubseteq q \cdot q_0$ or
$$aabaaaabaa = q_0 \cdot q_0 \sqsubseteq aabaaaab \cdot q_0 \,. \qquad \square$$

Moreover, in Example 2.5, $q \cdot q_0 \notin Q_q$. Thus our example shows also that $q \cdot P_q^*$ need not be contained in Q_q.

Example 2.6. Let $q := aba$. Then $m = 1$ and $P_q = \{ ab, aba\}$ is a code having a delay of decipherability 1. $\qquad \square$

2.5 Subword Complexity

In this section we investigate upper bounds on the subword complexity function $f(\xi, n)$ for quasiperiodic ω-words. If $\xi \in X^\omega$ is quasiperiodic with quasiperiod q then Proposition 2.3 and Corollary 2.3 show $\mathbf{infix}(\xi) \subseteq \mathbf{infix}(P_q^*)$. Thus,

$$f(\xi, n) \leq |\mathbf{infix}(P_q^*) \cap X^n| \text{ for } \xi \in P_q^\omega \,. \qquad (2.11)$$

Similarly to [23, Proposition 5.5], let $\xi_q := \prod_{v \in P_q^* \setminus \{e\}} v$. This implies $\mathbf{infix}(\xi_q) = \mathbf{infix}(P_q^*)$. Consequently, the tight upper bound on the subword complexity of quasiperiodic ω-words having a certain quasiperiod q is $f_q(n) := |\mathbf{infix}(P_q^*) \cap X^n|$. Observe that in view of Propositions 2.1 and 2.2 the identity

$$\mathbf{infix}(P_q^*) = \mathbf{infix}(R_q^*) = \mathbf{infix}(Q_q) \qquad (2.12)$$

holds.

    The asymptotic upper bound on the subword complexity $f_q(n)$ is obtained from

$$\lambda_q = \limsup_{n \to \infty} \sqrt[n]{|\mathbf{infix}(P_q^*) \cap X^n|} \,, \qquad (2.13)$$

that is, for large n, $f_q(n) \leq \lambda^n$ whenever $\lambda > \lambda_q$.

    The following facts are known from the theory of formal power series (cf. [5,19]). As $\mathbf{infix}(P_q^*)$ is a regular language the power series $\sum_{n \in \mathbb{N}} f_q(n) \cdot t^n$ is a rational series and, therefore, f_q satisfies a recurrence relation

$$f_q(n + k) = \sum_{i=0}^{k-1} a_i \cdot f_q(n + i)$$

with integer coefficients $a_i \in \mathbb{Z}$. Thus $f_q(n) = \sum_{i=0}^{k'-1} g_i(n) \cdot t_i^n$ where $k' \le k$, t_i are pairwise distinct roots of the polynomial $t^n - \sum_{i=0}^{k-1} a_i \cdot t^i$ and g_i are polynomials of degree not larger than k.

In the subsequent parts we estimate values characterising the exponential growth of the family $\left(|\mathbf{infix}(P_q^*) \cap X^n| \right)_{n \in \mathbb{N}}$. This growth mainly depends on the root of the largest modulus among the t_i and the corresponding polynomial g_i.

First we show that, independently of the quasiperiod q, the polynomial g_i is constant. Then we show that, for every quasiperiod q, a root of largest modulus is always positive and we estimate those quasiperiods for which this root is maximal.

In the remainder of this section we use, without explicit reference, known results from the theory of formal power series, in particular about generating functions of languages and codes which can be found in the literature, e.g. in [4,5] or [19].

2.5.1   *The subword complexity of a regular star language*

The language P_q^* is a regular star-language of special shape. Here we show that, generally, the number of subwords of regular star-languages grows only exponentially without a polynomial factor. We start with some easily derived relations between the number of words in a regular language and the number of its subwords.

Lemma 2.6. *If $L \subseteq X^*$ is a regular language then there is a $k \in \mathbb{N}$ such that*

$$|L \cap X^n| \le |\mathbf{infix}(L) \cap X^n| \le \sum_{i=0}^{k} |L \cap X^{n+i}|. \qquad (2.14)$$

If the finite automaton accepting L has k states then for every $w \in \mathbf{infix}(L)$ there are words u, v of length $\le k$ such that $u \cdot w \cdot v \in L$. Thus as a suitable k one may choose twice the number of states of an automaton accepting the language $L \subseteq X^*$.

A first consequence of Lemma 2.6 is that the identity

$$\limsup_{n \to \infty} \sqrt[n]{|L \cap X^n|} = \limsup_{n \to \infty} \sqrt[n]{|\mathbf{infix}(L) \cap X^n|} \qquad (2.15)$$

holds for regular languages $L \subseteq X^*$.

In order to derive the announced exponential growth we use Corollary 4 of [21] which shows that for every regular language $L \subseteq X^*$ there are constants $c_1, c_2 > 0$ and a $\lambda \ge 1$ such that

$$c_1 \cdot \lambda^n \le |\mathbf{pref}(L^*) \cap X^n| \le c_2 \cdot \lambda^n. \qquad (2.16)$$

A consequence of Lemma 2.6 is that Eq. (2.16) holds also (with a different constant c_2) for $\mathbf{infix}(L^*)$.

2.5.2 The subword complexity of Q_q

In this part we estimate the value λ_q of Eq. (2.13). In view of Eqs. (2.12) and (2.16) the value λ_q satisfies the inequality $c_1 \cdot \lambda_q^n \leq |\mathbf{infix}(P_q^*) \cap X^n| \leq c_2 \cdot \lambda_q^n$.

As P_q^* is a regular language Eqs. (2.13) and (2.15) show that $\lambda_q = \limsup_{n \to \infty} \sqrt[n]{|P_q^* \cap X^n|}$ which is the inverse of the convergence radius $\mathrm{rad}\, \mathfrak{s}_q^*$ of the power series $\mathfrak{s}_q^*(t) := \sum_{n \in \mathbb{N}} |P_q^* \cap X^n| \cdot t^n$. The series $\mathfrak{s}_q^*$ is also known as the structure generating function of the language P_q^*.

Since $\sqrt[*]{P_q}$ is a code, we have $\mathfrak{s}_q^*(t) = \frac{1}{1 - \mathfrak{s}_q(t)}$ where $\mathfrak{s}_q(t) := \sum_{v \in \sqrt[*]{P_q}} t^{|v|}$ is the structure generating function of the finite language $\sqrt[*]{P_q}$. As $\mathfrak{s}_q^*$ has non-negative coefficients Pringsheim's theorem shows that $\mathrm{rad}\, \mathfrak{s}_q^* = \lambda_q^{-1}$ is a singular point of $\mathfrak{s}_q^*$. Thus λ_q^{-1} is the smallest root of $1 - \mathfrak{s}_q(t)$. Hence λ_q is the largest positive root of the polynomial $\mathfrak{p}_q(t) := t^{|q|} - \sum_{v \in \sqrt[*]{P_q}} t^{|q| - |v|}$.

Remark 2.1. If the length of $q_0 = \min_{\sqsubseteq} \sqrt[*]{P_q}$ does not divide $|q|$ then $\mathfrak{p}_q(t)$ is the reversed polynomial of $1 - \mathfrak{s}_q(t)$, that is, has as roots exactly the inverses of the roots of $1 - \mathfrak{s}_q(t)$.

If $|q_0|$ divides $|q|$ then $q \notin \sqrt[*]{P_q}$ (cf. Lemma 2.4) and $\mathfrak{p}_q(t)$ has additionally the root 0 with multiplicity $|q| - |q'|$ where q' is the longest word in $\sqrt[*]{P_q}$.

Summarising our observations we obtain the following.

Lemma 2.7. *Let $q \in X^* \setminus \{e\}$. Then there are constants $c_{q,1}, c_{q,2} > 0$ such that the structure function of the language $\mathbf{infix}(P_q^*)$ satisfies*

$$c_{q,1} \cdot \lambda_q^n \leq |\mathbf{infix}(P_q^*) \cap X^n| \leq c_{q,2} \cdot \lambda_q^n$$

where λ_q is the largest (positive) root of the polynomial $\mathfrak{p}_q(t)$.

Remark 2.2. One could prove Lemma 2.7 by showing that, for each polynomial $\mathfrak{p}_q(t)$, its largest (positive) root has multiplicity 1. Referring to Corollary 4 of [21] (see Eq. (2.16)) we avoided these more detailed considerations of a particular class of polynomials.

2.5.3 *Quasiperiods of maximum subword complexity*

In this concluding part we are looking for those quasiperiods q which yield the largest value of λ_q among all quasiperiods thus answering Question 2 of [14]. All polynomials $\mathfrak{p}_q(t)$ are of the form $p(t) = t^n - \sum_{i \in M} t^i$ where $\emptyset \neq M \subseteq \{0, \ldots, n-1\}$.

We start with a general property of those polynomials.

Proposition 2.7. *Suppose* $p(t) = t^n - \sum_{i \in M} t^i$ *where* $\emptyset \neq M \subseteq \{0, \ldots, n-1\}$. *Then*

(1) $p(0) \leq 0$, $p(1) \leq 0$, $p(2) > 0$ *and* $p(t') < 0$ *for* $0 < t' < 1$.

(2) *If* $p(t') \geq 0$ *for some* $t' > 0$ *then* $p(t) > 0$ *for* $t > t'$.

(3) *Let* $t_{\max}$ *be the largest positive root of* $p(t)$. *If* $p(t') = 0$ *then* $|t'| \leq t_{\max}$.

Proof. The first assertion is obvious.

For the proof of the second one, let $t = (1 + \varepsilon) \cdot t'$ where $\varepsilon > 0$ and observe that $p((1 + \varepsilon) \cdot t') > (1 + \varepsilon)^n \cdot p(t')$.

The first assertion shows that $1 \leq t_{\max} < 2$. Then third assertion follows via $p(|t'|) = |t'|^n - \sum_{i \in M} |t'|^i \geq |t'|^n - |\sum_{i \in M} t'^i| = 0$ from the second one. $\square$

This yields the following fundamental property.

Corollary 2.6. *If* $t_{\max}$ *is the largest positive root of a polynomial* $p(t) = t^n - \sum_{i \in M} t^i$ *with* $\emptyset \neq M \subseteq \{0, \ldots, n-1\}$ *then* $t_{\max} \in [1, 2)$, *and* $p(t') \leq 0$ *if and only if* $t' \leq t_{\max}$, *for* $1 \leq t' < 2$.

Recall that $\mathbf{infix}(P_q^*) = \mathbf{infix}(Q_q)$. Moreover, $Q_q \subseteq Q_{\hat{q}}$ for some shorter quasiperiod $\hat{q}$ whenever q is not superprimitive. As Proposition 2.5 shows the latter is always the case if q_0 is not longer that $|q|/2$.

For quasiperiods q where q_0 is not longer that $|q|/2$ we have the following property. Consider the successive shortenings (see Section 2.3.3) $q^{(i)}$ of the quasiperiod q, that is $q^{(0)} := q$ and $q^{(i+1)} := \left(q^{(i)}\right)'$. This sequence trivially ends at least after $|q|$ steps with a shortening $\hat{q} = q^{(n)}$ for which $|\min_{\sqsubseteq} P_{\hat{q}}| > |\hat{q}|/2$. Moreover $Q_{q^{(1)}} \subseteq \cdots \subseteq Q_{\hat{q}}$ and its predecessor $q^{(n-1)}$ has $|q_0^{(n-1)}| \leq |q^{(n-1)}|/2$. In this situation we have the following.

Proposition 2.8. *Let* $q \in X^* \setminus \{e\}$ *be such that* $q = q_0^k \cdot \bar{q}$ *where* $\bar{q} \sqsubset q_0$ *and* $k \geq 2$. *If* $|\min_{\sqsubseteq} P_{\hat{q}}| > |\hat{q}|/2$ *for* $\hat{q} := q_0 \cdot \bar{q}$ *then* $\lambda_{\hat{q}} > \lambda_q$ *or* $P_q^* = \{q_0\}^*$.

Proof. Lemma 2.4 shows that $P_{\hat{q}} = \sqrt[*]{P_{\hat{q}}}$. Then $\mathfrak{p}_{\hat{q}}(t) = t^{|\hat{q}|} - \sum_{v \in P_{\hat{q}}} t^{|\hat{q}| - |v|} = t^{|\hat{q}|} - t^{(|\hat{q}| - |q_0|)} - \sum_{v \in P_{\hat{q}} \setminus \{q_0\}} t^{(|\hat{q}| - |v|)}$.

Via Lemma 2.2 and Corollary 2.5 we obtain the following relation between $\sqrt[*]{P_{\hat{q}}}$ and $\sqrt[*]{P_q}$

$$\sqrt[*]{P_q} = \{q_0\} \cup \{q_0^{k-1} \cdot v : v \in P_{\hat{q}} \setminus \{q_0\}\}.$$

If $P_{\hat{q}} = \{q_0\}$ then $\sqrt[*]{P_q} = \{q_0\}$ and, consequently $P_q^* = \{q_0\}^*$.

Let $P_{\hat{q}} \supset \{q_0\}$. This yields

$$\mathfrak{p}_q(t) = t^{|q|} - t^{(|q| - |q_0|)} - \sum_{v \in P_{\hat{q}} \setminus \{q_0\}} t^{(|q| - |q_0^{k-1}v|)}.$$

Since $\lambda_{\hat{q}}$ is a root of $\mathfrak{p}_{\hat{q}}(t)$ we have, in view of $q = q_0^{k-1} \cdot \hat{q}$,

$$0 = \lambda_{\hat{q}}^{k-1} \cdot \mathfrak{p}_{\hat{q}}(\lambda_{\hat{q}}) = \lambda_{\hat{q}}^{|q|} - \lambda_{\hat{q}}^{(|q| - |q_0|)} - \sum_{v \in P_{\hat{q}} \setminus \{q_0\}} \lambda_{\hat{q}}^{(|q| - |v|)}$$

$$< \lambda_{\hat{q}}^{|q|} - \lambda_{\hat{q}}^{(|q| - |q_0^{k-1}|)} - \sum_{v \in P_{\hat{q}} \setminus \{q_0\}} \lambda_{\hat{q}}^{(|q| - |q_0^{k-1}v|)} = \mathfrak{p}_q(\lambda_{\hat{q}}).$$

The assertion $\lambda_{\hat{q}} > \lambda_q$ follows with Corollary 2.6. $\qquad\square$

Thus every quasiperiod q having $|q_0|$ not longer than $|q|/2$ has $\lambda_q = 1$ or $\lambda_q < \lambda_{\hat{q}}$, and we may confine the subsequent considerations to estimate quasiperiods yielding maximal subword complexity to quasiperiods q satisfying $|q_0| > |q|/2$. In this case the corresponding polynomials $\mathfrak{p}_q(t)$ are of the form $t^n - \sum_{i \in M} t^i$ where $\emptyset \neq M \subseteq \{0, \ldots, \lfloor \frac{n-1}{2} \rfloor\}$.

Next we consider the positive roots of these polynomials. Define $p_n(t) := t^n - \sum_{i=0}^{\lfloor \frac{n-1}{2} \rfloor} t^i$.

Corollary 2.7. *For every $n \geq 1$ the polynomial $p_n(t)$ has the largest positive root among all polynomials $p(t) = t^n - \sum_{i \in M} t^i$ with $\emptyset \neq M \subseteq \{j : j \leq \frac{n-1}{2}\}$.*

Proof. This follows from $t'^n - \sum_{i=0}^{\lfloor \frac{n-1}{2} \rfloor} t'^i \leq p(t')$ when $1 \leq t' < 2$ and Corollary 2.6. $\qquad\square$

Corollary 2.7 allows us to restrict the further considerations to the polynomials $p_n(t)$.

Observe that $p_{2n+1}(t) = t^{2n+1} - \sum_{i=0}^{n} t^i$ and $p_{2n+2}(t) = t^{2n+2} - \sum_{i=0}^{n} t^i$.

Remark 2.3. It holds

$$\mathfrak{p}_{a^n b a^n}(t) = p_{2n+1}(t) \,, \text{ and}$$
$$\mathfrak{p}_{a^n b a^{n+1}}(t) = p_{2n+2}(t).$$

In particular, $\mathfrak{p}_{ba}(t) = t^2 - 1$ and $\mathfrak{p}_b(t) = t - 1$. So for all degrees ≥ 1 there are polynomials of the form $\mathfrak{p}_q(t)$.

In view of Remark 2.3 and Lemma 2.7 in the sequel the positive root $t_{\max}$ of $p_i(t)$ is denoted by λ_i. The roots λ_i can be ordered as follows.

Proposition 2.9. *Let* λ_i *be as above. Then*

(1) $\lambda_{2n-1} > \lambda_{2n+1}$ *for* $n \geq 3$, *and*
(2) $\lambda_{2n+1} > \lambda_{2n}$ *for* $n \geq 1$.

Proof. We have

$$t^{n-2} \cdot p_{2n+1}(t) - (t^n + 1) \cdot p_{2n-1}(t) = \sum_{i=0}^{n-3} t^i, \text{ for } n \geq 3. \qquad (2.17)$$

Then $\lambda_{2n-1}^{n-2} \cdot p_{2n+1}(\lambda_{2n-1}) = \sum_{i=0}^{n-3} \lambda_{2n-1}^i > 0$ for $n \geq 3$ and Corollary 2.6 yields the first assertion.

The second follows in a similar way from the identity $t \cdot p_{2n}(t) - 1 = p_{2n+1}(t)$. $\qquad\square$

The polynomials $p_1(t)$ and $p_2(t)$ have $\lambda_1 = \lambda_2 = 1$.

If $n = 2$ the identity Eq. (2.17) is still true as $p_5(t) = (t^2 + 1) \cdot p_3(t)$, that is, $\lambda_3 = \lambda_5$. Together with the inequalities of Proposition 2.9 this yields another proof of Lemma 18 in [17].

Lemma 2.8. *The polynomials* $t^3 - t - 1$ *and* $t^5 - t^2 - t - 1 = (t^2 + 1) \cdot (t^3 - t - 1)$ *have the largest positive roots among all polynomials* $\mathfrak{p}_q(t)$, $q \in X^* \setminus \{e\}$.
The ω-*words* $\xi_{aba} = \prod_{v \in P_{aba}^* \setminus \{e\}} v$ *and* $\xi_{aabaa} = \prod_{w \in P_{aabaa}^* \setminus \{e\}} w$ *are quasiperiodic* ω-*words having maximum subword complexity.*

We conclude with two remarks.

Remark 2.4.

(1) The positive root t_P of $\mathfrak{p}_{aba}(t)$ (or of $\mathfrak{p}_{aabaa}(t)$) is known as the smallest Pisot-Vijayaraghavan number, that is, a positive root > 1 of an irreducible polynomial (here $t^3 - t - 1$) with integer coefficients all of whose conjugates have modulus smaller than 1.
(2) In [18] several connections between the ω-languages P_{aba}^ω, P_{aabaa}^ω and the smallest Pisot number t_P are derived. In particular, it was shown that, for sufficiently large n, we have $f_{aba}(n) =$

$\text{INT}\left(\frac{2\cdot t_P^2+3\cdot t_P+2}{2\cdot t_P+3}\cdot t_P^n\right)$ and $f_{aabaa}(n) = \text{INT}\left(\frac{13\cdot t_P^2+16\cdot t_P+9}{5\cdot(2\cdot t_P+3)}\cdot t_P^n\right)$ where $\text{INT}(\alpha)$ is the integer closest to the real number α.

Here the coefficient $\frac{13\cdot t_P^2+16\cdot t_P+9}{5\cdot(2\cdot t_P+3)}$ for $aabaa$ is larger than the one for aba. This shows that the subword complexity of ξ_{aabaa} exceeds the one of ξ_{aba}.

Acknowledgement

My first acquaintance with Solomon Marcus was when I read his book *Teoretiko-mnozestvennyje modeli jazykov* [15] in early 1970s.

Fig. 2.1   Participants at DMTCS'01, Constanţa

But it was not until 2001 when I met him at the conference "Discrete Mathematics and Theoretical Computer Science 2001" organised by the "Ovidius" University of Constanţa, Romania.

Here his talk "Languages, Infinite Words and their Interaction", the content of which appeared in his papers [12,13] and [14] drew my attention to the subject of the present paper.

Two years later my joint paper with Solomon Marcus [7] was published.

Fig. 2.2   Professor Marcus presenting his talk in Caputh, September 2004

In 2004 I met Solomon Marcus again at the small conference on "Automata and Formal Languages" in Caputh organised by the Computer Science group of the Potsdam University. There he presented the talk "Contextual Grammars as a Bridge Between the Analytical and the Generative Approach to Natural Languages".

References

[1] J.-P. Allouche and J. Shallit, *Automatic sequences.* Cambridge University Press, Cambridge (2003), doi:10.1017/CBO9780511546563, http://dx.doi.org/10.1017/CBO9780511546563.

[2] A. Apostolico, M. Farach and C. S. Iliopoulos, Optimal superprimitivity testing for strings, *Inform. Process. Lett.* **39**, 1, pp. 17–20

(1991), doi:10.1016/0020-0190(91)90056-N http://dx.doi.org/10.1016/0020-0190(91)90056-N.

[3] J. Berstel and J. Karhumäki, Combinatorics on words: a tutorial, *Bulletin of the EATCS* **79**, pp. 178–228 (2003).

[4] J. Berstel and D. Perrin, *Theory of codes, Pure and Applied Mathematics*, Vol. 117. Academic Press Inc., Orlando, FL (1985).

[5] J. Berstel and C. Reutenauer, *Rational series and their languages, EATCS Monographs on Theoretical Computer Science*, Vol. 12. Springer-Verlag, Berlin (1988), ISBN 3-540-18626-3.

[6] V. Bruyère, L. M. Wang and L. Zhang, On completion of codes with finite deciphering delay, *European J. Combin.* **11**, 6, pp. 513–521 (1990).

[7] C. S. Calude, S. Marcus and L. Staiger, A topological characterization of random sequences, *Inform. Process. Lett.* **88**, 5, pp. 245–250 (2003), doi:10.1016/j.ipl.2003.07.002, http://dx.doi.org/10.1016/j.ipl.2003.07.002, reprinted in S. Marcus. *Words and Languages Everywhere*, Polimetrica, Milano, 2007, pp. 357–364.

[8] J. Cassaigne and F. Nicolas, Factor complexity, in *Combinatorics, automata and number theory, Encyclopedia Math. Appl.*, Vol. 135. Cambridge Univ. Press, Cambridge, pp. 163–247 (2010).

[9] H. Fernau, K. Reinhardt and L. Staiger, Decidability of code properties, *Theor. Inform. Appl.* **41**, 3, pp. 243–259 (2007), doi:10.1051/ita:2007019, http://dx.doi.org/10.1051/ita:2007019.

[10] F. Levé and G. Richomme, Quasiperiodic infinite words: Some answers (column: Formal language theory), *Bulletin of the EATCS* **84**, pp. 128–138 (2004).

[11] F. Levé and G. Richomme, Quasiperiodic Sturmian words and morphisms, *Theor. Comput. Sci.* **372**, 1, pp. 15–25 (2007).

[12] S. Marcus and G. Păun, Infinite (almost periodic) words, formal languages and dynamical systems, *Bulletin of the EATCS* **54**, pp. 224–231 (1994).

[13] S. Marcus, Bridging two hierarchies of infinite words, *J. UCS* **8**, 2, pp. 292–296 (2002).

[14] S. Marcus, Quasiperiodic infinite words (column: Formal language theory), *Bulletin of the EATCS* **82**, pp. 170–174 (2004).

[15] S. Markus, *Set-theoretic Models of Languages.* Izdat. "Nauka", Moscow (1970), [In Russian], Translated from the English by M. V. Arapov, Edited and with an appendix by Ju. A. Šreĭder.

[16] L. Mouchard, Normal forms of quasiperiodic strings, *Theoret. Comput. Sci.* **249**, 2, pp. 313–324 (2000), doi:10.1016/S0304-3975(00)00065-7, http://dx.doi.org/10.1016/S0304-3975(00)00065-7.

[17] R. Polley and L. Staiger, The maximal subword complexity of quasiperiodic infinite words, in I. McQuillan and G. Pighizzini (eds.), *DCFS, Electr. Proc. Theor. Comput. Sci. (EPTCS)*, Vol. 31, pp. 169–176 (2010).

[18] R. Polley and L. Staiger, Quasiperiods, subword complexity and the smallest Pisot number. *J. Autom. Lang. Comb.* **21**, 1-2, pp. 93–106 (2016).

[19] A. Salomaa and M. Soittola, *Automata-theoretic aspects of formal power series*, Texts and Monographs in Computer Science. Springer-Verlag, New York (1978).

[20] H.-J. Shyr, *Free Monoids and Languages*, 3rd edn. Hon Min Book Company, Taichung (2001).

[21] L. Staiger, The entropy of finite-state ω-languages, *Problems Control Inform. Theory/Problemy Upravlen. Teor. Inform.* **14**, 5, pp. 383–392 (1985).

[22] L. Staiger, On infinitary finite length codes, *RAIRO Inform. Théor. Appl.* **20**, 4, pp. 483–494 (1986).

[23] L. Staiger, Kolmogorov complexity and Hausdorff dimension, *Inform. and Comput.* **103**, 2, pp. 159–194 (1993), doi:10.1006/inco.1993.1017, http://dx.doi.org/10.1006/inco.1993.1017.

[24] L. Staiger, Asymptotic subword complexity, in H. Bordihn, M. Kutrib and B. Truthe (eds.), *Languages Alive, Lecture Notes in Computer Science*, Vol. 7300. Springer, Heidelberg, pp. 236–245 (2012), doi:10.1007/978-3-642-31644-9_16.

Chapter 3

Early Romanian Contributions to Algebra and Polynomials

Doru Ştefănescu

Department of Theoretical Physics, Mathematics,
Optics, Spectroscopy, Plasma and Lasers
University of Bucharest, Romania
doru.stefanescu@gmail.com

Abstract. We present earlier contributions of Romanian mathematicians to algebra and the analytic theory of polynomials in the first decade of the 20th century. Included are results of Anton Davidoglu, Gheorghe Ţiţeica and Traian Lalescu about polynomials, binary quadratic forms and Galois theory.

3.1 Introduction

When I was a student at the University of Bucharest during the seventies, the general opinion was that the first significant original algebra results in Romania were obtained by Dan Barbilian (1895–1961). In the eighties, professor Solomon Marcus (1925–2016) in a discussion with my PhD advisor professor Nicolae Radu (1931–2001), noted that actually the first algebra research papers published by Romanian mathematicians were written three decades earlier, by Traian Lalescu (1882–1929). Professor Radu mentioned that to me, being a little astonished by the fact that Lalescu — known for his pioneering work on integral equations, should be the first Romanian algebraist. He asked me to check this information. So I have looked at all publications of Traian Lalescu and found that Solomon Marcus was right. In fact, Lalescu had published in the first decade of the 20th century four papers on algebraic subjects.

Later I discovered that Gheorghe Ţiţeica (1873–1939) and Anton

37

Davidoglu (1876–1958) also published papers on polynomials, studying problems that today are related to numerical algebraic geometry.

In the nineties, I met Solomon Marcus during a visit at the University of Auckland. We found various common subjects of conversation, many of them on the history and philosophy of science and, especially, on the history and philosophy of mathematics. A concrete result of these discussions was a joint paper with Cristian Calude and the possibility to work together on other historical subjects. Professor Marcus was particularly interested by the history of Romanian mathematics [17].

I told him about my lecture on the algebraic work of Traian Lalescu and he encouraged me to write a paper about Lalescu's contributions to Galois theory and to the theory of polynomials.

I wold like to dedicate this presentation of the contributions of Țițeica, Davidoglu and Lalescu in algebra and the analytic theory of polynomials, to the memory of professor Solomon Marcus.

3.2   Early Romanian contributions to the study of polynomials

At the beginning of the 20th century, Gheorghe Țițeica and Anton Davidoglu published results on the number of solutions of polynomial systems. This happened during their PhD studies in Paris, and their work was influenced by a paper of Émile Picard ([19], 1892).

3.2.1   *Historical context*

The problem of computation of the number of solutions of a system of polynomials was studied at the end of the 19th century by Kronecker [9] and Picard [19].

Țițeica and Davidoglu defended their theses in Mathematics in 1899, respectively 1900, at Sorbonne, Paris. It is quite probable that they have known the work of Picard during their studies in Paris.

Davidoglu and Țițeica applied the results of Picard to the computation of the number of roots of a system of polynomials. Davidoglu published two papers on this topic, and Țițeica one paper. They stated theorems on the number of roots of multiplicity larger than 2.

We note that the results of Davidoglu and Țițeica were published in *C. R. Ac. Sci. Paris* and were presented by Émile Picard.

3.2.2 Picard's result

In his memoir from 1895, Émile Picard [20] gave a related formula for the computation of the number of simple roots of a polynomial in a given interval.

He proved that his integral formula, even if it does not give explicitly the number of roots, allows to obtain estimates that lead to the exact computation of this number.

Theorem 3.1 (Picard, 1895). *The number of roots of polynomial f in the interval (a, b) is given by*

$$-\frac{1}{\pi} \int_a^b \frac{\varepsilon(ff'' - f'^2)}{f^2\varepsilon^2 + f'^2}\, dx + \frac{1}{\pi} \arctan \frac{\varepsilon f'(b)}{f(b)} - \frac{1}{\pi} \arctan \frac{\varepsilon f'(a)}{f(a)}\,,$$

where arctan *is between* $-\pi/2$ *and* $\pi/2$ *and* ε *is "small enough".*

Țițeica's Theorem

The main result of Țițeica on polynomials was published in 1901 in [23]. Țițeica addresses the problem of finding the number of solutions of a system of univariate polynomials.

Theorem 3.2 (Țițeica). *Let f be a univariate polynomial with real coefficients. The number of its double roots in the interval (a, b) is equal to*

$$\frac{1}{2\pi} \int_a^b \left(P(u, \varepsilon) - P(u, -\varepsilon) \right) du\,,$$

where $P(u, \varepsilon)$ is defined by

$$\frac{-f'(u - \varepsilon)\left(f'(u + \varepsilon) + f''(u + \varepsilon)\right) + f''(u - \varepsilon)\left(f(u + \varepsilon) + f'(u + \varepsilon)\right)}{\left(f(u + \varepsilon) + f'(u + \varepsilon)\right)^2 + f'^2(u - \varepsilon)}$$

with "small enough" ε.

This is equivalent to the following formula for the number of double roots:

$$\frac{1}{2\pi} \lim_{\varepsilon \to 0} \int_a^b \left(P(u, \varepsilon) - P(u, -\varepsilon) \right) du\,.$$

Davidoglu's Theorem

A result related to those of Picard and Țițeica was published by Davidoglu:

Theorem 3.3 (Davidoglu). *If f is a univariate polynomial with real coefficients, the number of its double roots in the interval (a, b) is*

$$-\frac{1}{2\pi} \lim_{\varepsilon \to 0} \int_a^b Q(f, \varepsilon) \, dx \,,$$

where

$$Q(f, \varepsilon) = \frac{f'^2 - f'' + \varepsilon^2(f'f''' - f''^2)}{f'^2 + (f + \varepsilon^2 f'')^2} - \frac{f'^2 - f'' - \varepsilon^2(f'f''' - f''^2)}{f'^2 + (f - \varepsilon^2 f'')^2} \,.$$

The Theorem of Davidoglu was published in [6]. He obtained other results on the number of roots of polynomials in [7].

Remark. Like the results of Kronecker and Picard, Theorems 3.2 and 3.3 lead, in specific examples, to huge formulas.

3.3 The algebraic work of Traian Lalescu

Traian Lalescu (1882–1929) is well known for his pioneering work on integral equations. He is the author of one of the first monographs on integral equations. Lalescu obtained a PhD at Sorbonne, Paris for the thesis "Sur l'équation de Volterra" ([14], 1908).

During his studies in Paris he was also interested in algebraic subjects and published four papers on Galois theory and on the study of univariate polynomials [10–13]. One of them is devoted to the trinomial equations and the other two to the study of binary quadratic forms. The fourth is a memoir on Galois theory.

Trinomial equation

Theorem 3.4. *If the degree of the polynomial $f(X) = X^n + kaX + a$ is prime, where $a \in \mathbb{C}$ and $k = n/(n-1)^{\frac{n-1}{2}}$, then its Galois group is symmetric.*

Lalescu has proved that the monodromy group is symmetric, and from this it follows that the Galois group should be symmetric.

Such arguments were frequently used by algebraists around 1900. We assume that Traian Lalescu has not known the dissertation of A. Kneser

([15], 1884). Kneser in fact uses the monodromy group for studying the irreducibility.

Lalescu also gave an elegant proof to the following theorem of Hilbert.

Theorem 3.5. *The Galois group of a trinomial is symmetric for an infinity of values of the parameter a.*

3.4 Lalescu's contribution to Galois Theory

The scope of the memoir of Lalescu was the presentation of the general Galois theory for polynomials, starting from the basic property of the Galois group that describes the rationality domain of an algebraic equation. His proof makes use of the fundamental theorem of symmetric functions and of a theorem of Lagrange.

Lalescu considers that "the method of Galois is one of discovery". Related papers on the general Galois theory were published around 1900 also by Sörderberg ([22], 1888), Picard ([20], 1895), Borel–Drach ([2], 1895), Drach (1898) and Vessiot ([24], 1904).

Lalescu's interest in Galois Theory was probably stimulated by a memoir of Vessiot, which proposes a Galois Theory for homogeneous linear differential equations. A historical account on the Picard-Vessiot theory is given by E. R. Kolchin ([8], 1949). The differential equations were in the core of Lalescu's studies in Paris.

In fact, Lalescu explains in his memoir that he studied Vessiot's method for using Galois Theory in the study of homogeneous linear differential equations. The use of group theory in the study of differential equations was one of the challenges of the second half of 19th century. A pioneer of this approach was Sophus Lie. He published in collaboration with F. Engel a treatise on the theory of transformation groups and their applications to the study of differential equations. However, as remarked by Hans Wussing ([25], 1984), the actual formulation of a *"Galois theory of differential equations is due to É. Picard and É. Vessiot, in their works of 1883, 1887, respectively 1895"*.

In the introduction of his memoir Lalescu mentioned a paper of J. T. Sörderberg ([22], 1888). The statement of Sörderberg is the following:

Theorem 3.6. *If an algebraic equation has no multiple roots, there exists a unique group of substitutions having the following two properties:*

(1) Any rational functions of the roots that takes rational values, is invariable with respect to the substitutions of the group.

(2) Reciprocally, any rational function of the roots whose value is invariable with respect to the substitutions of the group, is expressed rationally by the known quantities.

Sörderberg calls the group in Theorem 3.6 the *Galois group* of the equation.

The result of Söderberg was extended successively by É. Borel–J. Drach ([2], 1895), E. T. Vessiot ([24], 1904) and finally by T. Lalescu ([13], 1907).

3.4.1 *Lalescu's statement*

Theorem 3.7. *All the elements in the field of degree N of an equation satisfy the total or partial resolvents of degree N or a divisor of N. The resolvents of degree N are total and normal.*

The algebraic equation considered above is only one of the rings[1] in the chain of the equations which are resolvents of its fields and among which there is an established intimate link, translated in the links of their groups: if the roots of the total resolvent are known, the roots of all the other are deduced rationally and the Galois groups of the other equations are formed through permutations of their roots, if there are applied to their rational expressions the permutations of the Galois group of the known equation. In particular the groups of the resolvents are isomorphic.

Lalescu's memoir on Galois Theory was discussed by I. Schur in the abstracting journal *Jajrbch für Mathematik* (see *JFM* 39.0203.02, 1908). Schur explains that Lalescu considered a polynomial having only simple roots in a field K and its Galois group G and proved the fundamental Theorem of Galois Theory avoiding the use of resolvents. The result of Galois states that every rational function of the roots with coefficients from K which is invariant to all permutations of G, is an element from field K. This fundamental theorem of Galois theory is generally proved using the Galois resolvent of the equation $f(x) = 0$. Another proof was given by Sörderberg [22]. The paper simplifies this proof and shows how, on the basis of the fundamental theorem, the rest of the main results of Galois theory can be developed without significantly preferring the Galois resolvent of the equation over the other resolvents.

---

[1]Here "ring" does not mean the algebraic structure of ring but an element of a chain!

3.5 Representation of numbers and composition of binary quadratic forms

Traian Lalescu also published two other algebra papers [11, 12], concerning the composition of binary quadratic forms and the representation of integers by such forms. This is still today a central problem in algebraic number theory and class field theory, see F. Lemmermayer [16]. The problem addressed by Lalescu was to establish which integers are represented by a given primitive binary quadratic form. Franz Lemmermeyer considers that *"answering this seemingly innocent question quickly leads us into areas that were (and still are) important for the development of algebraic number theory: reciprocity laws and class fields"*.

We note that the papers of Lalescu on quadratic forms were cited recently, more than one hundred years after their publication, see F. Lemmermeyer ([16], 2010) and F. Pintore ([21], 2015).

Lalescu considers the group of primitive classes.[2] He considers two integers, m and n, represented by the classes K_m and K_n.

In the first paper [11] he reminds that two binary quadratic forms $F_1 = (a_1, b_1, c_1) = a_1 x^2 b_1 xy + c_1 y^2$ and $F_2 = (a_2, b_2, c_2) = a_2 x^2 b_2 xy + 2_1 y^2$ are composable if they have the same determinant D if the a_1, a_2 and $\frac{1}{2}(b_1 + b_2)$ have no common divisor. The forms F_1 and F_2 are equivalent if and only if there exist integers x, y such that

$$x^2 - Dy^2 = 4a_1 a_2, \ x + b_1 y \equiv 0 \pmod{2a_1}, \ x - b_2 y \equiv 0 \pmod{2a_2}.$$

In the second paper on quadratic forms [12] he starts from the fact that if the integers m, n are properly represented by the classes K_m, respectively K_n, of primitive forms of square-free determinant D, then mn is represented by the composite class $K_m \cdot K_n$.

The question is to establish if such a representation is proper or not. He considers first numbers prime to $2D$. Using the representations

$$m = a_1^{\alpha_1} \cdots a_k^{\alpha_k} b_1^{\beta_1} \cdots b_p^{\beta_p},$$

$$n = a_1^{\alpha_1'} \cdots a_k^{\alpha_k'} c_1^{\gamma_1} \cdots c_q^{\gamma_q}$$

the expressions for the 2^{p+q} classes representing properly m, respectively n, are

$$K_m = K_{a_1}^{\pm \alpha_1} \cdots K_{a_k}^{\pm \alpha_k} K_{b_1}^{\pm \beta_1} \cdots K_{b_q}^{\pm \beta_q},$$

---

[2]In fact, of binary quadratic forms.

$$K_n = K_{a_1}^{\pm\alpha_1'} \cdots K_{a_k}^{\pm\alpha_k'} K_{c_1}^{\pm\gamma_1} \cdots K_{c_q}^{\pm\gamma_q} ,$$

where K_λ and $K_{-\lambda}$ are two opposite classes which represent properly the prime λ.

He obtains 2^{p+k} distinct proper representations of the number m, respectively 2^{q+k} distinct proper representations of n. He finally deduces that the product mn has exactly 2^{p+q+k} proper representations by classes of determinant d. He remarks that there are $(2^k - 1)2^{p+q+k}$ improper representations deduced from the resulting representation of the product mn.

Lalescu finally proves that a divisor d of D is represented properly only by the ambiguous class $dx^2 - \delta y^2$ and that no power of d is represented properly by forms of determinant D.

We mention also another result in the paper [12] of Lalescu:

Proposition 3.1. *If a divisor of D is involved both in m and n, the composed representation will be improper. However, if the numbers m and n are co-prime with D and are not divisible by the factors of D, and if the other conditions are satisfied, the composed representation is proper.*

Let us note that in the time when Lalescu published his papers on quadratic forms, the problems concerning quadratic forms were in the core of algebra and number theory. For example, in 1910, F. Mertens (in *Über die Koeffizienten und Irreduktibilität der Transformationsgleichungen der elliptischen Funktionen mit singulärem Modul,* Wien. Ber. **119**, 1493–1556) considered a problem related to Lalescu's approach, namely primitive positive quadratic forms

$$f = \left(a, \frac{b}{\sigma}, c \right) = ax^2 + \frac{2b}{\sigma}xy + cy^2 , \quad \text{with} \quad \sigma \in \{1, 2\} ,$$

for which $D = b^2 - \sigma^2 ac$ is negative. Other approaches were given by L. Aubry ([1], 1913) and H. Brandt ([3], 1914).

The results of Lalescu were presented in the third volume of the *History of Numbers* of L. E. Dickson [5].

Dedication. To the memory of Professor Solomon Marcus.

References

[1] L. Aubry. Composition des formes quadratiqes, *Intérm. des mathématiciens* **20**, 6–7 (1913).

[2] É. Borel, J. Drach. *Introduction à la théorie des nombres*, Nony, Paris (1895).

[3] H. Brandt. Komposition der binären quadratischen Formen relativ einer Grundform, *J. für Math.*, **150**, 1–46 (1919).

[4] C. Calude, S. Marcus, D. Ștefănescu. The Creator versus its creation, From Scotus to Gödel, in Collegium Logicum, *Annals of the Gödel Society*, vol. 3, Prague, 1–10 (1999).

[5] L. E. Dickson. *History of the history of numbers*, vol. I–III, Carnegie Institute, Washington (1919, 1920, 1923).

[6] A. Davidoglu. Sur le nombre des racines communes à plusieurs équations simultanées, *C. R. Ac. Sci. Paris*, **133**, 784–786 (1901).

[7] A. Davidoglu. Sur le nombre des racines communes à plusieurs équations, *C. R. Ac. Sci. Paris*, **133**, 784–786 (1901).

[8] E. R. Kolchin. *Algebraic matrice groups and the Picard–Vessiot theory of homogeneous linear differential equations*, Ann. Math., **49**, 1–42 (1949).

[9] L. Kronecker. Über Systeme von Funktionen mehrerer Variabeln, *Berl. Monatsber.*, 159–193, 688–698 (1869).

[10] T. Lalesco. Sur le groupe des équations trinômes, *Bull. Soc. Math. de France*, **35**, 75–76 (1907).

[11] T. Lalesco. Sur la représentation des nombres par les classes de formes à un déterminant donné, *Bull. Soc. Math. de France*, **35**, 248–252 (1907).

[12] T. Lalesco. Sur la composition des formes quadratiques, *Nouv. Ann. Math.*, (4), **7**, 145–150 (1907).

[13] T. Lalesco. La théorie générale de Galois, *Ann. Fac. de Toulouse*, **10**, 113–123 (1908).

[14] T. Lalesco. *Sur l'équation de Volterra*, Univ. Sorbonne, Paris (1908).

[15] A. Kneser. *Irreductibilität und Monodromiegruppe algebraischer Gleichungen*, Dissertation, Berlin (1884).

[16] F. Lemmermeyer, *Binary Quadratic Forms An Elementary Approach to the Arithmetic of Elliptic and Hyperelliptic Curves*, Technical Report (2010).

[17] S. Marcus. Mathematics in Romanian Culture and Society, plenary report at the 6th Congress of Romanian Mathematicians, June 28–July 4, 2007, Bucharest, Romania (2007). http://www.imar.ro/~purice/conferences/Cong-6/Plenary/Plenary.html.

[18] S. Marcus. *Words and Languages everywhere*, Polimetrica, Milano (2007).

[19] É. Picard. Sur le nombre des racines communes à plusieurs équations, *J. Math. Pures et Appl.*, IV–ème série, **8**, 5–24 (1892).

[20] É. Picard. Sur l'extension des ideés de Galois à la théorie de Galois des équations differrentielles, *Cr. Ac. Sci. Paris*, **121**, 789–792 (1895).

[21] F. Pintore. *Binary quadratic forms, elliptic curves and Schoof's algorithm*, PhD thesis, University of Trento (2015).

[22] J. T. Sörderberg. Démonstration du théorème fondamental de Galois dans la théorie algébrique des équations, *Acta Math.*, **11**, 297–302 (1888).

[23] G. Țiţeica. Sur le nombre des racines communes à plusieurs équations, *C. R. Ac. Sci. Paris*, 918–920, **133**, (1901).

[24] M. E. Vessiot. Sur la théorie de Galois et ses diverses applications, *Ann. École Normale Sup.*, **21** (3), 9–29 (1904).

[25] Hans Wussing. *The Genesis of Abstract Group Concept*, Dover, (1984).

Chapter 4

Distributed Compression through the Lens of Algorithmic Information Theory: A Primer

Marius Zimand
Department of Computer and Information Sciences
Towson University, Baltimore, MD, USA
mzimand@towson.edu

Abstract. Distributed compression is the task of compressing correlated data by several parties, each one possessing one piece of data and acting separately. The classical Slepian-Wolf theorem [SW73] shows that if data is generated by independent draws from a joint distribution, that is by a memoryless stochastic process, then distributed compression can achieve the same compression rates as centralised compression when the parties act together. Recently, the author [Zim17] has obtained an analogue version of the Slepian-Wolf theorem in the framework of Algorithmic Information Theory (also known as Kolmogorov complexity). The advantage over the classical theorem, is that the AIT version works for individual strings, without any assumption regarding the generative process. The only requirement is that the parties know the complexity profile of the input strings, which is a simple quantitative measure of the data correlation. The goal of this paper is to present in an accessible form that omits some technical details the main ideas from the reference [Zim17].

4.1 On busy friends wishing to share points

Zack has three good friends, Alice, Bob, and Charles, who share with him every piece of information they have. One day, Alice, Bob, and Charles, *separately*, observe three *collinear* points A, respectively B and C, in the 2-dimensional affine space over the field with 2^n elements. Thus, each one of Alice, Bob, and Charles possesses $2n$ bits of information, giving the two coordinates of their respective points. Due to the geometric relation, collectively, they have $5n$ bits of information, because given two points the third one can be described with just one coordinate. They want to email the points to Zack, without wasting bandwidth, that is by sending approximately $5n$ bits, where "approximately" means that they can afford an overhead of $O(\log n)$ bits. Clearly, if they collaborate, they can send exactly $5n$ bits. The problem is that they have busy schedules, and cannot find a good time to get together and thus they have to compress their points in isolation. How many bits do they need to send to Zack? Let us first note some necessary requirements for the compression lengths. Let n_A be the number of bits to which Alice compresses her point A, and let n_B and n_C have the analogous meaning for Bob and Charles. It is necessary that

$$n_A + n_B + n_C \geq 5n,$$

because Zack needs to acquire $5n$ bits. It is also necessary that

$$n_A + n_B \geq 3n, n_A + n_C \geq 3n, n_B + n_C \geq 3n,$$

because if Zack gets somehow one of the three points, he still needs $3n$ bits of informations from the other two points. And it is also necessary that

$$n_A \geq n, n_B \geq n, n_C \geq n,$$

because if Zack gets somehow two of the three points, he still needs n bits of informations from the remaining point.

We will see that any numbers n_A, n_B and n_C satisfying the above necessary conditions, are also sufficient up to a small logarithmic overhead, in the sense that there are probabilistic compression algorithms such that if n_A, n_B and n_C satisfy these conditions, then Alice can compress point A to a binary string p_A of length $n_A + O(\log n)$, Bob can compress point B to a binary string p_B of length $n_B + O(\log n)$, Charles can compress point C to a binary string p_C of length $n_C + O(\log n)$, and Zack can with high probability reconstruct the three points from p_A, p_B and p_C. Moreover, the compression does not use the geometric relation between the points, but only the correlation of information in the points, as expressed in the very flexible framework of algorithmic information theory.

4.2   Algorithmic information theory

Algorithmic Information Theory (AIT), initiated independently by Solomonoff [Sol64], Kolmogorov [Kol65], and Chaitin [Cha66], is a counterpart to the Information Theory (IT), initiated by Shannon. In IT the central object is a random variable X whose realisations are strings over an alphabet Σ. The Shannon entropy of X is defined by

$$H(X) = \sum_{x \in \Sigma} P(X = x) \, (1/\log P(X = x)).$$

The entropy $H(X)$ is viewed as the amount of information in X, because each string x can be described with $\lceil 1/\log P(X = x) \rceil$ bits (using the Shannon code), and therefore $H(X)$ is the expected number of bits needed to describe the outcome of the random process modelled by X.

AIT dispenses with the stochastic generative model, and defines the complexity of an individual string x as the length of its shortest description. For example, the string $x_1 = 00000000000000000000000000000000$ has low complexity because it can be succinctly described as "2^5 zeros." The string $x_2 = 10110000010101110101010011011100$ is a 32-bit string obtained using random atmospheric noise (according to random.org), and has high complexity because it does not have a short description.

Formally, given a Turing machine M, a string p is said to be a *program* (or a *description*) of a string x, if M on input p prints x. We denote the length of a binary string x by $|x|$. The *Kolmogorov complexity* of x relative to the Turing machine M is

$$C_M(x) = \min\{|p| \mid p \text{ is a program for } x \text{ relative to } M\}.$$

If U is universal Turing machine, then for every other Turing machine M there exists a string m such that $U(m, p) = M(p)$ for all p, and therefore for every string x,

$$C_U(x) \le C_M(x) + |m|.$$

Thus, if we ignore the additive constant $|m|$, the Kolmogorov complexity of x relative to U is minimal. We fix a universal Turing machine U, drop the subscript U in $C_U(\cdot)$, and denote the complexity of x by $C(x)$. We list below a few basic facts about Kolmogorov complexity:

(1) For every string x, $C(x) \le |x| + O(1)$, because a string x is trivially described by itself. (Formally, there is a Turing machine M that, for every x, on input x prints x.)

(2) Similarly to the complexity of x, we define the complexity of x conditioned by y as $C(x \mid y) = \min\{|p| \mid U \text{ on input } p \text{ and } y \text{ prints } x\}$.

(3) Using some standard pairing function $\langle \cdot, \cdot \rangle$ that maps pair of strings into single strings, we define $C(x, y)$ the complexity of a pair of strings (and then we can extend to tuples with larger arity) by $C(x, y) = C(<x, y>)$.

(4) We use the convenient shorthand notation $a \leq^+ b$ to mean that $a \leq b + O(\log(a+b))$, where the constant hidden in the $O(\cdot)$ notation only depends on the universal machine U. Similarly $a \geq^+ b$ means $a \geq b - O(\log(a + b))$, and $a =^+ b$ means ($a \leq^+ b$ and $a \geq^+ b$).

(5) The chain rule in information theory states that $H(X, Y) = H(X) + H(Y \mid X)$. A similar rule holds true in algorithmic information theory: for all x and y, $C(x, y) =^+ C(x) + C(y \mid x)$.

4.3 Distributed compression, more formally

We present the problem confronting Alice, Bob, Charles (the senders) and Zack (the receiver) in an abstract and formal setting. We assume that each one of Alice, Bob, and Charles has n bits of information, which, in concrete terms, means that Alice has an n-bit binary string x_A, Bob has an n-bit binary string x_B, and Charles has an n-bit binary string x_C. We also assume that the 3-tuplet (x_A, x_B, x_C) belongs to a set $S \subseteq \{0,1\}^n \times \{0,1\}^n \times \{0,1\}^n$, which defines the way in which the information is correlated (for example, S may be the set of all three collinear points) and that all parties (i.e., Alice, Bob, Charles, and Zack) know S. Alice is using an encoding function $E_A : \{0,1\}^n \to \{0,1\}^{n_A}$, Bob is using an encoding function $E_B : \{0,1\}^n \to \{0,1\}^{n_B}$, Charles is using an encoding function $E_C : \{0,1\}^n \to \{0,1\}^{n_C}$, and Zack is using a decoding function $D : \{0,1\}^{n_A} \times \{0,1\}^{n_B} \times \{0,1\}^{n_C} \to \{0,1\}^n$. Ideally, the requirement is that for all (x_A, x_B, x_C) in S, $D(E_A(x_A), E_B(x_B), E_C(x_C)) = (x_A, x_B, x_C)$. However, since typically the encoding functions are probabilistic, we allow the above equality to fail with probability bounded by some small ε, where the probability is over the random bits used by the encoding functions. Also, sometimes, we will be content if the encoding/decoding procedures work, not for all, but only for "most" 3-tuples in S (i.e., with probability close to 1, under a given probability distribution on S).

Our focus in this paper is to present distributed compression in the framework of Algorithmic Information Theory, but let us present first the point of view of Information Theory, where the problem has been studied early on. The celebrated classical theorem of Slepian and Wolf [SW73] characterises the possible compression rates n_A, n_B and n_C for the case of *memoryless* sources. The memoryless assumption means that (x_A, x_B, x_C) are realisations of random variables (X_A, X_B, X_C), which consist of n independent copies of a random variable that has a joint distribution $P(b_1, b_2, b_3)$ on triples of bits. In other words, the generative model for (x_A, x_B, x_C)

is a stochastic process that consists of n independent draws from the joint distribution, such that Alice observes x_A, the sequence of first components in the n draws, Bob observes x_B, the second components, and Charles observes x_C, the third components. A stochastic process of this type is called 3-DMS (Discrete Memoryless Source). By Shannon's Source Coding Theorem, if n' is a number that is at least $H(X_A, X_B, X_C)$ and if Alice, Bob, and Charles put their data together, then, for every $\varepsilon > 0$, there exists an encoding/decoding pair E and D, where E compresses $3n$-bit strings to $(n' + \varepsilon n)$-bit strings and $D(E(X_A, X_B, X_C)) = (X_A, X_B, X_C)$ with probability $1 - \varepsilon$, provided n is large enough. The second part of Shannon's Source Coding Theorem shows that this is essentially optimal because if the data is compressed to length smaller than $H(X_A, X_B, X_C) - \varepsilon n$ (for constant ε), then the probability of correct decoding goes to 0. The Slepian-Wolf Theorem shows that such a compression can also be done if Alice, Bob, and Charles compress separately. Actually, it describes precisely the possible compression lengths. Note that if the three senders compress separately to lengths n_A, n_B and n_C as indicated above, then it is essentially necessary that $n_A + n_B + n_C \geq H(X_A, X_B, X_C) - \varepsilon n$, $n_A + n_B \geq H(X_A, X_B \mid X_C) - \varepsilon n$ (because even if Zack has X_C, he still needs to receive a number of bits equal to the amount of entropy in X_A and X_B conditioned by X_C), $n_A \geq H(X_A \mid X_B, X_C) - \varepsilon n$ (similarly, even if Zack has X_B and X_C, he still needs to receive a number of bits equal to the amount of entropy in X_A conditioned by X_B and X_C), and there are the obvious other necessary conditions obtained by permuting A, B and C. The Slepian-Wolf Theorem shows that for 3-DMS these necessary conditions are, essentially, also sufficient, in the sense that the slight change of $-\varepsilon n$ into $+\varepsilon n$ allows encoding/decoding procedures. Thus, in the next theorem we suppose that $n_A + n_B + n_C \geq H(X_A, X_B, X_C) + \varepsilon n$, and similarly for the other relations.

Theorem 4.1 (Slepian-Wolf Theorem [SW73]). *Let (X_A, X_B, X_C) be a 3-DMS, let $\varepsilon > 0$, and let n_A, n_B, n_C satisfy the above conditions (with $+\varepsilon n$ instead of $-\varepsilon n$). Then there exist encoding functions $E_A : \{0, 1\}^n \to \{0, 1\}^{n_A}, E_B : \{0, 1\}^n \to \{0, 1\}^{n_B}, E_C : \{0, 1\}^n \to \{0, 1\}^{n_C}$ and a decoding function $D : \{0, 1\}^{n_A} \times \{0, 1\}^{n_B} \times \{0, 1\}^{n_C} \to \{0, 1\}^n$ such that $Prob[D(E(X_A, X_B, X_C)) = (X_A, X_B, X_C)] \geq 1 - O(\varepsilon)$, provided n is large enough.*

There is nothing special about three senders, and indeed the Slepian-Wolf theorem holds for any number ℓ of senders, where ℓ is a constant, and for sources which are ℓ-DMS over any alphabet Σ. This means that the senders compress $(x_1, \ldots, x_\ell)$, which is realisation of random variables $(X_1, \ldots, X_\ell)$, obtained from n independent draws from a joint distribution $p(a_1, \ldots, a_\ell)$, with each a_i ranging over the alphabet Σ. The i-th sender observes the realisation x_i of X_i, and uses an encoding function $E_i : \Sigma^n \to \Sigma^{n_i}$. Suppose that the compression lengths n_i, $i = 1, \ldots, \ell$, satisfy $\sum_{i \in V} n_i \geq H(X_V \mid X_{\overline{V}}) + \varepsilon n$, for every subset $V \subseteq \{1, \ldots, \ell\}$ (where if $V = \{i_1, \ldots, i_t\}$, X_V denotes the tuple $(X_{i_1}, \ldots, X_{i_t})$, and $\overline{V}$ denotes $\{1, \ldots, \ell\} - V$). Then the Slepian-Wolf theorem for ℓ-DMS states that there are $E_1, \ldots, E_\ell$ of the above type, and $D : \Sigma^{n_1} \times \ldots \times \Sigma^{n_\ell} \to \Sigma^n$ such that $D(E_1(X_1), \ldots, E_\ell(X_\ell)) = (X_1, \ldots, X_\ell)$ with probability $1 - \varepsilon$.

As pointed out above, the Slepian-Wolf theorem shows the surprising and remarkable fact that, for memoryless sources, distributed compression can be done at an optimality level that is on a par with centralised compression. On the weak side, the memoryless property means that there is a lot of independence in the generative process: the realisation at time i is independent of the realisation at time $i - 1$. Intuitively, independence helps distributed compression. For example, in the limit case in which the senders observe realisations of fully independent random variables, then, clearly, it makes no difference whether compression is distributed or centralised. The Slepian-Wolf theorem has been extended to sources that are stationary and ergodic [Cov75], but these sources are still quite simple, and intuitively realisations which are temporally sufficiently apart are close to being independent.

One may be inclined to believe that the optimal compression rates of distributed compression in the theorem are caused by the independence properties of the sources. However, this is not so, and we shall see that in fact the Slepian-Wolf phenomenon does not require any type of independence. Even more, it works without any generative model. For that we need to work in the framework of Kolmogorov complexity (AIT).

Let us recall the example from Section 4.1: Alice, Bob, and Charles observe separately, respectively, the collinear points A, B, C. Even without assuming any generative process for the three points, we can still express their correlation using Kolmogorov complexity. More precisely, their correlation is described by the Kolmogorov complexity profile, which consists of 7 numbers, giving the complexities of all non-empty subsets of $\{A, B, C\}$:

$$(C(A), C(B), C(C), C(A, B), C(A, C), C(B, C), C(A, B, C)).$$

Let us consider the general case, in which the three senders have, respectively, n-bit strings x_A, x_B, x_C having a given complexity profile $(C(x_V) \mid V \subseteq \{x_A, x_B, x_C\}, V \neq \emptyset)$ (where x_V is the notation convention that we used for the ℓ-senders case of the Slepian-Wolf theorem). What are the possible compression lengths, so that Zack can decompress and obtain (x_A, x_B, x_C) with probability $(1 - \varepsilon)$?

To answer this question, for simplicity, let us consider the case of a single sender, Alice. She wants to use a probabilistic encoding function E such that there exists a decoding function D with the property that for all n, and for all n-bit strings x, $D(E(x)) = x$, with probability $1 - \varepsilon$. A lower bound on the length $|E(x)|$ is given in the following lemma.

Lemma 4.1. *Let E be a probabilistic encoding function, and D be a decoding function such that for all strings x, $D(E(x)) = x$, with probability $(1 - \varepsilon)$. Then for every k, there is a string x with $C(x) \leq k$, such that $|E(x)| \geq k + \log(1 - \varepsilon) - O(1)$.*

Proof:
Fix k and let $S = \{x \mid C(x) \leq k\}$. It can be shown that for some constant c, $|S| \geq 2^{k-c}$, where $|S|$ is the size of S (the idea is that the first string which is not in S can be described with $\log|S| + O(1)$ bits). Since for every $x \in S$, $D(E(x, \varrho)) = x$ with probability $1 - \varepsilon$ over the randomness ϱ, there is some fixed randomness ϱ such that $D(E(x, \varrho)) = x$, for a fraction of $1 - \varepsilon$ of the x's in S. Let $S' \subseteq S$ be the set of such strings x. Thus, $|S'| \geq (1 - \varepsilon)|S| \geq (1 - \varepsilon)2^{k-c}$ and the function $E(\cdot, \varrho)$ is one-to-one on S' (otherwise decoding would not be possible). Therefore the function $E(\cdot, \varrho)$ cannot map all S' into strings of length $k + \log(1 - \varepsilon) - (c + 1)$.

In short, if for every x, $D(E(x)) = x$ with probability $1 - \varepsilon$, then for infinitely many x it must be the case that $|E(x)| \geq C(x) + \log(1-\varepsilon) - O(1)$. In other words, if we ignore the small terms, it is not possible to compress to length less than $C(x)$.

In the same way, similar lower bounds can be established for the case of more senders. For example, let us consider three senders that use the probabilistic encoding functions E_A, E_B and E_C: if there is a decoding function D such that for every (x_A, x_B, x_C),

$$D(E_A(x_A), E_B(x_B), E_C(x_C)) = (x_A, x_B, x_C), \quad \text{with probability } 1 - \varepsilon,$$

(where the probability is over the randomness used by the encoding procedures) then for infinitely many (x_A, x_B, x_C)

$$|E_A(x_A)| + |E_B(x_B)| + |E_C(x_C)| \geq C(x_A, x_B, x_C) + \log(1 - \varepsilon) - O(1),$$
$$|E_A(x_A)| + |E_B(x_B)| \geq C(x_A, x_B \mid x_C) + \log(1 - \varepsilon) - O(1),$$
$$|E_A(x_A)| \geq C(x_A \mid x_B, x_C) + \log(1 - \varepsilon) - O(1),$$

and similar relations hold for any permutation of A, B and C. As we did above, it is convenient to use the notation convention that if V is a subset of $\{A, B, C\}$, we let x_V denote the tuple of strings with indices in V (for example, if $V = \{A, C\}$, then $x_V = (x_A, x_C)$). Then the above relations can be written concisely as

$$\sum_{i \in V} |E_i(x_i)| \geq C(x_V \mid x_{\{A,B,C\}-V}) + \log(1-\varepsilon) - O(1), \text{ for all } V \subseteq \{A, B, C\}.$$

The next theorem — Kolmogorov complexity form of Slepian-Wolf coding — is the focal point of this paper. It shows that the above necessary conditions regarding the compression lengths are, essentially, also sufficient.

Theorem 4.2 ([Zim17]). *There exist probabilistic algorithms E_A, E_B, E_C, a deterministic algorithm D, and a function $\alpha(n) = O(\log n)$ such that for every n, for every tuple of integers (n_A, n_B, n_C), and for every tuple of n-bit strings (x_A, x_B, x_C) if*

$$\sum_{i \in V} n_i \geq C(x_V \mid x_{\{A,B,C\}-V}), \text{ for all } V \subseteq \{A, B, C\}, \qquad (4.1)$$

then

(a) E_A on input x_A and n_A outputs a string p_A of length at most $n_A + \alpha(n)$, E_B on input x_B and n_B outputs a string p_B of length at most $n_B + \alpha(n)$, E_C on input x_C and n_C outputs a string p_C of length at most $n_C + \alpha(n)$,

(b) D on input (p_A, p_B, p_C) outputs (x_A, x_B, x_C), with probability $1 - 1/n$.

We present the proof of this theorem in the next section, but for now, we make several remarks:

- Compression procedures for *individual* inputs (i.e., without using any knowledge regarding the generative process) have been previously designed using the celebrated Lempel-Ziv methods [LZ76, Ziv78]. Such methods have been used for distributed compression as well [Ziv84, DW85, Kuz09]. For such procedures two kinds of optimality have been established, both valid for infinite sequences and thus having an asymptotic nature. First, the procedures achieve a compression length that is asymptotically equal to the so-called finite-state complexity, which is the minimum length that can be achieved by finite-state encoding/decoding procedures. Secondly, the compression rates are asymptotically optimal in case the infinite sequences are generated by sources that are stationary and ergodic [WZ94]. In contrast, the compression in Theorem 4.2 applies to finite strings and achieves a compression length close to minimal description length. On the other hand, the Lempel-Ziv approach has lead to efficient compression algorithms that are used in practice.

- At the cost of increasing the "overhead" $\alpha(n)$ from $O(\log n)$ to $O(\log^3 n)$, we can obtain compression procedures E_A, E_B and E_C that run in polynomial time. On the other hand, the decompression procedure D is slower than any computable function. This is unavoidable at this level of optimality (compression at close to minimum description length) because of the existence of *deep strings*. (Informally, a string x is deep if it has a description p of small length but the universal machine takes a long time to produce x from p.)

- The theorem is true for any number ℓ of senders, where ℓ is an arbitrary constant. We have singled out $\ell = 3$ because this case allows us to present the main ideas of the proof in a relatively simple form.

- Romashchenko [Rom05] (building on an earlier result of Muchnik [Muc02]) has obtained a Kolmogorov complexity version of Slepian-Wolf, in which the encoding and the decoding functions use $O(\log n)$ of extra information, called *help bits*. The above theorem eliminates the help bits, and is, therefore, fully effective. The cost is that the encoding procedure is probabilistic and thus there is a small error probability. The proof of Theorem 4.2 is inspired from Romashchenko's approach, but the technical machinery is quite different.

- The classical Slepian-Wolf theorem can be obtained from the Kolmogorov complexity version because if X is memoryless, then with probability $1 - \varepsilon$, $H(X) - c_\varepsilon\sqrt{n} \leq C(X) \leq H(X) + c_\varepsilon\sqrt{n}$, where c_ε is a constant that only depends on ε.

4.4   Proof sketch of Theorem 4.2

The central piece in the proof is a certain type of bipartite graph with a low congestion property. We recall that in a bipartite graph, the nodes are partitioned in two sets, L (the left nodes) and R (the right nodes), and all edges connect a left node to a right node. We allow multiple edges between two nodes. In the graphs that we use, all left nodes have the same degree, called the left degree. Specifically, we use bipartite graphs G with $L = \{0,1\}^n$, $R = \{0,1\}^m$ and with left degree $D = 2^d$. We label the edges outgoing from $x \in L$ with strings $y \in \{0,1\}^d$. We typically work with a family of graphs indexed on n and such a family of graphs is *computable* if there is an algorithm that on input (x, y), where $x \in L$ and $y \in \{0,1\}^d$, outputs the y-th neighbour of x. Some of the graphs also depend on a rational $0 < \delta < 1$. A constructible family of graphs is *explicit* if the above algorithm runs in time $\text{poly}(n, 1/\delta)$.

We now introduce informally the notions of a *rich owner* and of a *graph with the rich owner property*. Let $B \subseteq L$. The B-degree of a right node is the number of its neighbours that are in B. Roughly speaking a left node is a rich owner with respect to B, if most of its right neighbours are "well-behaved," in the sense that their B-degree is not much larger than $|B| \cdot D/|R|$, the average right degree when the left side is restricted to B. One particularly interesting case, which is used many times in the proof, is when most of the neighbours of a left x have B-degree 1, i.e., when x "owns" most of its right neighbours. A graph has the rich owner property if, for all $B \subseteq L$, most of the left nodes in B are rich owners with respect to B. In the formal definition below, we replace the average right degree with a value which may look arbitrary, but since in applications, this value is approximately equal to the average right degree, the above intuition should be helpful.

The precise definition of rich ownership depends on two parameters k and δ.

Definition 4.1. Let G be a bipartite graph as above and let B be a subset of L. We say that $x \in B$ is a (k, δ)-rich owner with respect to B if the following holds:

- *small regime case:* If $|B| \leq 2^k$, then at least $1 - \delta$ fraction of x's neighbours have B-degree equal to 1, that is they are not shared with any other nodes in B. We also say that $x \in B$ owns y with respect to B if y is a neighbour of x and the B-degree of y is 1.

- *large regime case:* If $|B| > 2^k$, then at least a $1 - \delta$ fraction of x's neighbours have B-degree at most $(2/\delta^2)|B| \cdot D/2^k$.

If x is not a (k, δ)-rich owner with respect to B, then it is said to be a (k, δ)-poor owner with respect to B.

Definition 4.2. A bipartite graph $G = (L = \{0,1\}^n, R = \{0,1\}^m, E \subseteq L \times R)$ has the (k, δ)-rich owner property if for every set $B \subseteq L$ all nodes in B, except at most $\delta|B|$ of them, are (k, δ)-rich owners with respect to B.

The following theorem provides the type of graph that we use.

Theorem 4.3. *For every natural numbers n and k and for every rational number $\delta \in (0, 1]$, there exists a computable bipartite graph $G = (L, R, E \subseteq L \times R)$ that has the (k, δ)-rich property with the following parameters: $L = \{0,1\}^n$, $R = \{0,1\}^{k+\gamma(n/\delta)}$, left degree $D = 2^{\gamma(n/\delta)}$, where $\gamma(n) = O(\log n)$.*

There also exists an explicit *bipartite graph with the same parameters except that the overhead is $\gamma(n) = O(\log^3 n)$.*

The graphs in Theorem 4.3 are derived from randomness extractors. The computable graph is obtained with the probabilistic method, and we sketch the construction in Section 4.5. The explicit graph relies on the extractor from [RRV99] and uses a combination of techniques from [RR99], [CRVW02], and [BZ14].

Let us proceed now to the proof sketch of Theorem 4.2. *We warn the reader that for the sake of readability, we skip several technical elements. In particular, we ignore the loss of precision in $=^+, \leq^+, \geq^+$, and we treat these relations as if they were $=, \leq, \geq$.*

Recall that the input procedures E_A, E_B and E_C have as inputs, respectively, the pairs $(x_A, n_A), (x_B, n_B), (x_C, n_C)$, where x_A, x_B, x_C are n-bit strings, and n_A, n_B, n_C are natural numbers. The three encoding procedures use, respectively the graphs G_A, G_B and G_C, which have, respectively, the $(n_A + 1, 1/n^2)$, $(n_B + 1, 1/n^2)$, $n_C + 1, 1/n^2)$ rich owner property. Viewing the strings x_A, x_B, x_C as left nodes in the respective graphs, the encoding procedures pick p_A, p_B, p_C as random neighbours of x_A, x_B, x_C (see Figure 4.2).

We need to show that if n_A, n_B, n_C satisfy the inequalities (4.1), then it is possible to reconstruct (x_A, x_B, x_C) from (p_A, p_B, p_C) with high probability (over the random choice of (p_A, p_B, p_C)). The general idea is to identify computable enumerable subsets B_1, B_2, B_3 of left nodes in the three graphs, which are in the "small regime," and which contain respectively x_A, x_B, x_C

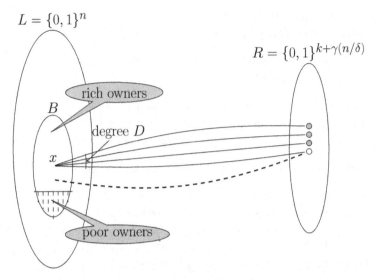

$L = \{0,1\}^n$

$R = \{0,1\}^{k+\gamma(n/\delta)}$

rich owners

B

degree D

x

poor owners

Fig. 4.1 Graph with the (k, δ) rich owner property. If $|B| \leq 2^k$ (small regime), a left node x is a rich owner with respect to B if it owns $(1 - \delta)$ of its neighbours; if $|B| > 2^k$ (large regime), if $(1 - \delta)$ of its neighbours have B-degree close to the average right B-degree. For every $B \subseteq L$, $(1 - \delta)$ fraction of B are rich owners. In the figure, the grey neighbours are owned by x, and the white neighbour is not owned.

as rich owners. Then p_A has x_A as its single neighbour in B_1, and therefore x_A can be obtained from p_A by enumerating the elements of B_1 till we find one that has p_A as a neighbour (x_B, x_C are obtained similarly).

We shall assume first that the decoding procedure D knows the 7-tuple $(C(x_V) \mid V \subseteq \{A, B, C\}, V \neq \emptyset)$, i.e., the complexity profile of (x_A, x_B, x_C).

The proof has an inductive character, so let us begin by analysing the case when there is a single sender, then when there are two senders, and finally when there are three senders.

1 Sender. We show how to reconstruct x_A from p_A, assuming $C(x_A) \leq n_A$. Let

$$B_1 = \{x \in \{0,1\}^n \mid C(x) \leq C(x_A)\}.$$

Since the size of B_1 is bounded by $2^{C(x_A)+1} \leq 2^{n_A+1}$, it follows that B_1 is in the small regime in G_A. The number of poor owners with respect to B_1 in G_A is at most $(1/n^2) \cdot 2^{C(x_A)+1} \approx 2^{C(x_A)-2\log n}$, and it can be shown that any poor owner can be described by $C(x_A) - \Omega(\log n)$ bits (essentially by its rank in some fixed standard ordering of the set of poor owners). Therefore the complexity of a poor owner is strictly less than $C(x_A)$ and thus x_A is a

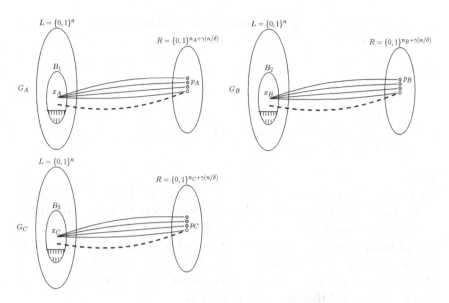

Fig. 4.2   The encoding/decoding procedures. The senders use graphs G_A, G_B, G_C with the rich owner property, and then encode x_A, x_B, x_C by random neighbours p_A, p_B, p_C. The receiver uses B_1, B_2, B_3 in the small regime in the respective graphs, for which x_A, x_B, x_C are rich owners, and reconstructs x_A, x_B, x_C as the unique neighbours of p_A, p_B, p_C in B_1, B_2, B_3.

rich owner with respect to B_1, as needed to enable its reconstruction from p_A.

2 Senders. We show how to reconstruct x_A, x_B from p_A, p_B, assuming $C(x_A \mid x_B) \leq n_A, C(x_B \mid x_A) \leq n_B, C(x_A, x_B) \leq n_A + n_B$.

If $n_A \geq C(x_A)$, then x_A can be reconstructed from p_A as in the *1 Sender* case. Next, since $n_B \geq C(x_B \mid x_A)$, x_B can be reconstructed from x_A and p_B, similar to the *1 Sender* case.

So let us assume that $C(x_A) > n_A$. Let

$$B_2 = \{x \in \{0,1\}^n \mid C(x \mid p_A) \leq C(x_B \mid p_A)\}.$$

We show below that (1) B_2 is in the small regime in G_B, and (2) that it can be effectively enumerated. Since $x_B \in B_2$, and since it is a rich owner with respect to B_2 (by a similar argument with the one used for x_A in the *1 Sender* case), this implies that x_B can be reconstructed from p_A, p_B, and next x_A can be reconstructed from x_B and p_A, as in the *1 Sender* case (because $n_A \geq C(x_A \mid x_B)$).

It remains to prove the assertions (1) and (2) claimed above. We establish the following fact.

Fact 1.

   (a) $C(p_A) =^+ n_A$.
   (b) $C(p_A, x_B) =^+ C(x_A, x_B)$.
   (c) $C(x_B \mid p_A) =^+ C(x_A, x_B) - n_A$.
   (d) $C(x_B \mid p_A) \leq^+ n_B$.

Proof:
(a) By the same argument used above, x_A is still a rich owner with respect to B_1, but B_1 is now in the large regime. This implies that with probability $1 - (1/n^2)$, p_A has, for some constant c, $2^{C(x_A) - n_A + c \log n}$ neighbours in B_1, one of them being x_A. The string x_A can be constructed from p_A and its rank among p_A's neighbours in B_1. This implies $C(x_A) \leq^+ C(p_A) + (C(x_A) - n_A)$, and thus, $C(p_A) \geq^+ n_A$. Since $|p_A| \leq^+ n_A$, it follows that $C(p_A) \leq^+ n_A$, and therefore, $C(p_A) =^+ n_A$.

   (b) The "$\leq^+$" inequality holds because p_A can be obtained from x_A and $O(\log n)$ bits which describe the edge (x_A, p_A) in G_A. For the "$\geq^+$" inequality, let

$$B_1' = \{x \in \{0,1\}^n \mid C(x \mid x_B) \leq C(x_A \mid x_B)\}.$$

B_1' is in the small regime in G_A (because $|B_1'| \leq 2^{C(x_A \mid x_B) + 1} \leq 2^{n_A + 1}$), and x_A is a rich owner with respect to B_1' (because, as we have argued above, poor owners, being few, have complexity conditioned by x_B, less than $C(x_A \mid x_B)$). So, x_A can be constructed from x_B (which is needed for the enumeration of B_1') and p_A, and therefore, $C(x_A, x_B) \leq C(p_A, x_B)$.

   (c) $C(x_B \mid p_A) =^+ C(p_A, x_B) - C(p_A) =^+ C(x_A, x_B) - n_A$, by using the chain rule, and (a) and (b).

   (d) $C(x_B \mid p_A) =^+ C(x_A, x_B) - n_A \leq^+ (n_A + n_B) - n_A = n_B$, by using (c) and the hypothesis.
Now the assertions (1) and (2) follow, because by Fact 1, (d), B_2 is in the small regime, and by Fact 1 (c), the decoding procedure can enumerate B_1 since it knows $C(x_A, x_B)$ and n_A.

   Finally, we move to the case of three senders.

   3 Senders. This is the case stated in Theorem 4.2. We show how to reconstruct x_A, x_B, x_C from p_A, p_B, p_C, if n_A, n_B, n_C satisfy the inequalities (4.1). We can actually assume that $C(x_A) > n_A$, $C(x_B) > n_B$,

$C(x_C) > n_C$, because otherwise, if for example $C(x_A) \leq n_A$, then x_A can be reconstructed from p_A as in the *1 Sender* case, and we have reduced to the case of two senders. As in the *2 Senders* case, it can be shown that $C(p_A) =^+ n_A$, $C(p_B) =^+ n_B$, $C(p_C) =^+ n_C$.

There are two cases to analyse.

Case 1. $C(x_B \mid p_A) \leq n_B$ or $C(x_C \mid p_A) \leq n_C$. Suppose the first relation holds. Then x_B can be reconstructed from p_A, p_B, by taking the small regime set for G_B,

$$B_2' = \{x \in \{0,1\}^n \mid C(x \mid p_A) \leq n_B\},$$

for which x_B is a rich owner, and, therefore, with high probability owns p_B. In this way, we reduce to the *2 Senders* case.

Case 2. $C(x_B \mid p_A) > n_B$ and $C(x_C \mid p_A) > n_C$. We show the following fact.

Fact 2.

(a) $C(x_B \mid x_C, p_A) \leq^+ n_B$ and $C(x_C \mid x_B, p_A) \leq^+ n_C$,
(b) $C(x_B, x_C \mid p_A) \leq^+ n_B + n_C$.

Proof:
(a) First note that $C(x_C, p_A) =^+ C(p_A) + C(x_C \mid p_A) \geq^+ n_A + n_C$. Then

$$\begin{aligned}
C(x_B \mid x_C, p_A) &=^+ C(x_B, x_C, p_A) - C(x_C, p_A) \\
&\leq^+ C(x_A, x_B, x_C) - C(x_C, p_A) \\
&\leq^+ (n_A + n_B + n_C) - (n_A + n_C) = n_B.
\end{aligned}$$

The other relation is shown in the obvious similar way.

(b)

$$\begin{aligned}
C(x_B, x_C \mid p_A) &=^+ C(x_B, x_C, p_A) - C(p_A) \\
&\leq^+ C(x_A, x_B, x_C) - C(p_A) \\
&\leq^+ (n_A + n_B + n_C) - n_A = n_B + n_C.
\end{aligned}$$

Fact 2 shows that, given p_A, the complexity profile of x_B, x_C satisfies the requirements for the *2 Senders* case, and therefore these two strings can be reconstructed from p_A, p_B, p_C. Next, since $n_A \geq C(x_A \mid x_B, x_C)$, x_A can be reconstructed from p_A, x_B, x_C, as in the *1 Sender* case.

Thus, both in Case 1 (which actually consists of two subcases Case 1.1 and Case 1.2) and in Case 2, x_A, x_B, x_C can be reconstructed. There is still a problem: the decoding procedure needs to know which of the cases actually holds true. In the reference [Zim17], it is shown how to determine which case holds true, but here we present a solution that avoids this.

The decoding procedure launches parallel subroutines according to all three possible cases. The subroutine that works in the scenario that is correct produces (x_A, x_B, x_C). The subroutines that work with incorrect scenarios may produce other strings, or may not even halt. How can this troublesome situation be solved? Answer: by hashing. The senders, in addition to p_A, p_B, p_C, use a hash function h, and send $h(x_A), h(x_B), h(x_C)$. The decoding procedure, whenever one of the parallel subroutines outputs a 3-tuple, checks if the hash values of the tuple match $(h(x_A), h(x_B), h(x_C))$, and stops and prints that output the first time there is a match. In this way, the decoding procedure will produce with high probability (x_A, x_B, x_C).

Hashing. For completeness, we present one way of doing the hashing. By the Chinese Remainder Theorem, if u_1 and u_2 are n-bit numbers (in binary notation), then $u_1 \bmod p = u_2 \bmod p$ for at most n prime numbers p. Suppose there are s numbers $u_1, \ldots, u_s$, having length n in binary notation and we want to distinguish the hash value of u_1 from the hash values of $u_2, \ldots, u_s$ with probability $1 - \varepsilon$. Let $t = (1/\varepsilon)sn$ and consider the first t prime numbers $p_1, \ldots, p_t$. Pick i randomly in $\{1, \ldots, t\}$ and define $h(u) = (p_i, u \bmod p_i)$. This *isolates* u_1 from $u_2, \ldots, u_s$, in the sense that, with probability $1 - \varepsilon$, $h(u_1)$ is different from any of $h(u_2), \ldots, h(u_s)$. Note that the length of $h(u)$ is $O(\log n + \log s + \log(1/\varepsilon))$. In our application above, $s = 3$, corresponding to the three parallel subroutines, and ε can be taken to be $1/n^2$, and thus the overhead introduced by hashing is only $O(\log n)$ bits.

Removing the assumption that the decoding procedure knows the inputs' complexity profile. So far, we have assumed that the decoding procedure knows the complexity profile of x_A, x_B, x_C. This assumption is lifted using a hash function h, akin to what we did above to handle the various cases for *3 Senders*. The complexity profile $(C(x_V) \mid V \subseteq \{A, B, C\}, V \neq \emptyset\}$ is a 7-tuple, with all components bounded by $O(n)$. The decoding procedures launches $O(n^7)$ subroutines performing the decoding operation with known complexity profile, one for each possible value of the complexity profile. The subroutine using the correct value of the complexity profile will output (x_A, x_B, x_C) with high probability, while the other ones may produce different 3-tuples, or may not even halt. Using the hash values $h(x_A), h(x_B), h(x_C)$ (transmitted by senders together with p_A, p_B, p_C), the decoder can identify the correct subroutine in the same way as presented above. The overhead introduced by hashing is $O(\log n)$.

4.5 Constructing graphs with the rich owner property

We sketch the construction needed for the *computable* graph in Theorem 4.3. Recall that we use bipartite graphs of the form $G = (L = \{0,1\}^n, R = \{0,1\}^m, E \subseteq L \times R)$, in which every left node has degree $D = 2^d$, and for every $x \in L$, the edges outgoing from x are labeled with strings from $\{0,1\}^d$. The construction relies on randomness extractors, which have been studied extensively in computational complexity and the theory of pseudorandom objects. A graph of the above type is said to be a (k, ε) extractor if for every $B \subseteq L$ of size $|B| \geq 2^k$ and for every $A \subseteq R$,

$$\left| \frac{|E(B, A)|}{|B| \cdot D} - \frac{|A|}{|R|} \right| \leq \varepsilon, \tag{4.2}$$

where $|E(B, A)|$ is the number of edges between vertices in B and vertices in A. In a (k, ε) extractor, any subset B of left nodes of size at least 2^k, "hits" any set A of right nodes like a random function: The fraction of edges that leave B and land in A is close to the density of A among the set of right nodes. It is not hard to show that this implies the rich owner property in the large regime. To handle the small regime, we need graphs that maintain the extractor property when we consider prefixes of right nodes. Given a bipartite graph G as above and $m' \leq m$, the m'-prefix graph G' is obtained from G by merging right nodes that have the same prefix of length m'. More formally, $G' = (L = \{0,1\}^n, R' = \{0,1\}^{m'}, E' \subseteq L \times R')$ and $(x, z') \in E'$ if and only if $(x, z) \in E$ for some extension z of z'. Recall that we allow multiple edges between two nodes, and therefore the merging operation does not decrease the degree of left nodes.

Lemma 4.2. *For every $k \leq n$, and every $\varepsilon > 0$, there exists a constant c and a computable graph $G = (L = \{0,1\}^n, R = \{0,1\}^k, E \subseteq L \times R)$ with left degree $D = cn/\varepsilon^2$ such that for every $k' \leq k$, the k'-prefix graph $G' = (L = \{0,1\}^n, R' = \{0,1\}^{k'}, E' \subseteq L \times R')$ is a (k', ε) extractor.*

Proof:
We show the existence of a graph with the claimed properties using the probabilistic method. Once we know that the graph exists, it can be constructed by exhaustive search. For some constant c that will be fixed later, we consider a random function $f : \{0,1\}^n \times \{0,1\}^d \to \{0,1\}^k$. This defines the bipartite graph $G = (L = \{0,1\}^n, R = \{0,1\}^k, E \subseteq L \times R)$ in the following way: (x, z) is an edge labeled by y if $f(x, y) = z$. For the analysis, let us fix $k' \in \{1, \ldots, k\}$ and let us consider the graph $G' = (L, R', E' \subseteq L \times R')$

that is the k'-prefix of G. Let $K' = 2^{k'}$ and $N = 2^n$. Let us consider $B \subseteq \{0,1\}^n$ of size $|B| \geq K'$, and $A \subseteq R'$. For a fixed $x \in B$ and $y \in \{0,1\}^d$, the probability that the y-labeled edge outgoing from x lands in A is $|A|/|R'|$. By the Chernoff bounds,

$$\text{Prob}\left[\left|\frac{|E'(B,A)|}{|B| \cdot D} - \frac{|A|}{|R'|}\right| > \varepsilon\right] \leq 2^{-\Omega(K' \cdot D \cdot \varepsilon^2)}.$$

The probability that relation (4.2) fails for some $B \subseteq \{0,1\}^{k'}$ of size $|B| \geq K'$ and some $A \subseteq R'$ is bounded by $2^{K'} \cdot \binom{N}{K'} \cdot 2^{-\Omega(K' \cdot D \cdot \varepsilon^2)}$, because A can be chosen in $2^{K'}$ ways, and we can consider that B has size exactly K' and there are $\binom{N}{K'}$ possible choices of such B's. If $D = cn/\varepsilon^2$ and c is sufficiently large, the above probability is less than $(1/4)2^{-k'}$. Therefore the probability that relation (4.2) fails for some k', some B and some A is less than $1/4$. It follows, that there exists a graph that satisfies the hypothesis.

Let $G = (L, R, E \subseteq L \times R)$ be the (k, ε)-extractor from Lemma 4.2. Let $\delta = (2\varepsilon)^{1/2}$. As hinted in our discussion above, by manipulating relation (4.2), we can show that for every $B \subseteq L$ of size $|B| > 2^k$, $(1-\delta)$ fraction of nodes in B are rich owners with respect to B. This proves the rich owner property for sets in the large regime. If B is in the small regime, then B has size $2^{k'}$ for some $k' < k$ (for simplicity, we assume that the size of B is a power of two). Let us consider G', the k'-prefix of G. As above, in G', $(1-\delta)$ fraction of elements x in B are rich owners with respect to B. Recall that this means that if x is a rich owner then $(1 - \delta)$ fraction of its neighbours have B-degree bounded by s, where $s = (2/\delta^2)|B| \cdot D/|R'| = O(n/\varepsilon^3)$. Using the same hashing technique, we can "split" each edge into poly(n/ε) new edges. More precisely, an edge (x, z) in G' is transformed into $\ell = (1/\delta)sn$ new edges, $(p_1, x \bmod p_1, z), \ldots, (p_\ell, x \bmod p_\ell, z)$, where, as above, p_i is the i-th prime number. If x is a rich owner then $(1-2\delta)$ of its "new" neighbours (obtained after splitting) have B-degree equal to one, as desired, because hashing isolates x from the other neighbours of z. The B-degree of these right nodes continues to be one also in G, because when merging nodes to obtain G' from G, the right degrees can only increase. Note that the right nodes in G have as labels the k-bit strings, and after splitting we need to add to the labels the hash values $(p_i, x \bmod p_i)$, which are of length $O(\log n/\varepsilon)$, and this is the cause for the $O(\log n/\delta)$ overhead in Theorem 4.3.

The *explicit* graph in Theorem 4.3 is obtained in the same way, except that instead of the "prefix" extractor from Lemma 4.2 we use the Raz-Reingold-Vadhan extractor [RRV99].

4.6 Note

This paper is dedicated to the memory of Professor Solomon Marcus. In the 1978 freshman Real Analysis class at the University of Bucharest, he asked several questions (on functions having pathological properties regarding finite variation). This has been my first contact with him, and, not coincidentally, also the first time I became engaged in a type of activity that resembled mathematical research. Over the years, we had several discussions, on scientific but also on rather mundane issues, and each time, without exception, I was stunned by his encyclopaedic knowledge on diverse topics, including of course various fields of mathematics, but also literature, social sciences, philosophy, and whatnot.

> The utilitarian function of mathematics is in most cases a consequence of its cognitive function, but the temporal distance between the cognitive moment and the utilitarian one is usually imprevisible.

Solomon Marcus

References

[BZ14]   Bruno Bauwens and Marius Zimand. Linear list-approximation for short programs (or the power of a few random bits). In *IEEE 29th Conference on Computational Complexity, CCC 2014, Vancouver, BC, Canada, June 11–13, 2014*, pages 241–247. IEEE, 2014.

[Cha66]   G. Chaitin. On the length of programs for computing finite binary sequences. *Journal of the ACM*, 13:547–569, 1966.

[Cov75]   Thomas M. Cover. A proof of the data compression theorem of Slepian and Wolf for ergodic sources (corresp.). *IEEE Transactions on Information Theory*, 21(2):226–228, 1975.

[CRVW02]   M. R. Capalbo, O. Reingold, S. P. Vadhan, and A. Wigderson. Randomness conductors and constant-degree lossless expanders. In John H. Reif, editor, *STOC*, pages 659–668. ACM, 2002.

[DW85]   G. Dueck and L. Wolters. The Slepian-Wolf theorem for individual sequences. *Problems of Control and Information Theory*, 14:437–450, 1985.

[Kol65]   A.N. Kolmogorov. Three approaches to the quantitative definition of information. *Problems Inform. Transmission*, 1(1):1–7, 1965.

[Kuz09]   S. Kuzuoka. Slepian-Wolf coding of individual sequences based on ensembles of linear functions. *IEICE Trans. Fundamentals*, E92-A(10):2393–2401, 2009.

[LZ76]   A. Lempel and J. Ziv. On the complexity of finite sequences. *IEEE Trans. Inf. Theory*, IT-22:75–81, 1976.

[Muc02]   Andrei A. Muchnik. Conditional complexity and codes. *Theor. Comput. Sci.*, 271(1-2):97–109, 2002.

[Rom05]   A. Romashchenko. Complexity interpretation for the fork network coding. *Information Processes*, 5(1):20–28, 2005. In Russian. Available in English as [Rom16].

[Rom16]   Andrei Romashchenko. Coding in the fork network in the framework of Kolmogorov complexity. *CoRR*, abs/1602.02648, 2016.

[RR99]   Ran Raz and Omer Reingold. On recycling the randomness of states in space bounded computation. In Jeffrey Scott Vitter, Lawrence L. Larmore, and Frank Thomson Leighton, editors, *STOC*, pages 159–168. ACM, 1999.

[RRV99]   R. Raz, O. Reingold, and S. Vadhan. Extracting all the randomness and reducing the error in Trevisan's extractor. In *Proceedings of the 30th ACM Symposium on Theory of Computing*, pages 149–158. ACM Press, May 1999.

[Sol64]   R. Solomonoff. A formal theory of inductive inference. *Information and Control*, 7:224–254, 1964.

[SW73]   D. Slepian and J.K. Wolf. Noiseless coding of correlated information sources. *IEEE Transactions on Information Theory*, 19(4):471–480, 1973.

[WZ94]   A.D. Wyner and J. Ziv. The sliding window Lempel-Ziv is asymptotically optimal. *Proc. IEEE*, 2(6):872–877, 1994.

[Zim17]   M. Zimand. Kolmogorov complexity version of Slepian-Wolf coding. In *STOC 2017*, pages 22–32. ACM, June 2017.

[Ziv78]   J. Ziv. Coding theorems for individual sequences. *IEEE Trans. Inform. Theory*, IT-24:405–412, 1978.

[Ziv84]   J. Ziv. Fixed-rate encoding of individual sequences with side information. *IEEE Trans. Inform. Theory*, IT-30:348–352–412, 1984.

PART 2

Integrals, Operators, AF Algebras, Proof Mining and Monotone Nonexpansive Mappings

Chapter 5

Monotonically Controlled Integrals

Thomas Ball[a] and David Preiss[b]
[a]Granary Wharf House
2 Canal Wharf, Leeds, United Kingdom, LS11 5PS
thomas.ball@lhasalimited.org
[b]Mathematics Institute, University of Warwick
Coventry CV4 7AL, United Kingdom
d.preiss@warwick.ac.uk

Abstract. The monotonically controlled integral defined by Bendová and Malý, which is equivalent to the Denjoy-Perron integral, admits a natural parameter $\alpha > 0$ thereby leading to the whole scale of integrals called α-monotonically controlled integrals. While the power of these integrals is easily seen to increase with increasing α, our main results show that their exact dependence on α is rather curious. For $\alpha < 1$ they do not even contain the Lebesgue integral, for $1 \leq \alpha \leq 2$ they coincide with the Denjoy-Perron integral, and for $\alpha > 2$ they are mutually different and not even contained in the Denjoy-Khintchine integral.

5.1 Introduction

The monotonically controlled integral, or (MC) integral, defined by Hana Bendová and Jan Malý in [1], is an interesting variant of nowadays rather abundant equivalent definitions of the Denjoy-Perron integral. It is defined as follows.

Definition 5.1. Let $I \subset \mathbb{R}$ be an open interval and $f, F : I \to \mathbb{R}$ be

The research leading to these results has received funding from the European Research Council under the European Union's Seventh Framework Programme (FP/2007-2013) / ERC Grant Agreement n.2011-ADG-20110209.

functions. We say that f is an (MC) *derivative* (monotonically controlled derivative) of F on I, or that F is an *indefinite* (MC) *integral* of f on I, if there exists a strictly increasing function $\varphi : I \to \mathbb{R}$ (which is called *control function* for the pair (F, f)) such that for each $x \in I$,

$$\lim_{y \to x} \frac{F(y) - F(x) - f(x)(y - x)}{\varphi(y) - \varphi(x)} = 0. \tag{5.1}$$

As Jan Malý pointed out, this definition invites introduction of a natural parameter thereby leading to the whole scale of α-monotonically controlled integrals, or (MC$_\alpha$) integrals, where $\alpha > 0$ is a parameter.

Definition 5.2. Let $I \subset \mathbb{R}$ be an open interval, $f, F : I \to \mathbb{R}$ be functions and $\alpha > 0$. We say that f is an (MC$_\alpha$) *derivative* of F on I, or that F is an *indefinite* (MC$_\alpha$) *integral* of f on I, if there exists a strictly increasing function $\varphi : I \to \mathbb{R}$ (which we call the α-control function for the pair (F, f)) such that for each $x \in I$,

$$\lim_{y \to x} \frac{F(y) - F(x) - f(x)(y - x)}{\varphi(x + \alpha(y - x)) - \varphi(x)} = 0.$$

The original (MC) integral is obtained for $\alpha = 1$ and, since (MC$_\alpha$) integrability implies (MC$_\beta$) integrability for $\beta > \alpha$, one of a number of natural questions, asked by Malý, is whether for $\alpha > 1$ the (MC$_\alpha$) integral is still equivalent to the Denjoy-Perron integral. Here we show that this is not the case, but that the situation is rather interesting: while for $\alpha \in [1, 2]$ the (MC$_\alpha$) integral is equivalent to the Denjoy-Perron (and so (MC)) integral, for $\alpha > 2$ the (MC$_\alpha$) integrals are mutually different and even are not contained in the Denjoy-Khintchine integral. Although the case $\alpha < 1$ is perhaps less interesting, we at least show that these integrals do not contain the Lebesgue integral. More precisely, our main results imply the following

Theorem 5.1. *On any open interval $I \subset \mathbb{R}$,*

(i) *There is a Lebesgue integrable function that is not (MC$_\alpha$) integrable for any $0 < \alpha < 1$.*

(ii) *For $1 \le \alpha \le 2$, the (MC$_\alpha$) integral coincides with the Denjoy-Perron integral.*

(iii) *For any $\alpha \ge 2$ there is a function which is not (MC$_\alpha$) integrable but is (MC$_\beta$) integrable for every $\beta > \alpha$.*

(iv) *There is a function that is (MC$_\alpha$) integrable for every $\alpha > 2$, but is not Denjoy-Khintchine integrable.*

In connection with (i) and (iv), standard examples show that there is a function that is (MC_α) integrable for any $\alpha < 1$ but not Lebesgue integrable, and a function that is (MC_α) integrable for any $\alpha > 2$ but not Denjoy-Khintchine integrable.

Theorem 5.1, sometimes in a stronger or more precise form, will be proved in the last part of this paper: (i) in Theorem 5.3, (ii) in Theorem 5.5, (iii) in Theorem 5.6, and (iv) in Theorem 5.7.

Before coming to the above results, we show in Section 5.2 some basic properties of these integrals, especially that the notion is reasonable, namely that two indefinite integrals of the same function differ by a constant. However we do not develop more advanced theory of these integrals.

The main results are stated and proved in Section 5.3. We first remind ourself with the notions used to give equivalent definitions of the Lebesgue, Denjoy-Perron and Denjoy-Khintchine integrals that we use to compare them with the (MC_α) integral. In addition to results stated in Theorem 5.1 we also show that bounded measurable functions are (MC_α) integrable for every $\alpha > 0$ and that every function that is (MC_α) integrable for some $\alpha > 0$ is Lebesgue integrable on some subinterval. In connection with the statement (ii) of Theorem 5.1 we reprove the result of Bendová and Malý [1] that the (MC) integral is equivalent to the Denjoy-Perron integral by showing directly its equivalence with Perron's original definition [6]. The argument in [1] is based on the definition of the Kurzweil-Henstock integral [4,5], which is known to be equivalent to the Denjoy-Perron integral. However, we should point out that our approach is close to Kurzweil's proof of equivalence of his integral (which later became the Kurzweil-Henstock integral) to the Perron integral. The closeness of the definition of the (MC) integral to Perron's definition is perhaps surprising, since [1] quotes as the intermediate step to their definition the variational integral of [3] which arose from Henstock's approach [4].

In this area, it is no wonder that most of our references are to the still best text on much of classical real analysis, *Theory of the Integral* by Stanisław Saks. As this book numbers paragraphs and results in each chapter separately, we will refer, for example, to VII(§5) for paragraph 5 in Chapter 7, or to Theorem VI(7.2) for Theorem (7.2) in Chapter 6.

As in [1], although this makes little difference, we are interested in indefinite integrals rather than in definite ones. In particular, by saying that a function is *integrable* we mean that it has an indefinite integral. Finally, we mention that we will use the terms *positive* for ≥ 0, *strictly positive* for > 0, and similarly *increasing* and *strictly increasing*.

5.2   Basic properties of (MC_α) integrals

We begin by remarking that it is immediate to see that if φ is an α-control function for (F, f), $c > 0$ and ψ is increasing, then $c\varphi + \psi$ is also an α-control function for (F, f). It follows that, if φ is an α-control function for (F, f), ψ is an α-control function for (G, g) and $a, b \in \mathbb{R}$, then $\varphi + \psi$ is a control function for $(aF + bG, af + bg)$. In other words, the (MC_α) integral is linear: If F and G are indefinite (MC_α) integrals of f and g, respectively, and $a, b \in \mathbb{R}$, then $aF + bG$ is an indefinite (MC_α) integral of $af + bg$.

Some simple basic properties of indefinite (MC_α) integrals are collected in the following statement.

Proposition 5.1. *Suppose $\alpha > 0$ and F is an indefinite (MC_α) integral of f on (a, b). Then*

  (i) *F is continuous on (a, b);*
  (ii) *F is an indefinite (MC_β) integral of f on (a, b) for every $\alpha > \beta$;*
  (iii) *$F'(x) = f(x)$ for almost every $x \in (a, b)$.*

Proof:
Let φ be an α-control function for the pair (F, f). Since φ is bounded on a neighbourhood of x, taking limit as $y \to 0$ in

$$F(y) = F(x) + f(x)(y - x)$$
$$+ \frac{F(y) - F(x) - f(x)(y - x)}{\varphi(x + \alpha(y - x)) - \varphi(x)}(\varphi(x + \alpha(y - x)) - \varphi(x))$$

gives

$$\lim_{y \to x} F(y) = F(x).$$

The second statement follows immediately from

$$\varphi(x + \alpha(y - x)) - \varphi(x) \le \varphi(x + \beta(y - x)) - \varphi(x).$$

For the third statement we observe that for every x at which φ is differentiable,

$$\lim_{y \to x} \frac{F(y) - F(x) - f(x)(y - x)}{y - x}$$
$$= \alpha \lim_{y \to x} \frac{F(y) - F(x) - f(x)(y - x)}{\varphi(x + \alpha(y - x)) - \varphi(x)} \lim_{y \to x} \frac{\varphi(x + \alpha(y - x)) - \varphi(x)}{\alpha(y - x)} = 0.$$

Since φ is differentiable almost everywhere, (iii) follows.

Proposition 5.2. *Suppose $F : (a, b) \to \mathbb{R}$ satisfies*

(i) $\limsup_{y \nearrow x} F(y) \leq F(x) \leq \limsup_{y \searrow x} F(y)$ *for every $x \in (a, b)$;*

(ii) *there are a strictly increasing $\varphi : (a, b) \to \mathbb{R}$ and $\alpha > 0$ such that for every $x \in (a, b)$ except at most countably many,*

$$\liminf_{h \searrow 0} \frac{F(x + h) - F(x)}{\varphi(x + \alpha h) - \varphi(x)} \geq 0. \tag{5.2}$$

Then F is increasing on (a, b).

Proof:

Fix $\tau > 0$ and notice that, since φ is increasing, $F_\tau := F + \tau \varphi$ also satisfies (i). We show that for every $x \in (a, b)$ at which (5.2) holds

$$\limsup_{h \searrow 0} \frac{F_\tau(x + h) - F_\tau(x)}{h} \geq 0. \tag{5.3}$$

Then [7, Theorem VI(7.2)] says that F_τ is increasing and the statement will follow by taking the limit as $\tau \to 0$.

Fix $x \in (a, b)$ at which (5.2) holds. Suppose first that there is a sequence $h_k \searrow 0$ such that

$$L := \lim_{k \to \infty} \frac{\varphi(x + \alpha h_k) - \varphi(x)}{h_k}$$

exists and is finite. Since the limit defining L consists of positive terms,

$$\limsup_{h \searrow 0} \frac{F_\tau(x + h) - F_\tau(x)}{h} \geq L \liminf_{k \to \infty} \frac{F(x + h_k) - F(x)}{\varphi(x + \alpha h_k) - \varphi(x)} \geq 0.$$

Suppose next that there is no L as above or, in other words, that φ has infinite right derivative at x. Let

$$u_k := \sup\{h \in [0, \delta] : \varphi(x + h) \geq \varphi(x) + kh\}.$$

Using that φ has infinite right derivative at x and is bounded by $\varphi(x + \delta)$, we see that $0 < u_k \leq (\varphi(x + \delta) - \varphi(x))/k$. Since φ is increasing, the definition of u_k implies $\varphi(x + u_k) \geq \varphi(x) + ku_k$. For sufficiently large k we have $\alpha u_k \in [0, \delta]$ and $\alpha u_k > u_k$, hence

$$\varphi(x + \alpha u_k) - \varphi(x) \leq k\alpha u_k \leq (\varphi(x + u_k) - \varphi(x))/\alpha$$

for large enough k. Passing to a subsequence of u_k, which we will denote h_k, we have $h_k \searrow 0$ and

$$L := \lim_{k \to \infty} \frac{\varphi(x + \alpha h_k) - \varphi(x)}{\varphi(x + h_k) - \varphi(x)}$$

exists and is finite. Hence

$$\limsup_{h \searrow 0} \frac{F_\tau(x+h) - F_\tau(x)}{\varphi(x+h) - \varphi(x)} \geq \tau + L \liminf_{k \to \infty} \frac{F(x+h_k) - F(x)}{\varphi(x+\alpha h_k) - \varphi(x)} \geq \tau > 0.$$

Consequently, in this case there are also arbitrarily small $h > 0$ such that $F_\tau(x+h) - F_\tau(x) > 0$, and so (5.3) holds as well. Hence (5.3) holds in both cases, and the proof is finished.

In order to see the connection with the monotonicity result of [7, Theorem VI(7.2)] on which its proof based, Proposition 5.2 is stated in considerably greater generality than we need to prove the following Theorem. However, we did not attempt to find its strongest version. For example, our proof would allow the φ to depend on x, and, rather obviously, one may replace the lim inf in (ii) by lim sup for $\alpha \leq 1$.

Theorem 5.2. *Suppose F is an indefinite (MC_α) integral of $f \geq 0$ on (a, b). Then F is increasing on (a, b).*

Proof:
This is immediate from Proposition 5.2, since its assumption (i) holds by continuity of F and (ii) holds with the α-control function for the pair (F, f) by the definition of the (MC_α) integral.

Corollary 5.1. *For any $\alpha > 0$, an indefinite (MC_α) integral of a function on an interval is unique up to an additive constant.*

Proof:
If F, G are two indefinite (MC_α) integrals of F, by linearity both $F - G$ and $G - F$ are indefinite (MC_α) integrals of zero. Hence $F - G$ and $G - F$ are both increasing by Theorem 5.2, showing that they differ by a constant.

5.3 Relations between the (MC_α), Lebesgue, Denjoy-Perron and Denjoy-Khintchine integrals

We begin by recalling notions related to the definitions or properties of the Lebesgue, Denjoy-Perron and Denjoy-Khintchine integrals that we use in our arguments. They all come from [7], where much more material on these integrals and notions may be found.

Definition 5.3. A real-valued function F defined on a set $E \subset \mathbb{R}$ is said to be

- of bounded variation (VB) on E if there is a constant $v \in [0, \infty)$ such that $\sum_i |F(b_i) - F(a_i)| \leq v$ for every sequence of non-overlapping intervals whose end-points belong to E,
- absolutely continuous (AC) on E if for every $\varepsilon > 0$ there is $\delta > 0$ such that for every sequence of non-overlapping intervals whose end-points belong to the set E, the inequality $\sum_i (b_i - a_i) < \delta$ implies $\sum_i |F(b_i) - F(a_i)| < \varepsilon$,
- generalized absolutely continuous (ACG) on E if it is continuous on E and E is the union of countably many sets on which F is absolutely continuous.

For the next definition we recall that the oscillation of a function F on a set is

$$\operatorname{osc}(F, E) := \sup_{x,y \in E} |F(x) - F(y)|.$$

Definition 5.4. Assuming in Definition 5.3 that F is defined on an interval containing E, and replacing $\sum_i |F(b_i) - F(a_i)|$ by $\sum_i \operatorname{osc}(F, [a_i, b_i])$ we obtain the notion of functions

- of bounded variation in the restricted sense (VB$_*$) on E,
- absolutely continuous in the restricted sense (AC$_*$) on E,
- generalized absolutely continuous in the restricted sense (ACG$_*$) on E,

respectively.

Although we do not need it, we point out the important results that ACG$_*$ functions are differentiable almost everywhere and ACG functions are approximately differentiable almost everywhere. For the definition of approximate derivative see [7, VII($\S$3)]; here we just need to know that if an ordinary derivative $F'(x)$ exists, then so does the approximate derivative $F'_{\mathrm{ap}}(x)$ and $F'_{\mathrm{ap}}(x) = F'(x)$.

Finally, we collect so called descriptive definitions of the three integrals that we use. Again, [7] is a reference for (often deep) proofs of equivalence to more usual definitions.

Fact 3. Suppose F and f are real-valued functions on $(a, b) \subset \mathbb{R}$.

- F is an indefinite Lebesgue integral of f on (a, b) if it is AC (or equivalently AC$_*$) on (a, b) and $F'(x) = f(x)$ for almost all $x \in (a, b)$,
- F is an indefinite Denjoy-Perron integral of f on (a, b) if it is ACG$_*$ on (a, b) and $F'(x) = f(x)$ for almost all $x \in (a, b)$,
- F is an indefinite Denjoy-Khintchine integral of f on (a, b) if it is ACG on (a, b) and $F'_{\mathrm{ap}}(x) = f(x)$ for almost all $x \in (a, b)$.

5.3.1 *Relations between Lebesgue and* (MC$_\alpha$) *integrals*

From Proposition 5.1 and the coincidence of the (MC) and Denjoy-Perron integral we know that (MC$_\alpha$) and Lebesgue integrals agree provided that they both exist. Here we show that in general the "both" cannot be replaced by existence of just one of them. In our first result we observe that the functions providing an example cannot be bounded.

Proposition 5.3. *Every measurable function that is locally bounded on (a, b) has an indefinite* (MC$_\alpha$) *integral on (a, b) for every $\alpha > 0$.*

Proof:
Let F be an indefinite Lebesgue integral of a bounded measurable function f on (a, b). Let $M := \{x : F'(x) = f(x)\}$ and $N = (a, b) \setminus M$. Since N has Lebesgue measure zero, there are open sets $(a, b) \supset G_k \supset N$ such that $|G_k| < 4^{-k}$. Define $\varphi_k(x) := 2^k |(a, x) \cap G_k|$ and $\varphi(x) := x + \sum_{k=1}^{\infty} \varphi_k(x)$. Clearly, φ is an increasing function on (a, b). We fix $\alpha > 0$ and show that φ is an α-control function for the pair (F, f).

If $x \in M$, (5.1) follows immediately from $F'(x) = f(x)$, since then

$$\limsup_{y \to x} \frac{|F(y) - F(x) - f(x)(y - x)|}{|\varphi(x + \alpha(y - x)) - \varphi(x)|}$$
$$\leq \lim_{y \to x} \frac{|F(y) - F(x) - f(x)(y - x)|}{\alpha|y - x|} = 0.$$

If $x \in N$, choose $c \in (0, \infty)$ such that $|f| \leq c$ on a neighbourhood of x. Then $|F(y) - F(x) - f(x)(y - x)| \leq 2c|y - x|$ and, given any $k \in \mathbb{N}$, we see that

$$\varphi(x + \alpha(y - x)) - \varphi(x) = 2^k \alpha(y - x)$$

for y close enough to x. Hence

$$\limsup_{y \to x} \frac{|F(y) - F(x) - f(x)(y - x)|}{|\varphi(y) - \varphi(x)|} \leq \lim_{y \to x} \frac{2c|y - x|}{2^k|y - x|} = 2^{-k-1}c.$$

Since k can be arbitrarily large, (5.1) follows.

The first part of the above proof also shows that, if $F'(x) = f(x)$ at every point $x \in (a, b)$, F is an indefinite (MC$_\alpha$) integral of f. Together with well known examples of non-absolutely integrable derivatives we get examples of functions that are (MC$_\alpha$) integrable for every $\alpha > 0$ but not Lebesgue integrable. For completeness, we record this in the following observation.

Observation 5.1. If F is everywhere differentiable on (a, b), then it is an indefinite (MC$_\alpha$) integral of F' for every $\alpha > 0$. Hence there are functions that are (MC$_\alpha$) integrable for every $\alpha > 0$ but not Lebesgue integrable.

The following Lemma provides the main building block in definition of a function that is Lebesgue but not (MC_α) integrable for any $0 < \alpha < 1$.

Lemma 5.1. *For any interval $J \subset \mathbb{R}$ and $0 < \varepsilon, \tau < 1$ there is a measurable function $f : \mathbb{R} \to [0, \infty)$ such that*

(i) $\int_{-\infty}^{\infty} f(x)\, dx \le \varepsilon$;

(ii) *there is a finite collection of intervals $[a_i, b_i] \subset J$ such that the intervals $[a_i, a_i + \tau(b_i - a_i)]$ are mutually disjoint and $\sum_i \int_{a_i}^{b_i} f(x)\, dx > 1/\varepsilon$.*

Proof:

We choose $\sigma \in (\tau, 1)$, an interval $[a, b] \subset J$ and $m \in \mathbb{N}$ such that $m > 1/\varepsilon^2$. For $i = 0, 1, \ldots, m$ we recursively define $a_0 := a$ and $a_i := a_{i-1} + \sigma(b - a_i)$ and notice that $a = a_0 < a_1 < \cdots < a_m < b$. Let

$$f(x) := \begin{cases} \varepsilon/(b - a_m) & x \in [a_m, b] \\ 0 & x \notin [a_m, b] \end{cases}.$$

Then (i) holds since $\int_{-\infty}^{\infty} f(x)\, dx = \varepsilon$ and to satisfy (ii) we may take the intervals $[a_i, b_i] := [a_i, b]$, $i = 0, \ldots, m - 1$. Indeed, with this choice we have $\sum_i \int_{a_i}^{b_i} f(x)\, dx = m\varepsilon > 1/\varepsilon$ and $a_i + \tau(b_i - a_i) < a_i + \sigma(b_i - a_i) = a_{i+1}$ which shows that the intervals $[a_i, a_i + \tau(b_i - a_i)]$ are mutually disjoint.

Theorem 5.3. *There is a Lebesgue integrable function $f : \mathbb{R} \to [0, \infty)$ that is, for any $0 < \alpha < 1$, not (MC_α) integrable on any interval $I \subset \mathbb{R}$.*

Proof:

Let r_k be an enumeration of all rational numbers, $\varepsilon_k := 2^{-k}$ and $\tau_k := 1 - 2^{-k}$. Obtain f_k from Lemma 5.1 used with these ε_k, τ_k and $I_k = (r_k - \varepsilon_k, r_k + \varepsilon_k)$. Since the function $\sum_{k=1}^{\infty} f_k$ is Lebesgue integrable, it is finite almost everywhere. Hence the set

$$N := \{x \in \mathbb{R} : \textstyle\sum_{k=1}^{\infty} f_k(x) = \infty\} \cup \{r_k : k = 1, 2, \ldots\}$$

is Lebesgue null. Choose a G_δ Lebesgue null set G containing N and define

$$f(x) := \begin{cases} \sum_{k=1}^{\infty} f_k(x) & x \notin G, \\ 0 & x \in G. \end{cases}$$

Then $f : \mathbb{R} \to [0, \infty)$ is Lebesgue integrable; let F be its indefinite Lebesgue integral.

Suppose $0 < \alpha < 1$ and f is (MC_α) integrable on some interval I. By Proposition 5.1, f is an (MC_α) derivative of F. Let φ be an α-control function for (F, f). For each $x \in N$ find $\delta_x > 0$ such that

$$|F(x + h) - F(x)| \le \varphi(x + \alpha h) - \varphi(x)$$

whenever $0 < h < \delta_x$.

Let $N_l := \{x \in G : \delta_x > 2^{-l}\}$ and infer from the Baire Category Theorem that there are $l \in \mathbb{N}$ and an interval $J = (u, v) \subset I$ such that $N_l \cap J$ is dense in J. Since $\varepsilon_k \to 0$ and $\tau_k \to 1$, the inequalities $\alpha < \tau_k$ and $\varphi(u) - \varphi(v) < 1/\varepsilon_k$ hold for all sufficiently large k. Using also that J contains $[r_k - \varepsilon_k, r_k + \varepsilon_k]$ for infinitely many k, we find $k > l$ such that $\alpha < \tau_k$, $\varphi(u) - \varphi(v) < 1/\varepsilon_k = 2^k$ and $[a, b] := [r_k - \varepsilon_k, r_k + \varepsilon_k] \subset J$.

Recalling that f_k has been found by using Lemma 5.1, we infer from its statement (ii) that there is a finite collection of intervals $[a_i, b_i] \subset (a, b)$ such that the intervals $[a_i, a_i + \tau_k(b_i - a_i)]$ are mutually disjoint and $\sum \int_{a_i}^{b_i} f_k(x)\, dx > 1/\varepsilon_k = 2^k$. Since $N_l \cap (a, b)$ is dense in (a, b) and $\alpha < \tau_k$, there are $x_i \in (a, b)$, $x_i \leq a_i$ close enough to a_i such that the intervals $[x_i, x_i + \alpha(b_i - x_i)]$ are also mutually disjoint. Recalling that $k > l$, we see that $b_i - x_i \leq 2\varepsilon_k \leq 2^{-l}$, so $\delta_{x_i} > 2^{-l} \geq b_i - x_i$ and the definition of δ_{x_i} implies

$$\varphi(x_i + \alpha(b_i - a_i)) - \varphi(x_j) \geq F(b_i) - F(x_i).$$

Since φ is increasing and $[x_i, x_i + \alpha(b_i - x_i)]$ are mutually disjoint subintervals of (u, v), we get

$$2^k > \varphi(v) - \varphi(u) \geq \sum_i (\varphi(x_i + \alpha(b_i - a_i)) - \varphi(x_j))$$

$$\geq \sum_i (F(b_i) - F(x_i))$$

$$\geq \sum_i \int_{x_i}^{b_i} f_k(x)\, dx > \sum_i \int_{a_i}^{b_i} f_k(x)\, dx > 2^k,$$

which is the desired contradiction.

The final result of this section may seem to be a good start for showing the equivalence of Denjoy-Perron and (MC_α) integrals for any $\alpha \geq 1$ by the methods stemming from Denjoy's original definition [2] of his integral. These methods have been used, for example, to show equivalence of the Denjoy and Perron integrals (see the proof of the Theorem of Hake-Alexandroff-Looman at [7, VIII(§3)]). However, the use of this idea to show equivalence of the (MC_α) and Denjoy-Perron integrals would need a similar statement with I replaced by any closed subset of I. This turned out to be possible when $1 \leq \alpha \leq 2$, and will lead us to the proof of Theorem 5.5, but for $\alpha > 2$ we actually used this information to guess how the counterexamples required in Theorem 5.1(iii) and (iv) may look like.

Proposition 5.4. *If, for some $\alpha > 0$, F is an indefinite (MC_α) integral of f on an interval I, there is a dense open subset G of I such that F*

is absolutely continuous on every component of G. Consequently, F is an indefinite Lebesgue integral of f on every component of G.

Proof:

It suffices to show that there is an interval $J \subset I$ on which F has bounded variation. Indeed, since $f = F'$ a.e., we infer from [7, Lemma IV(7.4)] that f is Lebesgue integrable on (a, b) and from Theorem 5.4 that F is an indefinite Lebesgue integral of f on J. The required set G is then obtained by a repeated use of this for suitable subintervals of I.

Let φ be an α-control function for (F, f) and for every $x \in I$ choose $\delta_x > 0$ such that $|F(y) - F(x) - f(x)(y - x)| \le |\varphi(x + \alpha(y - x)) - \varphi(x)|$ when $|y - x| \le \delta_x$. Let $Q_k := \{x \in I : |f(x)| \le k, \delta_x > 1/k\}$. Then $Q = \bigcup_{k=1}^{\infty} Q_k$, and hence by the Baire Category Theorem there is an open interval $(a, b) \subset I$ such that $Q_k \cap (a, b)$ is dense in (a, b). We diminish (a, b), if necessary, so that $b - a < 1/k$ and show

$$|F(y) - F(x)| \le |\gamma(y) - \gamma(x)| \text{ for } x, y \in (a, b), \qquad (5.4)$$

where $\gamma(x) = 2n(\varphi(x) + kx)$ and $n \in \mathbb{N}$ is the least integer greater than 3α.

To prove (5.4), suppose that $x, y \in (a, b)$, $x < y$ and $\varepsilon > 0$, and find $0 < \delta < (y - x)/6(1 + \alpha)$ such that $|F(u) - F(v)| < \varepsilon/2$ when $v = x, y$ and $|u - v| < \delta$. Use that Q_k is dense in (x, y) to find $x < x_0 < x_1 < \cdots < x_{2n} < y$ such that $x_i \in Q_k$ and $|x_i - (x + i(y - x)/2n)| < \delta$. If $1 \le i \le n$, we have

$$x_{i-1} + \alpha(x_i - x_{i-1}) < x + (i-1)(y - x)/2n + \delta + \alpha((y - x)/2n + \delta)$$
$$< x + (y - x)/2 + (y - x)/6 + (y - x)/6 + (y - x)/6$$
$$= y.$$

Since $x_{i-1} \in Q_k$ and $x_i - x_{i-1} < 1/k < \delta_{x_i}$, this and monotonicity of φ imply

$$|F(x_i) - F(x_{i-1})| \le \varphi(x_{i-1} + \alpha(x_i - x_{i-1})) - \varphi(x_{i-1}) + k(x_i - x_{i-1})$$
$$\le \varphi(y) - \varphi(x) + k(y - x)$$
$$\le (\gamma(y) - \gamma(x))/2n.$$

If $n < i \le 2n$, we similarly have $x_i - \alpha(x_i - x_{i-1}) \ge x$, and hence

$$|F(x_i) - F(x_{i-1})| \le |\varphi(x_i - \alpha(x_i - x_{i-1})) - \varphi(x_i)| + k(x_i - x_{i-1})$$
$$\le (\gamma(y) - \gamma(x))/2n.$$

Summing these inequalities gives $|F(x_{2n}) - F(x_0)| \leq \gamma(y) - \gamma(x)$, from which we infer

$$|F(y) - F(x)| \leq |F(x_{2n}) - F(x_0)| + |F(x_{2n}) - F(y)| + |F(x) - F(x_0)|$$
$$\leq \gamma(y) - \gamma(x) + 2\varepsilon$$

and, since $\varepsilon > 0$ is arbitrary, $|F(y) - F(x)| \leq |\gamma(y) - \gamma(x)|$.

Having thus finished the proof of (5.4), we use it together with the monotonicity of φ to infer that

$$\sum_i |F(u_i) - F(v_i)| \leq \sum_i (\gamma(v_i) - \gamma(u_i)) \leq \gamma(b) - \gamma(a)$$

for any mutually disjoint intervals (u_i, v_i) with end-points in (a, b). Consequently, F has bounded variation on (a, b), which, as explained at the beginning of this proof, implies the statement of the Proposition.

5.3.2 *Coincidence of* (MC) *and Denjoy-Perron integrals*

The coincidence the (MC) and Denjoy-Perron integrals, and so of the (MC_α) and Denjoy-Perron integrals when $\alpha = 1$ was proved in [1, Theorem 3] by Bendová and Malý. In their proof they used modern definitions of the Denjoy-Perron integral. Here we point out that it can be proved directly by using Perron's original definition of the Denjoy-Perron integral. For this, we first briefly recapitulate the definition of the indefinite Perron integral. Full information may be found in [7, VI(§6) and VIII(§3)].

Definition 5.5. Let f, F be functions defined on an open interval I. Then F is said to be an indefinite Perron integral of F on I if for every $\varepsilon > 0$ and a compact interval $J \subset I$ there are function $U, V : I \to \mathbb{R}$ such that

- $\underline{D}U(x) \geq f(x) \geq \overline{D}V(x)$ for every $x \in I$ and
- $|U(x) - F(x)| + |V(x) - F(x)| < \varepsilon$ for every $x \in J$.

Here

$$\underline{D}U(x) := \liminf_{y \to x} \frac{F(y) - F(x)}{y - x} \text{ and } \overline{D}U(x) := \limsup_{y \to x} \frac{F(y) - F(x)}{y - x}.$$

Theorem 5.4 (Bendová and Malý). *F is an indefinite* (MC) *integral of f on I if and only it is its indefinite Perron integral on I.*

Proof:
Write $I = \bigcup_{k=1}^{\infty} J_k$ where $J_k = [a_k, b_k]$ form an increasing sequence of compact intervals.

Let F be an indefinite (MC) integral of f on I and φ be a control function for (F, f). Given $\varepsilon > 0$, we let $U_\varepsilon := F + \varepsilon\varphi$ and $V_\varepsilon := F - \varepsilon\varphi$. For every $x \in I$ there is $\delta > 0$ such that $|y - x| < \delta$ implies

$$|F(y) - F(x) - f(x)(y - x)| \le \varepsilon|\varphi(y) - \varphi(x)|.$$

Rearranging this inequality gives $(U_\varepsilon(y) - U_\varepsilon(x))/(y - x) \ge f(x)$, which gives $\underline{D}U_\varepsilon(x) \ge f(x)$. A symmetric argument may be used to show that $\overline{D}V_\varepsilon(x) \le f(x)$. Finally, on each J_k we have

$$|U(x) - F(x)| + |V(x) - F(x)| \le 2\varepsilon \max(|\varphi(a_k)|, |\varphi(b_k)|).$$

Hence F is an indefinite Perron integral of f on I.

Assuming F is an indefinite Perron integral of f on I, for every $k \in \mathbb{N}$ there are U_k, V_k such that $\underline{D}U_k \ge f \ge \overline{D}V_k$ on I and $|U_k - V_k| \le 2^{-k}$ on J_k. Since $\underline{D}(U_k - V_j) \ge 0$, $U_k - V_j$ are increasing (see, for example, [7, Theorem VI(3.2)]), and so are also $U_k - F$ and $F - V_j$. Letting

$$\varphi(x) := x + \sum_{k=1}^{\infty} k(U_k(x) - V_k(x)),$$

which is well-defined since each $x \in I$ belongs to all but finitely many J_k, we show that φ is the required control function. Clearly, it is strictly increasing. For every $x \in I$ and $k \in \mathbb{N}$ there is $\delta > 0$ such that $0 < |y - x| < \delta$ implies

$$\frac{U_k(y) - U_k(x)}{y - x} \ge f(x) - 1/k \quad \text{and} \quad \frac{V_k(y) - V_k(x)}{y - x} \le f(x) + 1/k.$$

Hence

$$\frac{F(y) - F(x)}{y - x} - f(x) \le \frac{U_k(y) - U_k(x)}{y - x} - \frac{V_k(y) - V_k(x)}{y - x} + \frac{1}{k}$$
$$\le \frac{\varphi(y) - \varphi(x)}{k(y - x)}$$

and a symmetric argument gives

$$\frac{F(y) - F(x)}{y - x} - f(x) \ge \frac{V_k(y) - V_k(x)}{y - x} - \frac{U_k(y) - U_k(x)}{y - x} - \frac{1}{k}$$
$$\ge -\frac{\varphi(y) - \varphi(x)}{k(y - x)},$$

which shows that φ is a control function for (F, f).

5.3.3   *Relation between* (MC_α) *and Denjoy-Perron integrals*

Our main argument here shows that every (MC_2)-integrable function is Denjoy-Perron integrable, which together with the result of Bendová and Malý and Proposition 5.1 immediately implies that for $1 \leq \alpha \leq 2$ the (MC_α) and Denjoy-Perron integrals coincide.

Theorem 5.5. *For any $1 \leq \alpha \leq 2$, the (MC_α) integral on any interval I coincides with the Denjoy-Perron integral.*

Proof:
By Theorem 5.4 and Proposition 5.1 it suffices to show that every (MC_2) integrable function is Denjoy-Perron integrable. So suppose F is an indefinite (MC_2) integral of f on I. Denote by G the union of those open subintervals of I on which F is ACG_*. By the Lindelöf property of the real line, G is the union of a countable family of such subintervals, and so F is ACG_* on G. Since $F' = f$ almost everywhere, F is an indefinite Denjoy-Perron integral of f on each component of G. This means that if $G = (a, b)$, we are done; so assume $Q := (a, b) \setminus G \neq \emptyset$. Notice that Q has no isolated points by [7, Lemma VIII(3.1)]. We show that there is an interval $[a, b] \subset I$ such that $Q \cap (a, b) \neq \emptyset$ and

(a) f is Lebesgue integrable on Q;
(b) the series of the oscillations of F on the components of $(a, b) \setminus Q$ converges.

By Lemma 3.4 in [7, Chapter 7] this will imply that F is an indefinite Denjoy-Perron integral of f on (a, b). But then $(a, b) \subset G$, contradicting $Q \cap (a, b) \neq \emptyset$.

To find the interval (a, b), let φ be a 2-control function for (F, f) and for every $x \in I$ choose $\delta_x > 0$ such that $|F(y) - F(x) - f(x)(y - x)| \leq |\varphi(x + 2(y - x)) - \varphi(x)|$ when $|y - x| \leq \delta_x$. Let $Q_k := \{x \in Q : |f(x)| \leq k, \delta_x > 1/k\}$. Then $Q = \bigcup_{k=1}^{\infty} Q_k$, and hence by the Baire Category Theorem there is an open interval (a, b) such that $M := Q \cap (a, b) \neq \emptyset$ and $Q_k \cap M$ is dense in M. Since Q has no isolated points, we may diminish (a, b), if necessary, to guarantee $a, b \in M$ and $|b - a| < 1/k$. We show that

$$|F(y) - F(x)| \leq 2|\varphi(y) - \varphi(x)| + 2k|y - x| \text{ for } x, y \in M. \tag{5.5}$$

To prove this we use that $|y - x| < \delta_x$ to infer that

$$|F((x+y)/2) - F(x)| \leq |\varphi(y) - \varphi(x)| + |f(x)||y - x| \leq |\varphi(y) - \varphi(x)| + k|y - x|.$$

Similarly we have $|F((x + y)/2) - F(y)| \leq |\varphi(y) - \varphi(x)| + k|y - x|$. Hence

$$|F(y) - F(x)| \leq |F((x + y)/2) - F(x)| + |F((x + y)/2) - F(y)|$$
$$\leq 2|\varphi(y) - \varphi(x)| + 2k|y - x|,$$

as claimed.

Clearly, monotonicity of φ and (5.5) show that

$$\sum_i |F(u_i) - F(v_i)| \leq \sum_i (2|\varphi(v_i) - \varphi(u_i)| + 2k|v_i - u_i|)$$
$$\leq 2|\varphi(b) - \varphi(a)| + 2k|b - a|$$

for any mutually disjoint intervals (u_i, v_i) with end-points in M. Consequently, F has bounded variation on M and, since it is continuous, also on Q. (See [7, VII($\S$4)]). Since $f = F'$ a.e., we infer (a) from [7, Lemma VIII(2.1)] and [7, Lemma IV(7.4)].

For (b), consider any component (u, v) of $(a, b) \setminus Q$. If $x \in [u, (u + v)/2]$, then

$$|F(x) - F(u)| \leq |\varphi(u + 2(x - u)) - \varphi(u)| \leq \varphi(v) - \varphi(u),$$

and if $x \in [(u + v)/2, v]$, then

$$|F(x) - F(v)| \leq |\varphi(v + 2(x - v)) - \varphi(v)| \leq \varphi(v) - \varphi(u).$$

Using also (5.4), we get

$$|F(x) - F(u)| \leq 3(\varphi(v) - \varphi(u)) + 2k(y - x),$$

and hence the oscillation of F on (u, v) is at most $6(\varphi(v) - \varphi(u)) + 4k(y - x)$. The sum of these oscillations over the components of $(a, b) \setminus Q$ is therefore at most

$$6(\varphi(b) - \varphi(a)) + 4k(b - a),$$

showing that (b) holds and so proving the Theorem.

5.3.4   *Preliminaries to constructions for $\alpha > 2$*

As we already said in connection with Proposition 5.4, the examples we have to construct to show the cases of Theorem 5.1 when $\alpha > 1$ need a closed, necessarily nowhere dense, set on which the function we construct is not ACG$_*$, respectively ACG. The (ternary) Cantor set is a good candidate, especially when we recall that the corresponding Cantor function has a very quick increase when passing through the Cantor set, thereby providing a good choice for a control function. We will actually use the ternary Cantor set to prove Theorem 5.1(iii), but for the proof of Theorem 5.1(iv) we need a bit more room that we gain by using one of the Cantor type sets with base 5. We therefore fix notation for the construction of these sets with any odd base $q \geq 3$, although we will use it only for $q = 3$ and $q = 5$.

The Cantor type sets we use are defined in a standard way. Let $q = 2m+1$ be an odd integer. We recursively define collections of closed intervals $\mathscr{C}_k$, $k = 0, 1, 2, \ldots$ and collections of open intervals $\mathscr{R}_k$, $k = 1, 2, \ldots$ as follows.

Let $\mathscr{C}_0 := \{[0, 1]\}$. Whenever $\mathscr{C}_{k-1}$ has been defined, and $[u, v] \in \mathscr{C}_{k-1}$, we put into $\mathscr{C}_k$ the intervals $[u + j(v - u)/q, u + (j + 1)(v - u)/q]$ where $0 \leq j \leq q-1$ is even, and into $\mathscr{R}_k$ the intervals $(u + j(v-u)/q, u + (j+1)(v-u)/q)$ where $0 \leq j \leq q - 1$ is odd.

The (base q) Cantor set is then defined as $C := \bigcap_{k=0}^{\infty} C_k$ where C_k is the union of intervals from $\mathscr{C}$. We will use the following straightforward facts.

- $C_0 \supset C_1 \supset \cdots$
- $\mathscr{C}_k$ is the set of (connected) components of C_k.
- $\mathscr{R}_k$ is the set of components of $C_k \setminus C_{k-1}$.
- The set of components of $[0, 1] \setminus C$ is $\mathscr{R} := \bigcup_{k=1}^{\infty} \mathscr{R}_k$, where the union is disjoint.
- For $(u, v) \in \mathscr{R}_k$, both $u, v \in C$ and are end-points of intervals from $\mathscr{C}_k$.
- $\mathscr{C}_k$ consists of $(m + 1)^k$ disjoint closed intervals of length q^{-k}.
- $\mathscr{R}_k$ consists of $m(m + 1)^{k-1}$ disjoint open intervals of length q^{-k}.
- If $k > p$, an interval from $\mathscr{C}_p$ contains $m(m+1)^{k-p-1}$ intervals from $\mathscr{R}_k$.

We will also use the corresponding Cantor function $\psi : \mathbb{R} \to [0, 1]$, which is characterized by being continuous, increasing, constant on each component of $\mathbb{R} \setminus C$, and, for each k, mapping each interval from $\mathscr{C}_k$ onto an interval of length $(m + 1)^{-k}$. To define it, we may, for example, let $\psi_k(x) := (m+1)^{-k} q^k |(-\infty, x) \cap C_k|$, observe that $|\psi_k - \psi_{k-1}| \leq (m+1)^{-k}$ and define $\psi := \lim_{k \to \infty} \psi_k$.

5.3.5　(MC$_\alpha$) *integrabilities differ for* $\alpha \geq 2$

In this proof we will use the ternary Cantor set C, the collections of intervals $\mathscr{R}_k$ and $\mathscr{R}$ and the Cantor function ψ, as described in Section 5.3.4 when we take $q = 3$.

Lemma 5.2. *There are* $Q_J > 0$, $J \in \mathscr{R}$, *such that*

(i) $\lim_{k\to\infty} \max\{Q_j : J \in \mathscr{R}_k\} = 0$;

(ii) $\sum_{J\in\mathscr{R},\, J\subset I} Q_J = \infty$ *whenever* $I \subset (0,1)$ *is an open interval meeting* C.

(iii) *for every* $\eta > 0$,

$$Q_J \leq \eta \min(\psi(b + \eta(b-a)) - \psi(b), \psi(a) - \psi(a - \eta(b-a))) \quad (5.6)$$

holds for all but finitely many $J = (a,b) \in \mathscr{R}$.

Proof:

We let $k_l := 4^l$, define $Q_J := 2^{-k-2l}$ when $J \in \mathscr{R}_k$ and $k_{l-1} \leq k < k_l$ and notice that (i) holds.

For any open interval J meeting C there is $p \in \mathbb{N}$ such that J contains an interval from $\mathscr{C}_p$. It follows that for $k > p$, J contains at least 2^{k-p-1} intervals from $\mathscr{R}_k$. Choose $m \in \mathbb{N}$ such that $4^{m-1} > p$. Then, if $l \geq m$ and $k_{l-1} \leq k < k_l$, the sum of Q_J over those $J \in \mathscr{R}_k$ that are contained in J is at least $2^{-p-2l-1}$. Hence

$$\sum_{J\in\mathscr{R},\, J\subset J} Q_J \geq \sum_{l=m}^{\infty} \sum_{k=k_{l-1}}^{k_l-1} 2^{-p-2l-1}$$

$$= \sum_{l=m}^{\infty} 2^{-p-2l-1}(4^l - 4^{l-1}) \geq \sum_{l=m}^{\infty} 2^{-p-3} = \infty.$$

To prove (iii), suppose $\eta > 0$ and choose $n \in \mathbb{N}$ such that $2^{-n} < \eta$. Whenever $l \geq n$, $k_{l-1} \leq k < k_l$ and $J = (a,b) \in \mathscr{R}_k$, we notice that

$$b + \eta(b-a) \geq b + 2^{-n}3^{-k} \geq b + 3^{-k-n}$$

and so that b is the left-end point of an interval from $\mathscr{C}_{k+n}$ of length 3^{-k-n} that is mapped by ψ onto an interval of length 2^{-k-n}. Hence

$$\eta(\psi(b + \eta(b-a)) - \psi(b)) \geq 2^{-k-2n} \geq Q_J.$$

A symmetric argument shows $\eta(\psi(a) - \psi(a - \eta(b-a))) \geq Q_J$. Hence (5.6) holds for all $J \in \mathscr{R}_k$ when $k \geq n$, hence for all $J \in \mathscr{R}$ except finitely many.

Theorem 5.6. *For any interval* $I \subset \mathbb{R}$ *and* $\alpha \geq 2$ *there are functions* $f, F : \mathbb{R} \to \mathbb{R}$ *such that*

(i) F *is the Denjoy-Khintchine indefinite integral of* f *on* $\mathbb{R}$;

(ii) F *is the* (MC_β) *indefinite integral of* f *on* $\mathbb{R}$ *for every* $\beta > \alpha$;

(iii) f *is not* (MC_α) *integrable on* I.

Proof:
Without loss of generality we assume that I is an open interval containing $[0, 1]$. Let Q_J be as in Lemma 5.2. Choose a continuously differentiable function $\xi : \mathbb{R} \to [0, 1]$ with support in $[-1, 1]$ such that $\xi(x) = 1$ for $-1/2 \leq x \leq 1/2$. Let $\sigma := 1/\alpha$ and $\sigma_J := 3^{-k}\sigma$ for $J \in \mathscr{R}_k$. For $J = (a, b) \in \mathscr{R}$ let $u_J := a + \sigma(b - a)$ and define

$$\xi_J(x) := Q_J \xi((x - u_J)/(\sigma_J(b - a))) \text{ and } F(x) := \sum_{J \in \mathscr{R}} \xi_J(x).$$

Notice that the support of ξ_J is contained in $[u_J - \sigma_J(b-a), u_J + \sigma_J(b-a)]$ which, since $\sigma_J < \sigma \leq 1/2$ is contained in J. Since the intervals from $\mathscr{R}$ are mutually disjoint, the functions $F_k(x) := \sum_{l=1}^{k} \sum_{J \in \mathscr{R}_l} \xi_J(x)$ satisfy the inequality $|F - F_k| \leq \max_{l > k} \max\{Q_J : J \in J_k\}$. Hence Lemma 5.2(i) implies that F_k converge to F uniformly, and since F_k are continuous, so is F. Moreover, $F = 0$ outside $[0, 1]$ and $F = \xi_J$ on $J \in \mathscr{R}$; hence F is continuously differentiable on $\mathbb{R} \setminus C$ and we may define

$$f(x) := \begin{cases} F'(x) & \text{when } x \in \mathbb{R} \setminus C \\ 0 & \text{when } x \in C. \end{cases}$$

The first statement, that F is the Denjoy-Khintchine indefinite integral of f is straightforward. Since $F = 0$ on C, it is absolutely continuous on C and since it is continuously differentiable outside C, it is ACG also on $\mathbb{R} \setminus C$. So F is ACG on $\mathbb{R}$, continuous and $F' = f$ almost everywhere, which implies that indeed F is the Denjoy-Khintchine indefinite integral of f.

To prove the second statement, we let $\varphi(x) := x + \psi(x)$, observe that φ is strictly increasing and hence it suffices to show that for every $\beta > \alpha$, $x \in \mathbb{R}$ and $\varepsilon > 0$ there is $\delta > 0$ such that

$$|F(y) - F(x) - f(x)(y - x)| \leq \varepsilon |\varphi(x + \beta(y - x)) - \varphi(x)| \qquad (5.7)$$

whenever $y \in (x - \delta, x + \delta)$. So we fix $\beta > \alpha$, $x \in \mathbb{R}$ and $\varepsilon > 0$, and find such a δ. This is easy when $x \notin C$, since then $f(x) = F'(x)$ and so for small enough $\delta > 0$,

$$|F(y) - F(x) - f(x)(y - x)| \leq \varepsilon |y - x| \leq \varepsilon |\varphi(x + \beta(y - x)) - \varphi(x)|$$

for every $y \in (x - \delta, x + \delta)$.

So assume $x \in C$. Choose $\eta > 0$ such that $0 < \eta < \varepsilon$ and, recalling that $\sigma = 1/\alpha$ and $\beta > \alpha$, that also $\beta\sigma > (1 + \eta)$. By Lemma 5.2(iii) we find $0 < \kappa < \sigma - (1 + \eta)/\beta$ such that for every $J = (a, b) \in \mathscr{R}$ with $b - a < \kappa$,

$$Q_J \leq \eta \min(\psi(b + \eta(b - a)) - \psi(b), \psi(a) - \psi(a - \eta(b - a))). \qquad (5.8)$$

Since $\sigma_J \leq b - a \leq \kappa$, we also have

$$\beta(\sigma - \sigma_J) \geq 1 + \eta. \tag{5.9}$$

Let $\delta := \kappa\sigma/2$ and consider any $y \in (x - \delta, x + \delta)$. Since $F \geq 0$ and since $f(x) = F(x) = 0$, (5.7) reduces to showing that

$$F(y) \leq \varepsilon|\varphi(x + \beta(y - x)) - \varphi(x)|. \tag{5.10}$$

As this is obvious when $F(y) = 0$, we assume that $F(y) \neq 0$. Then there is $J = (a, b) \in \mathscr{R}$ such that $0 < F(y) \leq Q_J$ and

$$y \in [a + (\sigma - \sigma_J)(b - a), a + (\sigma + \sigma_J)(b - a)].$$

In particular we have $|x - y| \geq \sigma(b - a)/2$ since $x \notin J$, $\sigma - \sigma_J \geq \sigma/2$ and

$$1 - (\sigma + \sigma_J) \geq 1/2 - \sigma_J \geq \sigma - \sigma_J \geq \sigma/2.$$

Hence $\kappa\sigma/2 = \delta > |y - x| \geq \sigma(b - a)/2$, which gives $b - a < \kappa$ and hence (5.8) and (5.9) hold.

When $\alpha > 2$ the situations when $y > x$ and $y < x$ are not completely symmetric, so we continue by distinguishing these two cases.

Case $y > x$. Then $x \leq a < y$ and (5.9) gives

$$x + \beta(y - x) = x + \beta(a - x) + \beta(y - a)$$
$$\geq x + (a - x) + \beta(y - a) \geq a + \beta(\sigma - \sigma_J)(b - a) \geq b + \eta(b - a).$$

Hence

$$F(y) \leq Q_J \leq \eta(\psi(b + \eta(b - a)) - \psi(b))$$
$$\leq \eta(\psi(x + \beta(y - x)) - \psi(x)) \leq \varepsilon(\varphi(x + \beta(y - x)) - \varphi(x)).$$

Case $y < x$. Then $x \geq b$ and, using $\sigma \leq 1/2$ and (5.9) to infer

$$\beta(1 - \sigma - \sigma_J) \geq \beta(\sigma - \sigma_J) \geq \eta,$$

we get

$$x + \beta(y - x) = x - \beta(x - b) - \beta(b - y)$$
$$\leq x - (x - b) - \beta(b - y) \leq b - \beta(1 - \sigma - \sigma_J)(b - a) \leq a - \eta(b - a).$$

Hence

$$F(y) \leq Q_J \leq \eta(\psi(a) - \psi(a - \eta(b - a)))$$
$$\leq \eta(\psi(x) - \psi(x + \beta(y - x))) \leq \varepsilon|\varphi(x + \beta(y - x)) - \varphi(x)|.$$

In both cases we have proved that (5.10) holds for $y \in (x - \delta, x + \delta)$ as required, and we conclude that f is (MC_β) integrable.

It remains to show that f is not (MC_α) integrable on $(0,1)$. Arguing by contradiction and using Proposition 5.1, we assume that F is an indefinite (MC_α) integral of f on $(0,1)$. Then there is a strictly increasing function $\gamma : (0,1) \to \mathbb{R}$ such that for every $x \in (0,1)$ there is $\delta_x > 0$ such that for every $y \in (x, x + \delta_x)$,

$$|F(y) - F(x) - f(x)(y - x)| \leq \gamma(x + \alpha(y - x)) - \gamma(x).$$

Let $\Delta_k := \{x \in C \cap (0,1) : \delta_x > 1/k\}$. Since $C = \bigcup_{k=1}^{\infty} \Delta_k$, the Baire Category Theorem implies that there are $k \in \mathbb{N}$ and an open interval $J \subset (0,1)$ such that $J \cap C \neq \emptyset$ and $\Delta_k \cap J$ is dense in $C \cap J$. We diminish J if necessary to achieve $|J| < 1/k$ and choose an interval $[a, b] \subset J$ such that $(a, b) \cap C \neq \emptyset$.

By Lemma 5.2(ii) find $n \in \mathbb{N}$ and intervals $J_i = (a_i, b_i) \in \mathscr{R}$, $i = 1, \ldots n$ such that $(a_i, b_i) \subset (a, b)$ and $\sum_{i=1}^{n} Q_{J_i} > \gamma(b) - \gamma(a)$. Using that $a_i + \sigma(b_i - a_i) = u_{J_i}$, C has no isolated points and $a_i \in C \cap J$, we find $x_i \in C \cap J \cap \Delta_k$ so close to a_i that the intervals (x_i, b_i), $i = 1, \ldots, n$ are mutually disjoint and

$$y_i := x_i + \sigma(b_i - x_i) \in [u_{J_i} - \sigma_{J_i}(b_i - a_i)/2, u_{J_i} + \sigma_{J_i}(b_i - a_i)/2].$$

Hence $F(y_i) = Q_{J_i}$ and since $F(x_i) = f(x_i) = 0$,

$$
\begin{aligned}
Q_{J_i} = F(y_i) - F(x_i) - f(x_i)(y_i - x_i) \\
\leq \gamma(x_i + \alpha(y_i - x_i)) - \gamma(x_i) = \gamma(b_i) - \gamma(x_i),
\end{aligned}
$$

Finally, we use that γ is increasing to get

$$\gamma(b) - \gamma(a) \geq \sum_{i=1}^{n} (\gamma(b_i) - \gamma(x_i)) \geq \sum_{i=1}^{n} Q_{J_i} > \gamma(b) - \gamma(a),$$

which is the desired contradiction.

5.3.6 *Relation between* (MC_α) *and Denjoy-Khintchine integrals*

Since indefinite (MC_α) integrals are differentiable almost everywhere by Proposition 5.1(ii) but indefinite Denjoy-Khintchine integrals need not be differentiable almost everywhere (as an example one may take a continuous function that is everywhere approximately differentiable but not differentiable almost everywhere), we have

Observation 5.2. On any interval I there is a Denjoy-Khintchine integrable functions that is not (MC_α) integrable for any $\alpha > 0$.

For the opposite direction we need more work. To construct the required example, we will use the Cantor-type set C with base $q = 5$, its approximating sets C_k, the sets of intervals $\mathscr{C}_k$, $\mathscr{R}_k$ and $\mathscr{R}$, and the corresponding Cantor-type function ψ described in Section 5.3.4.

Theorem 5.7. *There is a function $f : \mathbb{R} \to \mathbb{R}$ that is (MC_α) integrable on $\mathbb{R}$ for every $\alpha > 2$ but is not Denjoy-Khintchine integrable on $[0,1]$.*

Proof:
For any interval $I = [a, b]$ and $0 < \tau < 1/2$ choose a continuously differentiable function $g_{I,\tau} : \mathbb{R} \to \mathbb{R}$ which is increasing on $(-\infty, (a+b)/2]$, decreasing on $[(a+b)/2, \infty)$ and satisfies

$$
g_{I,\tau}(x) = \begin{cases} 0 & x \le a + (1+\tau)(b-a)/5; \\ 0 & x \ge b - (1+\tau)(b-a)/5; \\ 1 & x \in [a + (2-\tau)(b-a)/5, b - (2-\tau)(b-a)/5]. \end{cases}
$$

We let $\sigma_k := 1/(k+1)$, $\tau_k := (k+1)/(2(k+2))$ and

$$
F(x) := \sum_{k=1}^{\infty} \sigma_k 3^{-k} \sum_{I \in \mathscr{C}_{k-1}} g_{I,\tau_k}(x).
$$

Since for each k, $\sum_{I \in \mathscr{C}_k} g_{I,\tau_k}(x)$ is continuous and bounded by one, F is the sum of a uniformly convergent series of continuous functions, and so it is continuous. We list the following easy but crucial properties of F.

(a) $|F(y) - F(x)| \le \sigma_k 3^{-k+1}$ whenever x, y belong to the same interval from $\mathscr{C}_{k-1}$;

(b) $|F(b) - F(a)| = \sigma_k 3^{-k}$ whenever (a, b) is an interval from $\mathscr{R}_k$;

(c) if $(a, b) \in \mathscr{R}_k$, then F is constant on $[a, a + \tau_k(b - a)]$ as well as on $[b - \tau_k(b - a), b]$.

(d) On each $J \in \mathscr{R}_k$ the sum defining F is finite, and hence F is continuously differentiable on $\mathbb{R} \setminus C$.

The property (d) allows us to define

$$
f(x) := \begin{cases} F'(x) & x \notin C; \\ 0 & x \in C. \end{cases}
$$

Fix for a while $\alpha > 2$, $x \in C$ and $\varepsilon > 0$. We show that there is $\delta > 0$ such that

$$
|F(y) - F(x)| \le \varepsilon(\psi(x + \alpha(y - x)) - \psi(x)) \tag{5.11}
$$

whenever $0 < y - x < \delta$. Since $F = 0$ on $[1, \infty)$, any $\delta > 0$ will do for $x = 1$. So we assume $x < 1$. To define δ, start by using that $\alpha > 2$ to find $l \in \mathbb{N}$ such that $\alpha > 2(1 + 5^{-l+1})$. Since $\tau_j \to 1/2$ and $\sigma_j \to 0$, there is $m \in \mathbb{N}$ such that $\alpha \tau_j > 1 + 5^{-l}$ and $\sigma_j 3^{l+2} < \varepsilon$ for $j \geq m$. Having done this, we let $\delta = \min(1 - x, 5^{-m-1})$.

We are now ready to prove that (5.11) indeed holds for $y \in (x, x + \delta)$. Given such y, find the least $k \geq 1$ for which there is an interval $(u, v) \in \mathscr{R}_k$ that is contained in (x, y). Clearly, $k > m$. To finish the argument, we distinguish three cases.

Case $y \in C_k$. Then x, y belong to the same interval from $\mathscr{C}_{k-1}$ since otherwise $k > 1$ and $[x, y]$ contains an interval from $\mathscr{R}_{k-1}$. Moreover,

$$x + \alpha(y - x) = x + \alpha(u - x) + \alpha(y - u) \geq u + \alpha(v - u).$$

Since $\alpha > 2$ and $v - u = 5^{-k}$, we infer that

$$[x + \alpha(y - x), x] \supset [u + \alpha(v - u), u] \supset [v, v + 5^{-k}].$$

Since $[v, v + 5^{-k}]$ belongs to $\mathscr{C}_k$, we conclude from (a) that

$$|F(y) - F(x)| \leq \sigma_k 3^{-k+1} = 3\sigma_k(\psi(v + 5^{-k}) - \psi(v))$$
$$\leq \tfrac{1}{2}\varepsilon(\psi(x + \alpha(y - x)) - \psi(x)).$$

In the remaining cases $y \notin C_k$. Since $y \in (0, 1)$, there is $1 \leq j \leq k$ such that $y \in (w, z)$ for some $(w, z) \in \mathscr{R}_j$. Since (x, y) contains an interval from $\mathscr{R}_k$ but does not contain any interval from any $\mathscr{R}_i$ with $i < k$, we have $w \in C_k$, $x < w$ and (x, w) contains an interval from $\mathscr{R}_k$. By the previous case,

$$|F(w) - F(x)| \leq \tfrac{1}{2}\varepsilon(\psi(x + \alpha(w - x)) - \psi(x)). \tag{5.12}$$

Case $y \notin C_k$ and $y - w \leq \tau_j 5^{-j}$. Then (c) implies that F is constant on $[w, y]$ and so (5.12) gives

$$|F(y) - F(x)| = |F(w) - F(x)| \leq \tfrac{1}{2}\varepsilon(\psi(x + \alpha(y - x)) - \psi(x)).$$

Case $y \notin C_k$ and $y - w > \tau_j 5^{-j}$. We use

$$\delta > y - x \geq y - w \geq \tau_j 5^{-j} \geq 5^{j-1}$$

to infer that $j > m$. Hence

$$[x, x + \alpha(y - x)] \supset [w, w + \alpha(y - w)] \supset [z, z + 5^{-j-l}].$$

Since $[z, z + 5^{-j-l}] \in \mathscr{C}_{j+l}$ and $[w, y]$ is contained in an interval from $\mathscr{C}_{j-1}$, (a) implies

$$|F(y) - F(w)| \leq \sigma_j 3^{-j+1} = \sigma_j 3^{l+1}(\psi(z + 5^{-j}) - \psi(z))$$
$$\leq \tfrac{1}{2}\varepsilon(\psi(x + \alpha(y - x)) - \psi(x)).$$

This and (5.12) give

$$|F(y) - F(x)| \leq |F(y) - F(w)| + |F(w) - F(x)|$$
$$\leq \varepsilon(\psi(x + \alpha(y - x)) - \psi(x)).$$

Having thus verified (5.11), we use it and $f(x) = 0$ (since $x \in C$) to conclude that

$$\lim_{y \searrow x} \frac{F(y) - F(x) - f(x)(y - x)}{\varphi(y) - \varphi(x)} = 0.$$

A symmetric argument shows

$$\lim_{y \nearrow x} \frac{F(y) - F(x) - f(x)(y - x)}{\varphi(y) - \varphi(x)} = 0.$$

Finally, if $x \notin C$, we infer from $|\varphi(y) - \varphi(x)| \geq |y - x|$ and $F'(x) = f(x)$ that

$$\limsup_{y \to x} \frac{|F(y) - F(x) - f(x)(y - x)|}{|\varphi(y) - \varphi(x)|}$$
$$\leq \lim_{y \to x} \frac{|F(y) - F(x) - f(x)(y - x)|}{|y - x|} = 0.$$

Hence F is an indefinite (MC_α) integral of f, as wanted.

It remains to show that f is not Denjoy-Khintchine integrable. Suppose the opposite and let H be its indefinite Denjoy-Khintchine integral. Notice that, in principle, H may be different from F. However, on each interval (a, b) from $\mathscr{R}$, both H and F are Lebesgue indefinite integrals of f and hence $H - F$ is constant on $[a, b]$. It follows that $H(b) - H(a) = F(b) - F(a)$, and so (b) holds with F replaced by H. This information will suffice for our arguments.

Since H is continuous, C is a union of closed sets on which it is AC. By the Baire Category Theorem, there is an open interval I meeting C such that H is AC on $I \cap C$. Find a component $[u, v]$ of some C_m contained in I. For $k \geq m$ the set $[u, v] \cap C_k$ has 3^{k-m} components and so $[u, v] \cap (C_{k+1} \setminus C_k)$ has $2 \cdot 3^{m-k}$ components. For each such component, say (u, v), we have $|H(v) - H(u)| = \sigma_{k+1} 3^{k+1}$ by validity of (b) for H.

Let (a_j, b_j) be an enumeration of the components of $[u, v] \setminus C$. Summing first over those (a_j, b_j) that are components of $C_{k+1} \setminus C_k$ and then over $k > m$, we get

$$\sum_{j=1}^{\infty} |H(b_j) - H(a_j)| = \sum_{k=m}^{\infty} 2\sigma_{k+1} 3^{k+1} 3^{m-k} = \sum_{k=m}^{\infty} 2\sigma_{k+1} 3^{m+1} = \infty.$$

This shows that H is not AC on $I \cap C$, and this contradiction shows that f is not Denjoy-Khintchine integrable.

References

[1] H. Bendová and J. Malý. An elementary way to introduce a Perron-like integral. *Ann. Acad. Sci. Fenn. Math.*, 36 (2011), no. 1, 153–164.

[2] A. Denjoy. Une extension de l'intégrale de M. Lebesgue. *C. R. Acad. Sci. Paris Sér. I Math.*, 154 (1912), 859–862.

[3] R. A. Gordon. The integrals of Lebesgue, Denjoy, Perron, and Henstock. Graduate Studies in Mathematics, volume 4, *American Mathematical Society, Providence, RI*, 1994.

[4] R. Henstock. Definitions of Riemann type of the variational integrals. *Proc. London Math. Soc.*, (3) 11 (1961), 402–418.

[5] J. Kurzweil. Generalized ordinary differential equations and continuous dependence on a parameter. *Czechoslovak Math. J.*, 7 (82) (1957), 418–449.

[6] O. Perron. Über den Integralbegriff. *Sitzungsber. Heidelberg Akad. Wiss. Klasse A*, 14 (1914), 1–16.

[7] S. Saks. Theory of the integral. Second revised edition. English translation by L. C. Young. With two additional notes by Stefan Banach. *Dover Publications Inc., New York*, 1964.

Chapter 6

Fine Properties of Duality Mappings

George Dincă
Faculty of Mathematics and Computer Science, University of Bucharest
14 Academiei Street, 010014 Bucharest, Romania
dinca@fmi.unibuc.ro

6.1 Introduction

This is not a very large survey. The title, the selected topics, and the structure of the paper are governed by some of G. H. Hardy's ideas, as exposed in his celebrated essay titled "A Mathematician's Apology", with a Foreword by C. P. Snow, Cambridge University Press, 1967 (first edition, 1940).

These ideas are the following.

1. It would be quite difficult now to find an educated man quite insensitive to the aesthetic appeal of mathematics. It may be very hard to define mathematical beauty, but that is just as true of beauty of any kind — we may not know quite what we mean by a beautiful poem, but that does not prevent us from recognising one when we read it.

G. H. Hardy, §10, p. 85

2. The "seriousness" of a mathematical theorem lies, not in its practical consequences, which are usually negligible, but in the *significance* of the mathematical ideas which connects. We may say, roughly, that a mathematical idea is "significant" if it can be connected, in a natural and illuminating way, with a large complex of other mathematical ideas. Thus a serious mathematical theorem, a theorem which connects significant ideas, is likely to lead to important advance in mathematics itself and even in other sciences.

G. H. Hardy, §11, p. 89

3. We can recognise a "significant" idea when we see it, ...; but this power of recognition requires a high degree of mathematical sophistication, and of that familiarity with mathematical ideas which comes only from many years spent in this company.

G. H. Hardy, §15, p. 103

4. The idea should be one which is a constituent in many mathematical constructs, which is used in the proof of theorems of many different kinds.

G. H. Hardy, §15, p. 104

5. A property common to too many objects can hardly be very exciting, and mathematical ideas also become dim unless they have plenty of individuality. Here at any rate I can quote Whitehead on my side: "it is the large generalisation, limited by a happy particularity, which is the fruitful conception".

G. H. Hardy, §16, p. 109

6.2 Duality mappings

The concept of the duality mapping was first introduced and studied by Beurling and Livingston [5] and generalised, extensively studied and applied by Browder [10], [11], [12], Laursen [38], Kato [36], Asplund [4], Dubinsky [26], Petryshyn [47]. For more references, see Browder [12] and de Figueiredo [16].

Beurling and Livingston had the elegance to justify the abstract definition of such a mapping by the necessity to give a natural proof for a result coming from the Fourier series theory for functions belonging to a Lebesgue space L^p, $1 < p < \infty$, where L^p denotes the space of measurable functions with period 2π and with norm

$$\|f\|_{L^p} = \left(\int_0^{2\pi} |f(x)|^p \, dx \right)^{1/p}.$$

Denote by

$$c_n(f) = \frac{1}{2\pi} \int_0^{2\pi} e^{-inx} f(x) \, dx$$

the Fourier coefficients of $f \in L^p$.

For any $0 < \alpha \le p$, define the operator $S_\alpha : L^p \to L^{p/\alpha}$,

$$S_\alpha f = |f|^{\alpha - 1} f.$$

In particular, S_{p-1} maps L^p onto its dual L^q, $\frac{1}{p} + \frac{1}{q} = 1$ and it is easily seen that

$$\langle S_{p-1} f, f \rangle = \|f\|_{L^p}^p,$$

and

$$\|S_{p-1}f\|_{L^q} = \|f\|_{L^p}^{p-1},$$

for all $f \in L^p$.

Here and in the remainder of this paper, if X is a normed space and X^* is its dual, $\langle\ ,\ \rangle$ stands for the duality pairing between X and X^*:

$$\langle x^*, x \rangle = x^*(x),$$

for all $x \in X$ and $x^* \in X^*$.

We then have:

Theorem 6.1. *Let the integers be partitioned into two disjoint sets A and A', neither of which is empty. Let p be a given exponent such that $1 < p < \infty$. Let $\{a_n; n \in A\}$ and $\{b_n; n \in A'\}$ be given sets of numbers such that, for some $g_0 \in L^p$ and for some $h_0 \in L^q$, $\frac{1}{p} + \frac{1}{q} = 1$,*

$$c_n(g_0) = a_n, \ n \in A,$$

$$c_n(h_0) = b_n, \ n \in A'.$$

Then there is a unique element $f \in L^p$ such that

$$c_n(f) = a_n, \ n \in A,$$

$$c_n(S_{p-1}f) = b_n, \ n \in A'.$$

Notice that for $p = 2$, $S_{p-1}f = f$ for all $f \in L^2$ and the above statement reduces to the following classical result:

If $(a_n)_{-\infty}^{\infty}$ is a given sequence of numbers such that $\sum_{n=-\infty}^{\infty} |a_n|^2 < \infty$, then there is a unique element $f \in L^2$ such that

$$c_n(f) = a_n \text{ for } n = 0, \pm 1, \pm 2, \ldots.$$

In what follows, the ideas of Beurling and Livingston are presented in a more general form, following Browder [9]. See also Asplund [4].

Let us remark that setting $\varphi(t) = t^{p-1}$, $t \geq 0$, the operator $S_{p-1} : L^p \to L^q = (L^p)^*$ has the following metric properties:

$$\langle S_{p-1}f, f \rangle = \varphi(\|f\|_{L^p}) \|f\|_{L^p}$$

and

$$\|S_{p-1}f\|_{(L^p)^*} = \varphi(\|f\|_{L^p}),$$

for all $f \in L^p$.

That suggested the following. Let there be given a function $\varphi : \mathbb{R}_+ \to \mathbb{R}_+$ which is continuous, strictly increasing, $\varphi(0) = 0$ and $\varphi(r) \to \infty$ as $r \to \infty$. (In the remainder of this paper, such a function will be called a "gauge function". Clearly $\varphi(t) = t^{p-1}$, $t \geq 0$ is such a function.) Does a mapping $J_\varphi : X = L^p \to X^* = L^q$, $\frac{1}{p} + \frac{1}{q} = 1$ satisfying the metric relations

$$\langle J_\varphi f, f \rangle = \varphi(\|f\|_X) \|f\|_X \tag{6.1}$$

and

$$\|J_\varphi f\|_{X^*} = \varphi(\|f\|_X) \tag{6.2}$$

exist?

We answer positively this question.

First, let us remark that from (6.1) and (6.2) it follows that J_φ must satisfy

$$J_\varphi 0_X = 0_{X^*}.$$

Secondly, if $f \neq 0_X$, by the Hahn-Banach Theorem, there exists $x^* \in X^*$ such that

$$\|x^*\|_{X^*} = 1 \text{ and } \langle x^*, f \rangle = \|f\|_X. \tag{6.3}$$

Recall that a Banach space X is said to be smooth at a nonzero $x \in X$ if there is a unique element $x^* \in X^*$ that satisfies $\|x^*\| = 1$ and $\langle x^*, x \rangle = \|x\|$. A Banach space X which is smooth at any nonzero $x \in X$, or, equivalently, at any point of the unit sphere $S(X) = \{x \in X; \|x\| = 1\}$ is said to be a smooth Banach space.

Since $X = L^p$ is a smooth Banach space (see further Theorem 6.7 and Theorem 6.12), for any $f \neq 0_X$ there is a unique element $x^* \in X^* = L^q$ such that conditions (6.3) are fulfilled.

Now, it is clear that the mapping $J_\varphi : X = L^p \to X^* = L^q$, $1 < p < \infty$, $\frac{1}{p} + \frac{1}{q} = 1$ defined by

$$J_\varphi 0_X = 0_{X^*}$$

$$J_\varphi f = \varphi(\|f\|_X) x^*, \text{ if } f \neq 0_X,$$

where x^* is the unique element in X^* satisfying (6.3), satisfies (6.1) and (6.2) and it is the unique mapping from L^p into L^q having these properties.

Obviously, the above existence and uniqueness result remains valid when replacing L^p, $1 < p < \infty$ by any smooth Banach space X and L^q, $\frac{1}{p} + \frac{1}{q} = 1$, by X^*.

Thus, the following definition is justified.

Definition 6.1. *Let X be a smooth Banach space, X^* its conjugate space, and let $\varphi : \mathbb{R}_+ \to \mathbb{R}_+$ be a gauge function. By* duality mapping on X corresponding to φ *we understand the mapping $J_\varphi : X \to X^*$, defined by*

$$J_\varphi x = \begin{cases} 0_{X^*} \text{ if } x = 0_X \\ \varphi\left(\|x\|\right) x^* \text{ if } x \neq 0_X, \end{cases} \tag{6.4}$$

where x^* is the unique element in X^* satisfying $\|x^*\| = 1$ and $\langle x^*, x \rangle = \|x\|$.

From the above definition it follows that J_φ satisfies

$$\langle J_\varphi x, x \rangle = \varphi\left(\|x\|\right) \|x\|, \tag{6.5}$$

and

$$\|J_\varphi x\| = \varphi\left(\|x\|\right), \tag{6.6}$$

for all $x \in X$.

If X is not a smooth Banach space, then some points $x \in X \backslash \{0_X\}$ for which the nonempty set $\{x^* \in X^*; \|x^*\| = 1$ and $\langle x^*, x \rangle = \|x\|\}$ is not a singleton could exist.

In that case, (6.4) suggests a definition of J_φ as a set valued mapping $J_\varphi : X \to 2^{X^*}$, defined as follows.

Definition 6.2. *Let X be a Banach space and let $\varphi : \mathbb{R}_+ \to \mathbb{R}_+$ be a gauge function. By* duality mapping on X corresponding to φ *we understand the mapping $J_\varphi : X \to 2^{X^*}$ defined by*

$$J_\varphi 0_X = \{0_{X^*}\},$$

$$J_\varphi x = \varphi\left(\|x\|\right) \{x^* \in X^*; \|x^*\| = 1, \langle x^*, x \rangle = \|x\|\}, \text{ if } x \neq 0_X,$$

or, equivalently,

$$J_\varphi x = \{u^* \in X^*; \langle u^*, x \rangle = \varphi\left(\|x\|\right) \|x\| \text{ and } \|u^*\| = \varphi\left(\|x\|\right)\} \tag{6.7}$$

for all $x \in X$.

By the Hahn-Banach Theorem again, the *domain of J_φ*, $\text{dom}(J_\varphi) := \{x \in X; J_\varphi x \neq \emptyset\}$, is the whole space X.

The duality mapping on X corresponding to the identity gauge function $\varphi(t) = t$, for all $t \geq 0$, will be called *normalized duality mapping on X* and it will be denoted by J. Thus $J : X \to X^*$ is defined by

$$Jx = \{u^* \in X^*; \langle u^*, x \rangle = \|x\|^2 \text{ and } \|u^*\| = \|x\|\}, \tag{6.8}$$

for all $x \in X$.

Clearly, if X is a smooth Banach space, Definition 6.2 reduces to the preceding Definition 6.1.

The main result in Beurling and Livingston [5] is the following:

Theorem 6.2. *Let X be a reflexive Banach space and let X^* be its dual space. Assume that both X and X^* are strictly convex. Let V be a closed subspace of X and let $V^\perp = \{x^* \in X^*; \langle x^*, v \rangle = 0, \forall v \in V\}$ be its annihilator. Let $\varphi : \mathbb{R}_+ \to \mathbb{R}_+$ be a gauge function and $J_\varphi : X \to X^*$ be the duality mapping on X corresponding to φ. If $x_0 \in X$ and $y_0 \in X^*$ are two elements, then*

$$J_\varphi (V + x_0) \cap (V^\perp + y_0)$$

is nonempty and reduces to a point.

This result not only leads to a natural proof of Theorem 6.1 but it also has many other important consequences.

Some remarks are in order before describing the principal steps of the proof.

First remark that, as a closed subspace in a reflexive space, V is reflexive itself.

Secondly, we recall the following theorem (due to Klee [37]), which illustrates the partial duality between strict convexity and smoothness.

Theorem 6.3. (a) *If X^* is strictly convex then X is smooth.*

(b) *If X^* is smooth then X is strictly convex.*

An immediate consequence of Klee's Theorem is the following:

Corollary 6.1. *Let X be a reflexive Banach space. Then X^* is strictly convex (smooth) if and only if X is smooth (strictly convex).*

It follows that both X and X^* appearing in the statement of Theorem 6.2 are strictly convex and smooth. Consequently, any duality mapping $J_\varphi : X \to X^*$ is single valued and so is any duality mapping $J_\varphi^* : X^* \to X^{**}$.

We state now one of the basic theorems of nonlinear analysis.

Theorem 6.4. (Minty-Browder) *Let X be a reflexive Banach space and let $T : X \to X^*$ be an operator having the following properties:*

a) *T is monotone, i.e.,*

$$\langle Tu - Tv, u - v \rangle \geq 0, \text{ for all } u, v \in X; \tag{6.9}$$

b) *T is demicontinuous, i.e.,*

$$u_n \to u \text{ (in } X) \Longrightarrow Tu_n \rightharpoonup Tu \text{ (in } X^*); \tag{6.10}$$

c) T *is strongly coercive, i.e.,*

$$\frac{\langle Tu, u \rangle}{\|u\|} \to \infty \ \ as \ \|u\| \to \infty. \tag{6.11}$$

Then T is surjective from X onto X^*.

In other words, for any $f \in X^*$, the equation $Tu = f$ has a solution. If, in addition, T is strictly monotone, i.e.,

$$\langle Tu - Tv, u - v \rangle > 0 \text{ for all } u, v \in X, \ u \neq v,$$

then T is a bijection of X onto X^*. That is, for any $f \in X^*$, the equation $Tu = f$ has a unique solution.

Next, we shall show that a duality mapping on a reflexive and smooth Banach space is an example of operator which satisfies all the hypotheses of Minty-Browder's Surjectivity Theorem.

Proposition 6.1. *If X is a smooth Banach space, the following are true.*

(a) *Any duality mapping $J_\varphi : X \to X^*$ is monotone in the Minty-Browder's sense, i.e.,*

$$\langle J_\varphi u - J_\varphi v, u - v \rangle \geq 0, \text{ for all } u, v \in X. \tag{6.12}$$

(b) *If, in addition, X is strictly convex, then any duality mapping $J_\varphi : X \to X^*$ is strictly monotone, i.e.,*

$$\langle J_\varphi u - J_\varphi v, u - v \rangle > 0 \text{ for all } u, v \in X, \ u \neq v. \tag{6.13}$$

(c) *Any duality mapping $J_\varphi : X \to X^*$ is strongly coercive, i.e.,*

$$\frac{\langle J_\varphi u, u \rangle}{\|u\|} \to \infty \ \ as \ \|u\| \to \infty. \tag{6.14}$$

Proof:

(a) The metric properties (6.5) and (6.6) that J_φ satisfies, easily imply:

$$\langle J_\varphi u - J_\varphi v, u - v \rangle \geq (\varphi(\|u\|) - \varphi(\|v\|))(\|u\| - \|v\|) \geq 0, \tag{6.15}$$

i.e., J_φ is monotone.

(b) Assume, by contradiction, that even if X is strictly convex, there could be $u, v \in X$, $u \neq v$, such that

$$0 = \langle J_\varphi u - J_\varphi v, u - v \rangle. \tag{6.16}$$

Then, by comparing (6.15) and (6.16), we infer that

$$(\varphi(\|u\|) - \varphi(\|v\|))(\|u\| - \|v\|) = 0. \tag{6.17}$$

Since φ is strictly increasing, it follows that $\|u\| = \|v\|$.

Since $u \neq v$ and $\|u\| = \|v\|$ we derive that both u and v are different from zero. Consequently, $J_\varphi u \neq 0_{X^*}$ and $J_\varphi v \neq 0_{X^*}$.

Now, rewrite (6.16) as

$$0 = [\langle J_\varphi u, u \rangle - \langle J_\varphi u, v \rangle] + [\langle J_\varphi v, v \rangle - \langle J_\varphi v, u \rangle]. \tag{6.18}$$

Since $\|u\| = \|v\|$, every square bracket in (6.18) is positive.

For example,

$$\langle J_\varphi u, u \rangle - \langle J_\varphi u, v \rangle = \varphi\left(\|u\|\right)\|u\| - \langle J_\varphi u, v \rangle$$

$$\geq \varphi\left(\|u\|\right)\|u\| - \varphi\left(\|u\|\right)\|v\| = 0.$$

Consequently, equality (6.18) holds if and only if

$$\langle J_\varphi u, u \rangle = \langle J_\varphi u, v \rangle \text{ and } \langle J_\varphi v, v \rangle = \langle J_\varphi v, u \rangle. \tag{6.19}$$

From (6.19) we derive that

$$\|J_\varphi u\| = \left\langle J_\varphi u, \frac{u}{\|u\|} \right\rangle = \left\langle J_\varphi u, \frac{v}{\|u\|} \right\rangle \tag{6.20}$$

and, similarly,

$$\|J_\varphi v\| = \left\langle J_\varphi v, \frac{v}{\|v\|} \right\rangle = \left\langle J_\varphi v, \frac{u}{\|v\|} \right\rangle.$$

According to (6.20), $J_\varphi u$ (which is a nonzero element in X^*) achieves its norm at two points, $\frac{u}{\|u\|}$ and $\frac{v}{\|u\|}$ of the unit sphere of X. Since X is strictly convex, this implies $u = v$, a contradiction.

(c) The result follows from

$$\frac{\langle J_\varphi u, u \rangle}{\|u\|} = \varphi\left(\|u\|\right) \to \infty \text{ as } \|u\| \to \infty.$$

Remark 6.1. *Point (b) of the above proposition tells us that, if X is a smooth and strictly convex Banach space, any duality mapping $J_\varphi : X \to X^*$, in particular the normalized duality mapping $J : X \to X^*$, is strictly monotone. We shall see later that a deeper connection between the strict convexity of a space and the strict monotonicity of the normalized duality mapping on such a space exists. This connection was first proved by Petryshyn and tells us that a Banach space (not necessarily smooth) is strictly convex if and only if the normalized duality mapping on X is strictly monotone.*

Notice that, in case X is not a smooth space, the normalized duality mapping on X is a set-valued mapping $J : X \to 2^{X^*}$ defined by (6.8) and the strict monotonicity of J means that for any $x, y \in X$, $x \neq y$, and any $u^* \in Jx$, $v^* \in Jy$, the following inequality holds:

$$\langle u^* - v^*, x - y \rangle > 0.$$

Proposition 6.2. *If X is reflexive and smooth, then any duality mapping $J_\varphi : X \to X^*$ is demicontinuous, i.e.,*

$$u_n \to u \Longrightarrow J_\varphi u_n \rightharpoonup J_\varphi u.$$

Proof:

Since $u_n \to u$, (u_n) is bounded. Since $\|J_\varphi u_n\| = \varphi(\|u_n\|)$, we infer that $(J_\varphi u_n)$ is bounded. Since X^* is reflexive and $(J_\varphi u_n) \subset X^*$ is bounded, in order to show that $J_\varphi u_n \rightharpoonup J_\varphi u$ it is sufficient to show that $J_\varphi u$ is the unique weakly cluster point to $(J_\varphi u_n)$ or, in other words, all the weak convergent subsequences of $(J_\varphi u_n)$ have the same weak limit, namely $J_\varphi u$. (Notice that by virtue of the reflexivity of X^* and the boundedness of $(J_\varphi u_n)$, weak convergent subsequences of $(J_\varphi u_n)$ exist.) Indeed, assume that a subsequence of $(J_\varphi u_n)$, also denoted by $(J_\varphi u_n)$, weakly converges to some $x^* \in X^*$. We shall show that

$$\langle x^*, u \rangle = \varphi(\|u\|)\|u\| \text{ and } \|x^*\| = \varphi(\|u\|)$$

and then, the uniqueness of the duality mapping corresponding to φ will entail that $x^* = J_\varphi u$.

Now, $J_\varphi u_n \rightharpoonup x^*$ implies

$$\|x^*\| \leq \liminf_n \|J_\varphi u_n\| = \liminf_n \varphi(\|u_n\|) = \varphi(\|u\|). \tag{6.21}$$

Also, $u_n \to u$ (in X) and $J_\varphi u_n \rightharpoonup x^*$ (in X^*) imply

$$\langle J_\varphi u_n, u_n \rangle \to \langle x^*, u \rangle \text{ as } n \to \infty.$$

On the other hand, since

$$\langle J_\varphi u_n, u_n \rangle = \varphi(\|u_n\|)\|u_n\| \to \varphi(\|u\|)\|u\|,$$

we obtain that

$$\langle x^*, u \rangle = \varphi(\|u\|)\|u\|. \tag{6.22}$$

From (6.21) and (6.22) we get

$$\|x^*\| = \varphi(\|u\|),$$

which completes the proof.

Theorem 6.4, Proposition 6.1 and Proposition 6.2 allow us to state the following:

Theorem 6.5. (a) *If X is a smooth and reflexive Banach space, any duality mapping $J_\varphi : X \to X^*$ is surjective, i.e., given any $f \in X^*$, there exists $u \in X$ such that $J_\varphi u = f$.*

(b) *If, in addition, X is strictly convex then any duality mapping J_φ : $X \to X^*$ is bijective, i.e., given any $f \in X^*$, there exists a unique element $u \in X$ such that $J_\varphi u = f$.*

Remark 6.2. *Since many differential operators are duality mappings on appropriate function spaces, the abstract existence result supplied by Theorem 6.5 turns out to be a powerful tool in proving existence results for some boundary value problems corresponding to such operators. Some selected examples will be given later.*

Remark 6.3. *Point (b) of Theorem 6.5 tells us that if X is reflexive and smooth, any duality mapping $J_\varphi : X \to X^*$ is surjective. We shall see later that a deeper connection between the reflexivity of a space X and the surjectivity property of any duality mapping $J_\varphi : X \to 2^{X^*}$ exists, without any smoothness assumption of X. Roughly, the celebrated James' characterisation of reflexivity of X it is equivalent to the surjectivity property of any duality mapping $J_\varphi : X \to 2^{X^*}$, i.e., for any $f \in X^*$, there is some $x \in X$ such that $J_\varphi x \ni f$.*

Now it's time to give
Proof:
[Proof of Theorem *6.2 (Beurling and Livingston)*] We follow Browder [9] and we mention that the Minty-Browder's Surjectivity Theorem (Theorem 6.4) represents the main tool which is involved in this proof.

The proof will be divided into three steps.

Step 1. Define $T : V \to V^*$ as follows:

$$Tu = i^* \left[J_\varphi \left(u + x_0 \right) - y_0 \right]$$

where $i : V \to X$, $i(u) = u$ for all $u \in V$ is the canonical injection from V into X and $i^* : X^* \to V^*$ is the adjoint mapping of i, i.e., $\forall x^* \in X^* \longrightarrow i^* x^* \in V^*$, where $i^* x^*$ is defined by

$$\langle i^* x^*, v \rangle_{V,V^*} = \langle x^*, i(v) \rangle_{X,X^*} = \langle x^*, v \rangle_{X,X^*}$$

for all $x \in V$.

In other words, for any $x^* \in X^*$, $i^* x^*$ represents the restriction of x^* to V.

By the Hahn-Banach Theorem, i^* is surjective and weak to weak continuous, i.e.,

$$x_n^* \rightharpoonup x^* \text{ (in } X^*) \Longrightarrow i^* x_n^* \rightharpoonup i^* x^* \text{ (in } V^*)$$

as $n \to \infty$.

Step 2. $T : V \to V^*$ satisfies all the hypotheses of the Minty-Browder Surjectivity Theorem. Indeed one has:

a) V is reflexive (as a closed subspace of a reflexive space) and strictly convex (as a subspace of a strictly convex space).

b) T is strictly monotone.

Let u_1 and u_2 be two different elements in V. Then one has:

$$\langle Tu_1 - Tu_2, u_1 - u_2 \rangle_{V,V^*}$$

$$= \langle i^* [J_\varphi (u_1 + x_0) - y_0] - i^* [J_\varphi (u_2 + x_0) - y_0], u_1 - u_2 \rangle_{V,V^*}$$

$$= \langle J_\varphi (u_1 + x_0) - y_0 - [J_\varphi (u_2 + x_0) - y_0], i (u_1 - u_2) \rangle_{X,X^*}$$

$$= \langle J_\varphi (u_1 + x_0) - J_\varphi (u_2 + x_0), u_1 - u_2 \rangle_{X,X^*}$$

$$= \langle J_\varphi (u_1 + x_0) - J_\varphi (u_2 + x_0), (u_1 - x_0) - (u_2 - x_0) \rangle_{X,X^*} > 0,$$

since $u_1 - x_0$ and $u_2 - x_0$ are two different elements in X, the space X is assumed to be strictly convex and, by Proposition 6.1, (b), any duality mapping on a strict convex Banach space is strictly monotone.

c) T is demicontinuous.

Let $(u_n) \subset V$ be (strongly) convergent to $u \in V$: $u_n \to u$ as $n \to \infty$. Since J_φ is semicontinuous on X (Proposition 6.2), $J_\varphi (u_n + x_0) - y_0 \rightharpoonup J_\varphi (u + x_0) - y_0$ in X^*. Since $i^* \in \mathcal{L} (X^*, V^*)$,

$$i^* [J_\varphi (u_n + x_0) - y_0] \rightharpoonup i^* [J_\varphi (u + x_0) - y_0] \text{ in } V^*,$$

that is $Tu_n \rightharpoonup Tu$ in V^*.

d) T is strongly coercive, i.e.,

$$\frac{\langle Tu, u \rangle_{V,V^*}}{\|u\|} \to \infty \text{ as } \|u\| \to \infty.$$

Indeed, one has:

$$\frac{\langle Tu, u \rangle_{V,V^*}}{\|u\|} = \frac{\langle J_\varphi (u + x_0) - y_0, u \rangle_{X,X^*}}{\|u\|}$$

$$= \frac{\langle J_\varphi (u + x_0) - y_0, (u + x_0) - x_0 \rangle_{X,X^*}}{\|u\|}$$

$$= \frac{\langle J_\varphi (u + x_0), u + x_0 \rangle_{X,X^*} - \langle J_\varphi (u + x_0), x_0 \rangle_{X,X^*} - \langle y_0, u \rangle_{X,X^*}}{\|u\|}$$

$$\geq \frac{\varphi\left(\|u + x_0\|\right) \|u + x_0\| - \|J_\varphi\left(u + x_0\right)\| \|x_0\| - \|y_0\| \|u\|}{\|u\|}$$

$$= \frac{\varphi\left(\|u + x_0\|\right) \|u + x_0\| - \varphi\left(\|u + x_0\|\right) \|x_0\| - \|y_0\| \|u\|}{\|u\|}$$

$$= \varphi\left(\|u + x_0\|\right) \left[\frac{\|u + x_0\|}{\|u\|} - \frac{\|x_0\|}{\|u\|}\right] - \|y_0\|.$$

Thus,

$$\frac{\langle Tu, u\rangle_{V,V^*}}{\|u\|} \geq \varphi\left(\|u + x_0\|\right) \left[\frac{\|u + x_0\|}{\|u\|} - \frac{\|x_0\|}{\|u\|}\right] - \|y_0\|. \tag{6.23}$$

As $\|u + x_0\| \to \infty$ and $\frac{\|u+x_0\|}{\|u\|} \to 1$ as $\|u\| \to \infty$, it follows from (6.23) that

$$\frac{\langle Tu, u\rangle_{V,V^*}}{\|u\|} \to \infty \text{ as } \|u\| \to \infty.$$

Step 3. From a), b), c) and d) in the preceding step, it follows that the Minty-Browder Surjectivity Theorem (Theorem 6.4) applies. Consequently, $T : V \to V^*$ is a bijection of V onto V^*. In particular, there is a unique $u \in V$ that satisfies:

$$i^*\left[J_\varphi\left(u + x_0\right) - y_0\right] = 0_{V^*}. \tag{6.24}$$

It follows from (6.24) that

$$\langle i^*\left[J_\varphi\left(u + x_0\right) - y_0\right], v\rangle_{V,V^*} = \langle J_\varphi\left(u + x_0\right) - y_0, v\rangle_{X,X^*} = 0,$$

for all $v \in V$, which reads as

$$J_\varphi\left(u + x_0\right) - y_0 \in V^\perp$$

or, equivalently

$$J_\varphi\left(u + x_0\right) \in V^\perp + y_0.$$

Thus,

$$J_\varphi\left(V + x_0\right) \cap \left(V^\perp + y_0\right)$$

is not empty.

Moreover, we shall show that $J_\varphi\left(V + x_0\right) \cap \left(V^\perp + y_0\right)$ reduces to a point.

Assume, by contradiction, that two different elements, $J_\varphi\left(u + x_0\right)$ and $J_\varphi\left(u' + x_0\right)$, with $u, u' \in V$, belong to $\left(V^\perp + y_0\right)$. Then, at least one of them, must be different from zero.

Let say that $J_\varphi (u + x_0) \neq 0_{X^*}$, which is equivalent with $u + x_0 \neq 0$.

Now, from $J_\varphi (u + x_0) \in V^\perp + y_0$ and $J_\varphi (u' + x_0) \in V^\perp + y_0$ it follows that $J_\varphi (u + x_0) - J_\varphi (u' + x_0) \in V^\perp$ or equivalently,

$$\langle J_\varphi (u + x_0) - J_\varphi (u' + x_0), v \rangle_{X,X^*} = 0, \qquad (6.25)$$

for all $v \in V$. In particular, $v = (u + x_0) - (u' + x_0) = u - u' \in V$ and, thus, it follows from (6.25) that

$$0 = \langle J_\varphi (u + x_0) - J_\varphi (u' + x_0), (u + x_0) - (u' + x_0) \rangle_{X,X^*}$$

$$\geq (\varphi (\|u + x_0\|) - \varphi (\|u' + x_0\|)) (\|u + x_0\| - \|u' + x_0\|) \geq 0.$$

We derive that

$$(\varphi (\|u + x_0\|) - \varphi (\|u' + x_0\|)) (\|u + x_0\| - \|u' + x_0\|) = 0,$$

and, since φ is strictly increasing, we conclude that

$$\|u + x_0\| = \|u' + x_0\| > 0$$

saying that $u' + x_0$ is different from zero too and, $J_\varphi (u' + x_0) \neq 0_{X^*}$. Moreover, $\|J_\varphi (u' + x_0)\| = \|J_\varphi (u + x_0)\|$.

Taking into account these new achievements, we go back to

$$0 = \langle J_\varphi (u + x_0) - J_\varphi (u' + x_0), (u + x_0) - (u' + x_0) \rangle$$

and rewrite it as

$$0 = [\langle J_\varphi (u + x_0), u + x_0 \rangle - \langle J_\varphi (u + x_0), u' + x_0 \rangle]$$

$$+ [\langle J_\varphi (u' + x_0), u' + x_0 \rangle - \langle J_\varphi (u' + x_0), u + x_0 \rangle]. \qquad (6.26)$$

Since any square bracket is positive, equality (6.26) holds if and only if each bracket equals zero, i.e.,

$$0 = [\langle J_\varphi (u + x_0), u + x_0 \rangle - \langle J_\varphi (u + x_0), u' + x_0 \rangle] \qquad (6.27)$$

and

$$0 = [\langle J_\varphi (u' + x_0), u' + x_0 \rangle - \langle J_\varphi (u' + x_0), u + x_0 \rangle]. \qquad (6.28)$$

From (6.28), it easily follows that

$$\langle J_\varphi (u' + x_0), u + x_0 \rangle = \langle J_\varphi (u' + x_0), u' + x_0 \rangle$$

$$= \|J_\varphi (u' + x_0)\| \|u' + x_0\| = \|J_\varphi (u' + x_0)\| \|u + x_0\|$$

$$= \|J_\varphi (u + x_0)\| \|u + x_0\| = \langle J_\varphi (u + x_0), u + x_0 \rangle. \qquad (6.29)$$

Let $\chi : X \to X^{**}$ be the canonical injection of X into X^{**}:

$$\langle \chi(x), x^* \rangle = \langle x^*, x \rangle \text{ for all } x \in X \text{ and } x^* \in X^*.$$

Then taking into account (6.29), one obtains:

$$\|\chi(u + x_0)\| = \|u + x_0\| = \left\langle \frac{J_\varphi(u' + x_0)}{\|J_\varphi(u' + x_0)\|}, u + x_0 \right\rangle$$

$$= \left\langle \frac{J_\varphi(u + x_0)}{\|J_\varphi(u + x_0)\|}, u + x_0 \right\rangle = \left\langle \chi(u + x_0), \frac{J_\varphi(u' + x_0)}{\|J_\varphi(u' + x_0)\|} \right\rangle$$

$$= \left\langle \chi(u + x_0), \frac{J_\varphi(u + x_0)}{\|J_\varphi(u + x_0)\|} \right\rangle.$$

We conclude that the nonzero element $\chi(u + x_0) \in X^{**}$ achieves its norm at two points of the unit sphere in X^*. Since X^* is strictly convex, we must have

$$\frac{J_\varphi(u' + x_0)}{\|J_\varphi(u' + x_0)\|} = \frac{J_\varphi(u + x_0)}{\|J_\varphi(u + x_0)\|}$$

and, since $\|J_\varphi(u' + x_0)\| = \|J_\varphi(u + x_0)\|$ we obtain $J_\varphi(u' + x_0) = J_\varphi(u + x_0)$, a contradiction.

We are now in a position to show how the Beurling-Livingston Theorem can be used to proving Theorem 6.2. First, the following lemma is needed.

Lemma 6.1. *Let the integers be partitioned into two disjoint sets A and A'. Let p be a given exponent such that $1 < p < \infty$. Define the following subspace of L^p:*

$$V := \{ f \in L^p; c_n(f) = 0 \text{ for all } n \in A \}. \tag{6.30}$$

Then one has:

(a) V is the closure of the subspace generated by $\{e^{ikt}; k \in A'\}$:

$$V = \overline{Sp[e^{ikt}; k \in A']}.$$

(b) The annihilator of V is given by

$$V^\perp = \left\{ h \in L^q; \frac{1}{p} + \frac{1}{q} = 1, c_n(h) = 0, n \in A' \right\}.$$

Proof:
(a) First we show that, as defined by (6.30), V is closed. Indeed, if $(f_k) \subset V$ and $f_k \to f$ in L^p, then from

$$|c_n(f_k) - c_n(f)| \le \|f_k - f\|,$$

it follows that $c_n(f) = 0$ for all $n \in A$, thus $f \in V$.

Now, for any $k \in A'$, $e^{ikt} \in V$. Indeed, it is clear that $e^{ikt} \in L^p$ for all $k \in A'$.

Moreover, for any $n \in A$,

$$c_n\left(e^{ikt}\right) = \frac{1}{2\pi}\int_0^{2\pi} e^{-int} \cdot e^{ikt} \mathrm{d}t = 0,$$

since $n \in A$, $k \in A'$ and the system $\left\{e^{int}; n = 0, \pm 1, \pm 2, \ldots\right\}$ is orthonormal in L^2. Thus $e^{ikt} \in V$ and, consequently, any finite linear combination of e^{ikt} belongs to V. From all these arguments we infer that

$$\overline{Sp\left[e^{ikt}; k \in A'\right]} \subset \overline{V} = V.$$

For the converse inclusion, let $f \in V$ be given. We have to show that there is a sequence contained in $Sp\left[e^{ikt}; k \in A'\right]$ converging to f. As for any $f \in L^p$,

$$\sum_{n=-k}^{k} c_n\left(f\right) e^{int} \to f\left(t\right) \text{ for a.e. } t \in [0, 2\pi]$$

as $k \to \infty$.

Since $c_n\left(f\right) = 0$ for $n \in A$, it follows that

$$\sum_{\substack{n=-k \\ n \in A'}}^{k} c_n\left(f\right) e^{int} \to f\left(t\right) \text{ for a.e. } t \in [0, 2\pi]$$

as $k \to \infty$, showing that $f \in \overline{Sp\left[e^{ikt}; k \in A'\right]}$.

Let $H := \left\{h \in L^q; \frac{1}{p} + \frac{1}{q} = 1, c_n\left(h\right) = 0, n \in A'\right\}$.

First we show that $H \subset V^\perp$, i.e., if h is an arbitrary element in H, then

$$\int_0^{2\pi} h\left(t\right) f\left(t\right) \mathrm{d}t = 0, \text{ for all } f \in V.$$

This is true for $f\left(t\right) = e^{ikt}$, $k \in A'$. Indeed, for any $k \in A'$,

$$\int_0^{2\pi} h\left(t\right) e^{ikt} \mathrm{d}t = c_k\left(h\right) = 0.$$

It follows from this that

$$\int_0^{2\pi} h\left(t\right) f\left(t\right) \mathrm{d}t = 0 \text{ for any } f \in Sp\left[e^{ikt}; k \in A'\right].$$

Finally, since

$$V = \overline{Sp\left[e^{ikt}; k \in A'\right]},$$

for any $f \in V$, there is a sequence $\left(f_n\right) \subset Sp\left[e^{ikt}; k \in A'\right]$ such that $f_n \to f$. Since $\int_0^{2\pi} h\left(t\right) f_n\left(t\right)\mathrm{d}t = 0$ for all n, it follows that $\int_0^{2\pi} h\left(t\right) f\left(t\right)\mathrm{d}t = 0$ too.

Conversely, $V^\perp \subset H$.

Let $h \in V^\perp$. Then,

$$\int_0^{2\pi} h\left(t\right) f\left(t\right) \mathrm{d}t = 0 \text{ for all } f \in V.$$

In particular, $\int_0^{2\pi} h\left(t\right) e^{ikt}\mathrm{d}t = 0$ for all $k \in A'$, that is $c_k\left(h\right) = 0$ for all $k \in A'$.

Proof:

[Proof of Theorem *6.1*] Now, by using the Beurling-Livingston Theorem (Theorem 6.4), the proof of Theorem 6.1 is as follows.

Under the hypotheses of Theorem 6.1, Theorem 6.4 applies with the following choice:

- $X = L^p$, $1 < p < \infty$, $X^* = L^q$, $\frac{1}{p} + \frac{1}{q} = 1$;
- $J_\varphi : L^p \to L^q$, the duality mapping corresponding to the gauge function $\varphi(t) = t^{p-1}$, $t \geq 0$;
- $V = \{g \in L^p; c_n(g) = 0, n \in A\}$.

According to Lemma 6.1, V is a closed subspace in L^p and its annihilator is given by

$$V^\perp = \{l \in L^q; c_n(l) = 0, n \in A'\}.$$

- $x_0 = g_0$, $y_0 = h_0$.

Then,

$$V + g_0 = \{f \in L^p; c_n(f) = c_n(g_0) = a_n, n \in A\}$$

$$V^\perp + h_0 = \{h \in L^q; c_n(h) = c_n(h_0) = b_n, n \in A'\}.$$

According to Theorem 6.4,

$$J_\varphi(V + g_0) \cap (V^\perp + h_0)$$

reduces to an element, i.e., there is a unique element $f \in V + g_0$ such that $J_\varphi f \in V^\perp + h_0$.

In other words, there is a unique $f \in L^p$ that satisfies

$$c_n(f) = c_n(g_0) = a_n \text{ for } n \in A$$

and

$$c_n(J_\varphi f) = c_n(h_0) = b_n \text{ for } n \in A'.$$

Since $\varphi(t) = t^{p-1}$, $c_n(J_\varphi f) = c_n(S_{p-1}f)$ and the proof is complete.

6.3 Equivalent definitions

Recall that a duality mapping on a Banach space X, corresponding to a gauge function φ, is defined by (see (6.7)):

$$X \ni x \to J_\varphi x = \{u^* \in X^*; \langle u^*, x \rangle = \|u^*\| \, \|x\|, \ \|u^*\| = \varphi(\|x\|)\} \in 2^{X^*}$$
$$(6.31)$$

or, equivalently

$$X \ni x \to J_\varphi x = \begin{cases} \{0_{X^*}\} & \text{if } x = 0_X; \\ \varphi(\|x\|)\{x^* \in X^*; \|x^*\| = 1, \langle x^*, x \rangle = \|x\|\} & \text{if } x \neq 0_X. \end{cases} \tag{6.32}$$

Furthermore, due to one of Asplund's results (cf. [4]), J_φ can be equivalently defined as

$$\forall x \in X, \ J_\varphi x = \partial F(x) \text{ where } F(x) = \int_0^{\|x\|} \varphi(t)\, dt. \tag{6.33}$$

Here, $\partial F(x)$ stands for the sub-differential at x of the convex and continuous functional F, in the sense of convex analysis, i.e.

$$\partial F : X \to 2^{X^*},$$

$$\partial F(x) = \{u^* \in X^*; F(y) - F(x) \geq \langle u^*, y - x \rangle \text{ for all } y \in X\}. \tag{6.34}$$

Remark that $\partial F(x) \neq \emptyset$ at any $x \in X$. This is due to the following theorem (see, e.g. [49, Section 1], [30], [35, Theorem 3.26 and Lemma 3.25]):

Theorem 6.6. *Let $(X, \|\ \|)$ be a Banach space, let $D \subset X$ be a nonempty open convex subset of X and let $F : D \to \mathbb{R}$ be a convex continuous function. Then one has:*

(a) *$(\partial F)(x)$ is nonempty, for all $x \in D$.*

(b) *Moreover,*

$$(\partial F)(x) = \left\{x^* \in X^*; (d^+ F)(x) \cdot h \geq \langle x^*, h \rangle, \forall h \in X\right\}$$

where,

$$(d^+ F)(x) \cdot h = \lim_{t \to 0_+} \frac{F(x + th) - F(x)}{t}.$$

Now, one of the most simple convex and continuous function on X is $F(x) = \|x\|, \ \forall x \in X$. By Theorem 6.6, $(\partial \|\ \|)(x) \neq \emptyset$ for any $x \in X$. In fact, simple computations show that:

$$\begin{aligned} &\text{(a) } (\partial \|\ \|)(0_X) = \{x^* \in X^*; \|x^*\| \leq 1\} = \overline{B}_{X^*}(0_{X^*}, 1) \\ &\text{(b) } (\partial \|\ \|)(x) = \{x^* \in X^*; \|x^*\| = 1, \langle x^*, x \rangle = \|x\|\} \text{ if } x \neq 0_X. \end{aligned} \tag{6.35}$$

Now, by comparing (6.32) and (6.35), another equivalent definition of J_φ is obtained, namely

$$J_\varphi x = \begin{cases} \{0_{X^*}\} & \text{if } x = 0_X; \\ \varphi(\|x\|)(\partial \|\ \|)(x) & \text{if } x \neq 0_X. \end{cases} \tag{6.36}$$

Formula (6.36) provides "the concrete form" of a duality mapping on a Banach space: if we are able to compute the sub-differential of the norm of that space, formula (6.36) allows us to "compute" the duality mapping on the same space.

Next we are interested in formulating some (at least sufficient) conditions ensuring that $(\partial \| \ \|)(x)$ is a singleton. To do that we first recall the following classical results (see, e.g. Phelps [49, Corollary, p. 20]).

Assume that D is an open convex subset of a Banach space X and $f : D \to \mathbb{R}$ is a convex function. Then one has:

a) if f is continuous at a point $x_0 \in D$ then f is continuous at any point $x \in D$ and $(\partial f)(x)$ is nonempty;

b) $(\partial f)(x)$ is a singleton if and only if f is Gâteaux differentiable at x and, in that case, $(\partial f)(x) = \{(df)(x)\}$ where the Gâteaux differential of f at x, $(df)(x) \in X^*$ is defined by

$$X \ni h \longrightarrow \langle (df)(x), h \rangle = \lim_{t \to 0} \frac{f(x + th) - f(x)}{t}.$$

Now, since $\lim_{t \to 0} \frac{\|th\|}{t}$ does not exist for $h \neq 0_X$, no Banach spaces with a Gâteaux differentiable norm at 0_X exist. On the contrary, there are important classes of Banach spaces whose norm is Gâteaux differentiable at any $x \neq 0_X$. For example, if $(X, (\ ,\ ), \| \ \|)$ is a Hilbert space then, at any $x \neq 0_X$, $(d \| \ \|)(x) = \frac{x}{\|x\|}$, in the sense that

$$\langle (d \| \ \|)(x), h \rangle = \left(\frac{x}{\|x\|}, h \right), \text{ for all } h \in X.$$

Next, by a space with a Gâteaux differentiable norm we will understand a Banach space whose norm is Gâteaux differentiable at any nonzero point of the space and usually we shall write $(\text{grad} \| \ \|)(x)$ instead of $(d \| \ \|)(x)$.

According to Vajnberg ([53, Lemma 2.5]) the Gâteaux gradient of the norm has the following metric properties:

$$\begin{aligned} &\|(\text{grad} \| \ \|)(x)\| = 1 \\ &\langle (\text{grad} \| \ \|)(x), x \rangle = \|x\| \\ &(\text{grad} \| \ \|)(\alpha x) = \text{sign} \alpha \, (\text{grad} \| \ \|)(x), \text{ for any } \alpha \neq 0. \end{aligned} \quad (6.37)$$

The following theorem summarizes some of the results discussed above.

Theorem 6.7. *Let* $(X, \| \ \|)$ *be a Banach space. The following statements are equivalent:*

(a) *Any duality mapping on X is single valued.*

(b) *The space $(X, \| \ \|)$ is smooth.*

(c) *At any nonzero $x \in X$, $(\partial \| \ \|)(x)$ is a singleton.*

(d) *The norm of X is Gâteaux differentiable.*

If any of the previous conditions (a)–(d) is satisfied, then, a duality mapping $J_\varphi : X \to X^*$ is defined by

$$J_\varphi x = \begin{cases} \{0_{X^*}\} & \text{if } x = 0_X; \\ \varphi\left(\|x\|\right)\left(\text{grad}\, \| \, \|\right)(x) & \text{if } x \neq 0_X. \end{cases} \tag{6.38}$$

With a different proof, the equivalence (b)$\Longleftrightarrow$(d) is contained in Diestel [19, Theorem 1 in Chapter Two]. By combining the results provided by Theorem 6.7 and the quoted theorem in Diestel [19] one can see that, we also have:

Corollary 6.2. *If any of conditions* (a)–(d) *is satisfied, then, we also have:*
(e) *every support mapping* $x \in X\backslash\{0_X\} \longrightarrow h\,(x) \in X^*\backslash\{0_{X^*}\}$ *is norm to weak-star continuous.*

Recall that a mapping $h : X\backslash\{0_X\} \longrightarrow X^*\backslash\{0_{X^*}\}$ is called a *supporting mapping* whenever

(i) $\|x\| = 1 \Longrightarrow \begin{cases} \|h\,(x)\| = 1 \\ \langle h\,(x)\,, x \rangle = 1 \end{cases}$;

(ii) $h\,(\lambda x) = \lambda h\,(x)$ for all $\lambda > 0$ and all $x \in X\backslash\{0_X\}$.

Example 6.1. *Taking into account the metric properties of the gradient of the norm (as given by (6.37)) we infer that, on a smooth Banach space, the normalized duality mapping* $x \in X\backslash\{0_X\} \longrightarrow Jx = \|x\|\left(\text{grad}\, \| \, \|\right)(x) \in X^*$ *is a supporting mapping.*

Consequently, we get:

Corollary 6.3. *On every smooth Banach space, the normalized duality mapping* $x \in X\backslash\{0_X\} \longrightarrow Jx = \|x\|\left(\text{grad}\, \| \, \|\right)(x) \in X^*$ *is norm to weak* continuous.*

Obviously, if in addition X is reflexive then the weak and the weak* topologies on X^* are the same and we find again the result supplied by Proposition 6.2.

6.4 Examples of duality mappings on some smooth function spaces

6.4.1 *On some methods to prove the smoothness of a Banach space*

Method A. Give a direct check to the definition of the smoothness, i.e., show that for any nonzero $x \in X$ there exists a unique element (depending on x) $x^* \in X^*$ that satisfies

$$\langle x^*, x \rangle = \|x\| \text{ and } \|x^*\| = 1. \tag{6.39}$$

Here is an example. Let $(H, (\, , \,))$ be a real Hilbert space and let x be a nonzero element in H. Let $\ell \in H^*$ be such that

$$\langle \ell, x \rangle = \|x\| \text{ and } \|\ell\| = 1. \tag{6.40}$$

For any $\ell \in H^*$ satisfying (6.40) let $w = w(\ell) \in H$ be the unique element in H "representing" ℓ, i.e. such that

$$\langle \ell, u \rangle = (w(\ell), u) \text{ for all } u \in H \text{ and } \|w(\ell)\|_H = \|\ell\|_{H^*} = 1. \tag{6.41}$$

We claim that $w(\ell) = \dfrac{x}{\|x\|}$ (which proves the uniqueness of ℓ). Assume the contrary: $w(\ell) = \dfrac{x}{\|x\|} + y$ with $y \neq 0_H$. Combining (6.40) and (6.41) we get:

$$\|x\| = \langle \ell, x \rangle = (w(\ell), x) = \left(\frac{x}{\|x\|} + y, x \right),$$

which implies $(y, x) = 0$.

Consequently, by Pythagoras's Theorem,

$$1 = \|w(\ell)\|^2 = \left\| \frac{x}{\|x\|} + y \right\|^2 = \left\| \frac{x}{\|x\|} \right\|^2 + \|y\|^2 = 1 + \|y\|^2.$$

Thus, $y = 0_H$ and $w(\ell) = \dfrac{x}{\|x\|}$.

We conclude that: for a given $x \in H \setminus \{0_H\}$, the unique linear and continuous functional $x^* \in H^*$ satisfying (6.39) is that defined by $u \in H \to \left(\dfrac{x}{\|x\|}, u \right)$. Thus H is smooth.

Method B. Show that the dual space X^* is strictly convex and then apply Klee's Theorem.

Next, the above strategy will be illustrated by considering two examples.

The first example. Let again $(H, (,))$ be a real Hilbert space. It is known that the dual space H^* may be viewed as a Hilbert space itself. That is because the dual norm $\|f\|_{H^*} = \sup\limits_{x \neq 0_H} \dfrac{\langle f, x \rangle}{\|x\|}$ may be regarded as being generated by the inner product $(f, g)_{H^*} = (u_f, u_g)_H$ where u_f (respectively u_g) are the unique elements in H representing f and g (according to Riesz's Theorem), i.e.,

$$\langle f, h \rangle = (h, u_f)_H \text{ for all } h \in H,$$

$$\langle g, h \rangle = (h, u_g)_H \text{ for all } h \in H.$$

On the other hand, from the *parallelogram law*, in any Hilbert space one has:

$$\left\| \frac{x+y}{2} \right\|^2 + \left\| \frac{x-y}{2} \right\|^2 = \frac{1}{2} \left(\|x\|^2 + \|y\|^2 \right).$$

It follows that if $\|x\| = \|y\| = 1$ and $x \neq y$, then one has

$$\left\| \frac{x+y}{2} \right\|^2 = 1 - \left\| \frac{x-y}{2} \right\|^2,$$

which implies that $\left\| \dfrac{x+y}{2} \right\| < 1$. Accordingly, any real Hilbert space is strictly convex.

We conclude that the dual space of any real Hilbert space is still a Hilbert space. Any real Hilbert space is strictly convex. Accordingly, the dual of any real Hilbert space is strictly convex. By Klee's Theorem, any real Hilbert space is smooth.

The second example. Let Ω be an open (thus measurable) subset of $\mathbb{R}^n$. Given any $1 < p < \infty$, we let $L^p(\Omega)$ denote the set formed by all (equivalence classes of) measurable functions $f : \Omega \to \mathbb{R}$ such that $|f|^p \in L^1(\Omega)$ or equivalently

$$\int_\Omega |f(x)|^p \, dx < \infty.$$

It is known that $L^p(\Omega)$ is a real vector space and the map

$$u \in L^p(\Omega) \longrightarrow \|u\|_{L^p} = \left(\int_\Omega |u(x)|^p \, dx \right)^{1/p}$$

is a norm on $L^p(\Omega)$. Moreover, the space $(L^p(\Omega), \| \; \|_{L^p})$, $1 < p < \infty$ is uniformly convex and thus reflexive.

By definition, a Banach space is said to be:

(a) *uniformly convex* if for any $\varepsilon \in (0, 2]$ there exists $\delta = \delta(\varepsilon) \in (0, 1]$ such that, for any $x, y \in X$ with $\|x\| = \|y\| = 1$ and $\|x - y\| \geq \varepsilon$, one has

$$\left\| \frac{x + y}{2} \right\| \leq 1 - \delta(\varepsilon);$$

(b) *locally uniformly convex* if

$$\left[\|x_n\| = \|x\| = 1 \text{ and } \left\| \frac{x_n + x}{2} \right\| \to 1 \right] \implies x_n \to x.$$

Theorem 6.8. (1) *Every uniformly convex Banach space is locally uniformly convex.*

(2) *Every locally uniformly convex Banach space is strictly convex.*

For the proof see Diestel [19].

For the proof of uniform convexity of $(L^p(\Omega), \|\ \|_{L^p})$ see, e.g. Adams [1, Corollary 2.29], Brezis [8, Theorem 4.10]. On the other hand, due to a well known theorem of Milman [41] and Pettis [48] every uniformly convex Banach space is reflexive. Thus, being uniformly convex, $(L^p(\Omega), \|\ \|_{L^p})$, $1 < p < \infty$ is reflexive. Now, the dual space of $(L^p(\Omega), \|\ \|_{L^p})$, $1 < p < \infty$ is $\left(L^{p'}(\Omega), \|\ \|_{L^{p'}} \right)$, with $\dfrac{1}{p} + \dfrac{1}{p'} = 1$ (hence $1 < p' < \infty$). By the above quoted result, $\left(L^{p'}(\Omega), \|\ \|_{L^{p'}} \right)$ is uniformly convex (which is "more" than strictly convex). By Klee's Theorem again, $(L^p(\Omega), \|\ \|_{L^p})$ is smooth.

Method C. According to Theorem 6.7, a Banach space $(X, \|\ \|)$ is smooth if and only if its norm is Gâteaux differentiable. Thus if we are able to show that, at any nonzero $x \in X$, the limit

$$\lim_{t \to 0} \frac{\|x + th\| - \|x\|}{t} \in \mathbb{R}$$

exists for all $h \in X$, then the smoothness of X is proven and if we explicitly compute the previous limit then we obtain an explicit formula for the gradient of the norm of X, namely, at any nonzero $x \in X$,

$$\langle (\text{grad} \|\ \|)(x), h \rangle = \lim_{t \to 0} \frac{\|x + th\| - \|x\|}{t}.$$

Consequently, according to (6.38) we will have an explicit formula for any duality mapping $J_\varphi : X \to X^*$.

Bearing in mind these arguments, next we pay some attention to the computation of the gradient of the norm in some important spaces of functions: the Lebesgue spaces $L^p(\Omega)$, $1 < p < \infty$, the Sobolev spaces $W_0^{1,p}(\Omega)$, $1 < p < \infty$, the Sobolev spaces with variable exponents $\left(U_{\Gamma_0}, \|\ \|_{0, p(\cdot), \nabla} \right)$, the space of periodic functions $W_T^{1,p}(0, T; \mathbb{R}^n)$, $1 < p < \infty$.

6.4.2 Some abstract results

We start by observing that in any Hilbert space $(H, (\ , \ ))$, if $(x_n)_{n=1}^{\infty}$ is a sequence in H and x is an element in H such that

$$x_n \rightharpoonup x \text{ and } \|x_n\| \to \|x\| \text{ as } n \to \infty \tag{6.42}$$

then $x_n \to x$ as $n \to \infty$.

Indeed, the parallelogram law gives us

$$\|x_n + x\|^2 + \|x_n - x\|^2 = 2 \left(\|x_n\|^2 + \|x\|^2 \right),$$

which yields to

$$\|x_n - x\|^2 = \|x_n\|^2 + \|x\|^2 - 2 (x_n, x). \tag{6.43}$$

Clearly, from (6.42) and (6.43) it follows that

$$\|x_n - x\| \to 0 \text{ as } n \to \infty.$$

The above simple remark concerning the Hilbert spaces justifies the following definition:

Definition 6.3. *We say that a real Banach space* $(X, \| \ \|)$ *possesses the* Kadeč-Klee *property if from*

$$(x_n)_{n=1}^{\infty} \subset X, x \in X, x_n \rightharpoonup x \text{ and } \|x_n\| \to \|x\|,$$

it follows that $x_n \to x$.

According to the above result, any real Hilbert space possesses the Kadeč-Klee property. But any Hilbert space is uniformly convex. Indeed, if $\|x\| = \|y\| = 1$ and $\|x - y\| \geq \varepsilon$ then, from the parallelogram law again,

$$\left\| \frac{x + y}{2} \right\|^2 + \left\| \frac{x - y}{2} \right\|^2 = \frac{1}{2} \left(\|x\|^2 + \|y\|^2 \right),$$

we derive that

$$\left\| \frac{x + y}{2} \right\| \leq 1 - \delta(\varepsilon), \text{ with } \delta(\varepsilon) = 1 - \sqrt{1 - \varepsilon^2/4}.$$

Thus a natural question arises: does any uniformly convex Banach space possess the Kadeč-Klee property?

The following theorem shows that even a stronger result holds.

Theorem 6.9. *Every locally uniformly convex Banach space possesses the* Kadeč-Klee *property.*

Proof:
Consider first the particular case

$$x_n \rightharpoonup x \text{ and } \|x_n\| = \|x\| = 1.$$

(In that case the assumption $\|x_n\| \to \|x\|$ is trivially satisfied.)

In order to show that $x_n \to x$ it would be sufficient to show that $\left\|\dfrac{x_n + x}{2}\right\| \to 1$ and to take into account that X is assumed to be locally uniformly convex.

Let $x^* \in X^*$ be such that $\|x^*\| = 1$ and $\langle x^*, x \rangle = \|x\| = 1$. Then one has

$$\left\langle x^*, \frac{x_n + x}{2} \right\rangle \le \left\|\frac{x_n + x}{2}\right\| \le 1. \tag{6.44}$$

On the other hand, since $x_n \rightharpoonup x$ we also have

$$\left\langle x^*, \frac{x_n + x}{2} \right\rangle \to \langle x^*, x \rangle = 1. \tag{6.45}$$

Clearly, from (6.44) and (6.45) one derives that $\left\|\dfrac{x_n + x}{2}\right\| \to 1$.

Consider now the general case

$$x_n \rightharpoonup x \text{ and } \|x_n\| \to \|x\|. \tag{6.46}$$

If $x = 0_X$, it is obvious that from $\|x_n\| \to \|0_X\| = 0$, it follows that $x_n \to x = 0_X$. Assume thus that in (6.46), $x \ne 0_X$. Then it obviously follows from (6.46) that

$$\frac{x_n}{\|x_n\|} \rightharpoonup \frac{x}{\|x\|}, \text{ with } \left\|\frac{x_n}{\|x_n\|}\right\| = \left\|\frac{x}{\|x\|}\right\| = 1.$$

According to the previously obtained result, $\dfrac{x_n}{\|x_n\|} \to \dfrac{x}{\|x\|}$ holds, which, in combination with $\|x_n\| \to \|x\|$ gives us $x_n \to x$.

6.4.3 *Fréchet differentiability of norms*

The following result is a classical one (see, e.g., Phelps [49, Corollary, p. 20]).

Theorem 6.10. *Let $(X, \|\ \|)$ be a Banach space, let $D \subset X$ be a nonempty open convex subset of X and let $f : D \to \mathbb{R}$ be a Fréchet differentiable convex function on D. Then, the map $x \in D \longrightarrow f'(x) \in X^*$ is norm to norm continuous.*

Thus, Fréchet differentiable convex functions are necessarily C^1.

Clearly, $X \backslash \{0_X\}$ is open but not convex. But, at any $x_0 \in X \backslash \{0_X\}$, there is some open ball $\mathcal{B}(x_0, r) \subset X \backslash \{0_X\}$ and Theorem 6.10 applies for $f(x) = \|x\|$ and $D = \mathcal{B}(x_0, r)$. Consequently, if the norm is Fréchet differentiable on $\mathcal{B}(x_0, r)$ then it is $\mathcal{C}^1$. That's why, conditions ensuring Fréchet differentiability of the norms are in order. Below, such a condition expressed in terms of duality mappings is given.

Theorem 6.11. *Let $(X, \| \ \|)$ be a Banach space. Then one has:*

(a) *Every duality mapping on X is single valued (i.e., $J_\varphi : X \to X^*$) and continuous if and only if the norm of X is Fréchet differentiable.*

(b) *A Gâteaux differentiable norm is a Fréchet differentiable one if and only if the map*

$$x \in X \backslash \{0_X\} \longrightarrow (\text{grad} \ \| \ \|)(x) \in S_{X^*}(0_{X^*}, 1)$$

is continuous.

Proof:

(a) Assume that $J_\varphi : X \to X^*$ and it is continuous. First, since J_φ is single-valued, X is smooth and J_φ is defined as

$$J_\varphi x = \begin{cases} \{0_{X^*}\} & \text{if } x = 0_X; \\ \varphi(\|x\|) (\text{grad} \ \| \ \|)(x) & \text{if } x \neq 0_X. \end{cases}$$

Obviously, since $\|J_\varphi x\| = \varphi(\|x\|) \to 0$ as $x \to 0_X$, we infer that any duality mapping on a smooth space is continuous at 0_X. That's why, assuming that $J_\varphi : X \to X^*$ is continuous we assume that

$$x \in X \backslash \{0_X\} \longrightarrow \|J_\varphi x\| (\text{grad} \ \| \ \|)(x)$$

is continuous. Let $(x_n) \subset X \backslash \{0_X\}$ such that $x_n \to x \in X \backslash \{0_X\}$. From $J_\varphi x_n \to J_\varphi x$ we infer that

$$\frac{J_\varphi x_n}{\|J_\varphi x_n\|} \to \frac{J_\varphi x}{\|J_\varphi x\|},$$

that is $(\text{grad} \ \| \ \|)(x_n) \to (\text{grad} \ \| \ \|)(x)$.

But the continuity of the Gâteaux differential implies the existence of the Fréchet differential and their coincidence. Thus, the norm of X is Fréchet differentiable.

Conversely, assume that the norm of X is Fréchet differentiable. Then, the space is smooth (or, equivalently, J_φ is single-valued). Furthermore, by Theorem 6.10, the norm is $\mathcal{C}^1$, i.e.

$$x \in X \backslash \{0_X\} \longrightarrow (\text{grad} \ \| \ \|)(x) \in S_{X^*}(0_{X^*}, 1)$$

is continuous. Consequently J_φ is continuous.

(b) Assume that the norm is Fréchet differentiable. By Theorem 6.10, the norm is $\mathcal{C}^1$, i.e.

$$x \in X \backslash \{0_X\} \longrightarrow (\text{grad} \, \| \, \|)(x) \in S_{X^*}(0_{X^*}, 1) \qquad (6.47)$$

is continuous.

Conversely, if (6.47) holds then, according to a classical result, the norm is Fréchet differentiable. Result (b) was obtained by Kadeč [34] and it is proved with a different technique (see also Vajnberg [53]).

6.4.4 Gâteaux and Fréchet differentiability of norms of some function spaces

6.4.4.1 *The space* $(L^p(\Omega), \| \, \|_{L^p})$, $1 < p < \infty$

Theorem 6.12. *Let Ω be an open subset of $\mathbb{R}^n$, let $1 < p < \infty$ and consider the Lebesgue space $(L^p(\Omega), \| \, \|_{L^p})$. Then one has:*

(a) *The mapping $u \in L^p(\Omega) \longrightarrow \|u\|_{L^p}$ is Fréchet differentiable and, at any nonzero $u \in L^p(\Omega)$, the Fréchet differential of $\| \, \|_{L^p}$ is given by*

$$\| \, \|'_{L^p}(u) = (\text{grad} \, \| \, \|_{L^p})(u) = \frac{|u|^{p-2}u}{\|u\|_{L^p}^{p-1}} \in L^{p'}(\Omega),$$

with $\dfrac{1}{p} + \dfrac{1}{p'} = 1$.

(b) *The mapping $u \in L^p(\Omega) \backslash \{0_{L^p}\} \longrightarrow \| \, \|'_{L^p}(u) \in L^{p'}(\Omega)$ is continuous. In other words the mapping $u \in L^p(\Omega) \backslash \{0_{L^p}\} \longrightarrow \|u\|_{L^p}$ is $\mathcal{C}^1$ at any nonzero $u \in L^p(\Omega)$.*

For a detailed proof and references see [53, §2.6].

6.4.4.2 *The space* $\left(W_0^{1,p}(\Omega), \| \, \|_{0,p,\nabla}\right)$, $1 < p < \infty$

In contrast to the case of Lebesgue spaces $L^p(\Omega)$, where Ω is an arbitrary open subset of $\mathbb{R}^n$, the smoothness of the Sobolev space $\left(W_0^{1,p}(\Omega), \| \, \|_{0,p,\nabla}\right)$, $1 < p < \infty$ and the formula providing the gradient of its norm are obtained by assuming that Ω *is a domain in* $\mathbb{R}^n$, i.e., Ω is a bounded connected open subset of $\mathbb{R}^n$ with a Lipschitz continuous boundary Γ, the set Ω being locally on the same side of Γ. A measure, denoted by $d\Gamma$, can be defined on Γ (see, e.g. Adams [1], Nečas [44], Ciarlet [13]).

Let Ω be a domain in $\mathbb{R}^n$ and let $1 < p < \infty$. We define the Sobolev space $W^{1,p}(\Omega)$ as consisting of those functions $u \in L^p(\Omega)$ that possess the distributional derivative $\dfrac{\partial u}{\partial x_i}$ also in $L^p(\Omega)$ for all $i = 1, 2, \ldots, n$, i.e.,

$$W^{1,p}(\Omega) = \left\{ u \in L^p(\Omega) ; \frac{\partial u}{\partial x_i} \in L^p(\Omega), \, i = 1, 2, \ldots, n \right\}.$$

For $u \in W^{1,p}(\Omega)$ we also write

$$\nabla u = \left(\frac{\partial u}{\partial x_1}, \frac{\partial u}{\partial x_2}, \ldots, \frac{\partial u}{\partial x_n} \right)$$

and we notice that if $u \in W^{1,p}(\Omega)$ then $|\nabla u| \in L^p(\Omega)$, $|\cdot|$ standing for the Euclidean norm in $\mathbb{R}^n$.

Each of the following mappings

$$u \in W^{1,p}(\Omega) \to \|u\|_{W^{1,p}} := \left(\|u\|_{L^p}^p + \sum_{i=1}^n \left\| \frac{\partial u}{\partial x_i} \right\|_{L^p}^p \right)^{1/p}, \tag{6.48}$$

$$u \in W^{1,p}(\Omega) \to \|u\|_{1,p} := \|u\|_{L^p} + \sum_{i=1}^n \left\| \frac{\partial u}{\partial x_i} \right\|_{L^p}, \tag{6.49}$$

$$u \in W^{1,p}(\Omega) \to \|u\|_{1,p,\nabla} := \|u\|_{L^p} + \||\nabla u|\|_{L^p}, \tag{6.50}$$

defines a norm on $W^{1,p}(\Omega)$ and all these norms are equivalent. For the proof see, e.g., Adams [1], Brezis [8], Ciarlet [13].

We define the space $W_0^{1,p}(\Omega)$ as being the closure of $\mathcal{C}_0^\infty(\Omega)$ in $W^{1,p}(\Omega)$, with respect to any of the equivalent norms (6.48), (6.49) or (6.50).

Notice that since $\mathcal{C}_0^\infty(\Omega)$ is contained in $W^{1,p}(\Omega)$ but it is not dense in $W^{1,p}(\Omega)$, $W_0^{1,p}(\Omega)$ is a closed proper subspace of $W^{1,p}(\Omega)$. It is also shown (see e.g., Adams [1], Brezis [8], Ciarlet [13]) that there is a unique operator $\text{tr} \in \mathcal{L}\left(W^{1,p}(\Omega), L^p(\partial\Omega) \right)$ such that $\text{tr} u = u |_{\partial\Omega}$ if $u \in \mathcal{C}^\infty(\overline{\Omega})$ (see, e.g. Ciarlet [13, Theorem 6.6-5] and the comments preceding this theorem). The space $W_0^{1,p}(\Omega)$ previously defined is nothing else but the kernel of this operator:

$$W_0^{1,p}(\Omega) = \ker \text{tr} = \left\{ u \in W^{1,p}(\Omega) ; \text{tr} u = 0_{L^p(\partial\Omega)} \right\}.$$

On $W_0^{1,p}(\Omega)$ the following *Poincaré-Friedrichs inequality* holds: there exists a constant $C = C(\Omega, p)$ such that

$$\|u\|_{L^p} \leq C \||\nabla u|\|_{L^p}, \text{ for all } u \in W_0^{1,p}(\Omega). \tag{6.51}$$

Due to this inequality, on $W_0^{1,p}(\Omega)$ all the norms (6.48), (6.49) and (6.50) induced from $W^{1,p}(\Omega)$ are equivalent to the norm

$$\|u\|_{0,p,\nabla} := \||\nabla u|\|_{L^p}, \text{ for all } u \in W_0^{1,p}(\Omega). \tag{6.52}$$

In what follows *the space* $W_0^{1,p}(\Omega)$ *will always be considered as endowed with the norm* $\|\ \|_{0,p,\nabla}$.

Theorem 6.13. (see, e.g. Adams [1, Theorem 3.5]) *As equipped with any of the usual norms* (6.48), (6.49) *or* (6.50), $W^{1,p}(\Omega)$ *is reflexive and separable.*

As a direct consequence of Theorem 6.13 we have:

Corollary 6.4. *The space* $\left(W_0^{1,p}(\Omega), \|\ \|_{0,p,\nabla}\right)$ *is reflexive, separable and uniformly convex.*

The next theorem supplies the smoothness of $\left(W_0^{1,p}(\Omega), \|\ \|_{0,p,\nabla}\right)$.

Theorem 6.14. *Let* Ω *be a domain in* $\mathbb{R}^n$, *let* $1 < p < \infty$ *and consider the space* $\left(W_0^{1,p}(\Omega), \|\ \|_{0,p,\nabla}\right)$. *Then one has:*

(a) *The mapping* $u \in W_0^{1,p}(\Omega) \setminus \{0\} \to \|u\|_{0,p,\nabla}$ *is Fréchet differentiable and, at any nonzero* $u \in W_0^{1,p}(\Omega)$, *the Fréchet derivative of* $\|\ \|_{0,p,\nabla}$ *is given by:*

$$\left\langle \|\ \|_{0,p,\nabla}'(u), h \right\rangle = \frac{1}{\|u\|_{0,p,\nabla}^{p-1}} \int_\Omega |\nabla u|^{p-2}\, \nabla u \cdot \nabla h\, dx,$$

for all $h \in W_0^{1,p}(\Omega)$.

(b) *The mapping* $u \in W_0^{1,p}(\Omega) \setminus \{0\} \to \|\ \|_{0,p,\nabla}'(u) \in \left(W_0^{1,p}(\Omega)\right)^*$ *is continuous. In other words, the mapping* $u \in W_0^{1,p}(\Omega) \setminus \{0\} \to \|u\|_{0,p,\nabla}$ *is Fréchet differentiable and* C^1.

For detailed proofs and references see [24].

6.4.4.3 *The space* $\left(U_{\Gamma_0}, \|\ \|_{0,p(\cdot),\nabla}\right)$

Before stating the main result, various definitions and basic properties related to Lebesgue and Sobolev spaces with variable exponents are needed.

For proofs and references, see [18].

Let Ω be a domain in $\mathbb{R}^N$. Given a function $p(\cdot) \in L^\infty(\Omega)$ that satisfies

$$1 \le p^- := \operatorname*{ess\,inf}_{x \in \Omega} p(x) \le p^+ := \operatorname*{ess\,sup}_{x \in \Omega} p(x),$$

the Lebesgue space $L^{p(\cdot)}(\Omega)$ *with variable exponent* $p(\cdot)$ is defined as

$$L^{p(\cdot)}(\Omega) := \{v : \Omega \to \mathbb{R};\ v \text{ is } dx\text{-measurable and}$$

$$\varrho_{0,p(\cdot)}(v) := \int_{\Omega} |v(x)|^{p(x)} \, dx < \infty \}.$$

Likewise, given a function $q(\cdot) \in L^{\infty}(\Gamma)$ that satisfies

$$1 \leq \operatorname*{ess\,inf}_{y \in \Gamma} q(y),$$

the Lebesgue space $L^{q(\cdot)}(\Gamma)$ *with variable exponent* $q(\cdot)$ is defined as

$$L^{q(\cdot)}(\Gamma) := \{v : \Gamma \to \mathbb{R}; \, v \text{ is } d\Gamma\text{-measurable and } \int_{\Gamma} |v(y)|^{q(y)} \, dy < \infty \}.$$

Theorem 6.15. *Let Ω be a domain in $\mathbb{R}^N$. Let $p(\cdot) \in L^{\infty}(\Omega)$ be such that $p^- \geq 1$. Equipped with the norm*

$$v \in L^{p(\cdot)}(\Omega) \to \|v\|_{0,p(\cdot)} := \inf \left\{ \lambda > 0; \, \int_{\Omega} \left| \frac{v(x)}{\lambda} \right|^{p(x)} \, dx \leq 1 \right\},$$

the space $L^{p(\cdot)}(\Omega)$ is a separable Banach space. If $p^- > 1$, the space $L^{p(\cdot)}(\Omega)$ is uniformly convex, and hence reflexive.

Given a function $p(\cdot) \in L^{\infty}(\Omega)$ that satisfies $p^- \geq 1$, the Sobolev space $W^{1,p(\cdot)}(\Omega)$ *with variable exponent* $p(\cdot)$ is defined as

$$W^{1,p(\cdot)}(\Omega) := \left\{ v \in L^{p(\cdot)}(\Omega); \, \partial_i v \in L^{p(\cdot)}(\Omega), \, 1 \leq i \leq N \right\},$$

where, for each $1 \leq i \leq N$, ∂_i denotes the distributional derivative operator with respect to the i-th variable.

Theorem 6.16. *Let Ω be a domain in $\mathbb{R}^N$. Let $p(\cdot) \in L^{\infty}(\Omega)$ be such that $p^- \geq 1$. Equipped with the norm*

$$v \in W^{1,p(\cdot)}(\Omega) \to \|v\|_{1,p(\cdot)} := \|v\|_{0,p(\cdot)} + \sum_{i=1}^{N} \|\partial_i v\|_{0,p(\cdot)},$$

the space $W^{1,p(\cdot)}(\Omega)$ is a separable Banach space. If $p^- > 1$, the space $W^{1,p(\cdot)}(\Omega)$ is reflexive.

Besides $\|\cdot\|_{1,p(\cdot)}$, another equivalent norm on $W^{1,p(\cdot)}(\Omega)$ is given by:

$$\|u\|_{1,p(\cdot),\nabla} := \|u\|_{0,p(\cdot)} + \||\nabla u|\|_{0,p(\cdot)}.$$

Theorem 6.17. *Let Ω be a domain in $\mathbb{R}^N$.*

(a) *Let $p(\cdot) \in L^{\infty}(\Omega)$ be such that $p^- \geq 1$. Since $W^{1,p(\cdot)}(\Omega) \hookrightarrow W^{1,1}(\Omega)$, the trace $\mathrm{tr}\,v$ on Γ of any function $v \in W^{1,p(\cdot)}(\Omega)$ is a well-defined function in the space $L^1(\Gamma)$.*

(b) *Let there be given a function* $p(\cdot) \in C\left(\overline{\Omega}\right)$ *that satisfies* $p^- > 1$. *Given any* $x \in \Gamma$, *let*

$$p^{\partial}(x) := \frac{(N-1)\,p(x)}{N - p(x)} \ \text{if } p(x) < N, \text{ and } p^{\partial}(x) := \infty \ \text{if } p(x) \geq N,$$

and let there be given a function $q(\cdot) \in C\left(\Gamma\right)$ *that satisfies*

$$1 \leq q(x) < p^{\partial}(x) \ \text{for each } x \in \Gamma.$$

Then, given any function $v \in W^{1,p(\cdot)}\left(\Omega\right)$, $\mathrm{tr}\,v \in L^{q(\cdot)}\left(\Gamma\right)$ *and the trace operator*

$$\mathrm{tr} : W^{1,p(\cdot)}\left(\Omega\right) \to L^{q(\cdot)}\left(\Gamma\right)$$

defined in this fashion is compact. Thus, in particular, the trace operator

$$\mathrm{tr} : W^{1,p(\cdot)}\left(\Omega\right) \to L^{p(\cdot)}\left(\Gamma\right)$$

is compact.

Now, the Fréchet differentiability of the norm $\|\ \|_{0,p(\cdot),\nabla}$ on U_{Γ_0} is given by:

Theorem 6.18. *Let* Ω *be a domain in* $\mathbb{R}^N$, $N \geq 2$, *let* Γ_0 *be a* $d\Gamma$-*measurable subset of* $\Gamma = \partial\Omega$ *that satisfies* $d\Gamma$-*meas* $\Gamma_0 > 0$, *let* $p(\cdot) \in C\left(\overline{\Omega}\right)$ *be such that* $p(x) > 1$ *for all* $x \in \overline{\Omega}$ *and let*

$$U_{\Gamma_0} := \left\{ u \in \left(W^{1,p(\cdot)}\left(\Omega\right), \|\cdot\|_{1,p(\cdot),\nabla} \right); \ \mathrm{tr}\,u = 0 \ \text{on } \Gamma_0 \right\}.$$

Then:

(a) *The space* U_{Γ_0} *is closed in* $\left(W^{1,p(\cdot)}\left(\Omega\right), \|\cdot\|_{1,p(\cdot),\nabla} \right)$; *consequently,* $\left(U_{\Gamma_0}, \|\cdot\|_{1,p(\cdot),\nabla} \right)$ *is a separable reflexive Banach space.*

(b) *The map*

$$u \in U_{\Gamma_0} \to \|u\|_{0,p(\cdot),\nabla} := \||\nabla u|\|_{0,p(\cdot)}$$

is a norm on U_{Γ_0} *equivalent with the norm* $\|\cdot\|_{1,p(\cdot),\nabla}$.

(c) *The norm* $\|u\|_{0,p(\cdot),\nabla}$ *is Fréchet-differentiable at any nonzero* $u \in U_{\Gamma_0}$ *and the Fréchet-differential of this norm at any nonzero* $u \in U_{\Gamma_0}$ *is given for any* $h \in U_{\Gamma_0}$ *by*

$$\left\langle \|\cdot\|'_{0,p(\cdot),\nabla}(u), h \right\rangle = \frac{\displaystyle\int_{\Omega\setminus\Omega_{0,u}} p(x) \frac{|\nabla u(x)|^{p(x)-2}\,\langle \nabla u(x), \nabla h(x)\rangle}{\|u\|_{0,p(\cdot),\nabla}^{p(x)-1}} \, dx}{\displaystyle\int_{\Omega} p(x) \frac{|\nabla u(x)|^{p(x)}}{\|u\|_{0,p(\cdot),\nabla}^{p(x)}} \, dx},$$

where $\Omega_{0,u} := \{x \in \Omega; |\nabla u(x)| = 0\}$.

(d) *If, in addition, the function* $p(\cdot) \in C\left(\overline{\Omega}\right)$ *satisfies* $p(x) \geq 2$ *for all* $x \in \overline{\Omega}$, *then the space* $(U_{\Gamma_0}, \|\cdot\|_{0,p(\cdot),\nabla})$ *is uniformly convex.*

For a detailed proof see [14].

Remark 6.4. *According to Theorem 6.16, $\left(W^{1,p(\cdot)}\left(\Omega\right),\|\cdot\|_{1,p(\cdot),\nabla}\right)$ is separable and reflexive. As a closed subspace of $\left(W^{1,p(\cdot)}\left(\Omega\right),\|\cdot\|_{1,p(\cdot),\nabla}\right)$, the space $\left(U_{\Gamma_0},\|\cdot\|_{1,p(\cdot),\nabla}\right)$ is thus also separable and reflexive.*

A result from Kadeč's (see [34, Theorem 3]) asserts that, if X is a Banach space with a separable dual, then X has an equivalent Fréchet-differentiable norm. Consequently, there exists a Fréchet-differentiable norm on U_{Γ_0} that is equivalent with the norm $\|\cdot\|_{1,p(\cdot),\nabla}$. Points (b) and (c) of Theorem 6.18 show that such a norm may be defined as $\|u\|_{0,p(\cdot),\nabla} = \||\nabla u|\|_{0,p(\cdot)}$ for all $u \in U_{\Gamma_0}$.

6.4.4.4 The space $\left(W_T^{1,p}, \|\ \|_{W_T^{1,p}}\right)$

Before stating the main result, some definitions and basic properties related to the space $\left(W_T^{1,p}, \|\ \|_{W_T^{1,p}}\right)$ are needed.

Let $\mathcal{C}_T^\infty$ be the space of indefinitely differentiable T-periodic functions from $\mathbb{R}$ into $\mathbb{R}^N$. We denote by $\langle\cdot,\cdot\rangle$ the inner product on $\mathbb{R}^N$ and by $\|\cdot\|$, the norm generated by this inner product.

A function $v \in L^1\left(0,T;\mathbb{R}^N\right)$ is called a weak derivative of a function $u \in L^1\left(0,T;\mathbb{R}^N\right)$ if for each $f \in \mathcal{C}_T^\infty$,

$$\int_0^T \langle u\left(t\right), f'\left(t\right)\rangle \, \mathrm{d}t = -\int_0^T \langle v\left(t\right), f\left(t\right)\rangle \, \mathrm{d}t. \tag{6.53}$$

The weak derivative of u will be denoted by $\dot{u}$ or $\dfrac{du}{dt}$. If $v = \dot{u}$ satisfies (6.53), then $\int_0^T v\left(s\right)\mathrm{d}s = 0$ and there is $c \in \mathbb{R}^N$ such that $u\left(t\right) = \int_0^t v\left(s\right)\mathrm{d}s + c$.

The Sobolev space $W_T^{1,p}$, $1 < p < \infty$, is the space of functions $u \in L^p\left(0,T;\mathbb{R}^N\right)$ having the weak derivative $\dot{u} \in L^p\left(0,T;\mathbb{R}^N\right)$. According to the previous results, if $u \in W_T^{1,p}$ then

$$u\left(t\right) = \int_0^t \dot{u}\left(s\right)\mathrm{d}s + c \text{ and } u\left(0\right) = u\left(T\right).$$

The norm over $W_T^{1,p}$ is defined by

$$\|u\|_{W_T^{1,p}}^p = \int_0^T \|u\left(t\right)\|^p \, \mathrm{d}t + \int_0^T \|\dot{u}\left(t\right)\|^p \, \mathrm{d}t.$$

It is a simple matter to verify that $W_T^{1,p}$ is a reflexive Banach space and $\mathcal{C}_T^\infty \subset W_T^{1,p}$. Let us also recall the following result (see Mawhin and Willem [40, Propositions 1.1 and 1.2].

Theorem 6.19. 1) *There exists $c > 0$ such that*

$$\|u\|_\infty \leq c \|u\|_{W_T^{1,p}}, \text{ for all } u \in W_T^{1,p}.$$

Moreover, if $\int_0^T u(t)\mathrm{d}t = 0$, then

$$\|u\|_\infty \leq c \|\dot{u}\|_{L^p(0,T;\mathbb{R}^N)}.$$

2) *If the sequence (u_k) converges weakly to u in $W_T^{1,p}$, then (u_k) converges uniformly to u on $[0,T]$.*

By Theorem 6.19, the injection of $W_T^{1,p}$ in $C\left([0,T];\mathbb{R}^N\right)$ is compact. Consequently, the injection of $W_T^{1,p}$ in $L^p\left(0,T;\mathbb{R}^N\right)$ is also compact.

Theorem 6.20. *If $1 < p < \infty$, then:*

(a) *the space $\left(W_T^{1,p}, \|\ \|_{W_T^{1,p}}\right)$ is uniformly convex and smooth;*

(b) *the gradient (in the Gâteaux sense) of $\|\ \|_{W_T^{1,p}}$-norm is defined as follows:*

$$\left(\nabla \|\ \|_{W_T^{1,p}}\right) : W_T^{1,p}\setminus\{0\} \to \left(W_T^{1,p}\right)^*,$$

$$\left\langle \left(\nabla \|\ \|_{W_T^{1,p}}\right)(u), v\right\rangle_{W_T^{1,p},\left(W_T^{1,p}\right)^*}$$

$$= \frac{1}{\|u\|_{W_T^{1,p}}^{p-1}} \left[\int_0^T \left\langle \|u(t)\|^{p-2} u(t), v(t)\right\rangle \mathrm{d}t + \int_0^T \left\langle \|\dot{u}(t)\|^{p-2} \dot{u}(t), \dot{v}(t)\right\rangle \mathrm{d}t\right],$$

for all $v \in W_T^{1,p}$.

For detailed proofs and references see [23].

6.5 Connecting duality mappings to significant mathematical ideas

6.5.1 *Duality mappings and monotonicity*

We have already seen that a duality mapping on a Banach space X, $J_\varphi : X \to 2^{X^*}$, is monotone. Thus, all the generic properties of monotone operators can be converted into corresponding properties of duality mappings. Here we offer an example leading to a classical question concerning the Hahn-Banach.

Theorem 6.21. (see [22]) *Let X be a separable Banach space. Then the set Z of points $x \in X\setminus\{0_X\}$ for which there exists more than one linear and continuous functional $x^* \in X^*$ that satisfies $\langle x^*, x\rangle = \|x\|$ and $\|x^*\| = 1$ has no interior. If, in addition, X is finite dimensional, this set has Lebesgue measure zero.*

The proof is as follows.

In [54], Zarantonello proved the following:

Theorem 6.22. [54, Theorem 1] *The set of points where a monotone operator* $T : X \to 2^{X^*}$ *from a separable Banach space into its dual is not single-valued has an empty interior. If the domain of T has a nonempty interior, the set is a F-sigma set; if, in addition, X is a finite dimensional space, the set has Lebesgue measure zero.*

A very detailed proof of Zarantonello's result may be found in Nirenberg [45, §5.3, p. 182].

Now, let X be separable and $J : X \to 2^{X^*}$ be the normalized duality mapping on X:

$$J0_X = \{0_{X^*}\},$$

$$Jx = \|x\| \{x^* \in X^*; \langle x^*, x \rangle = \|x\|, \|x^*\| = 1\}, \text{ if } x \neq 0_X.$$

We know that J is monotone. Applying Theorem 6.22 with $T = J$, $D(T) = D(J) = X$ we obtain that Z is a F-sigma set, i.e., Z is the union of a countable number of closed sets all without interior. Thus Z has no interior. Consequently, the complement set of Z in X is dense in X which implies

$$\{x \in X \backslash \{0_X\}; \text{ there exists a unique } x^* \in X^*$$

$$\text{with } \|x^*\| = 1 \text{ and } \langle x^*, x \rangle = \|x\|\}$$

is dense in X.

Now, taking into account Asplund's result, we see that duality mappings belong to a particular class of monotone operators, namely, any duality mapping is the subdifferential of a convex and continuous functional:

$$J_\varphi = \partial\psi, \ \psi(x) = \int_0^{\|x\|} \varphi(t) \, dt.$$

Thus, all generic properties of subdifferentials of convex and continuous functionals can be converted into corresponding properties of duality mappings. Here we offer an example leading to continuity properties of duality mappings.

The following result is a classical one (see, e.g., Phelps [49, Proposition 2.5]).

Theorem 6.23. *Let $(X, \| \ \|)$ be a Banach space. If D is an open convex subset of X and $f : D \to \mathbb{R}$ is continuous convex then the subdifferential* *map* $x \in D \longrightarrow \partial f(x) \in 2^{X^*}$ *is norm to weak* upper semicontinuous at any* $x \in D$, *i.e., for any weak* open set* V *containing* $\partial f(x)$ *and every* $(x_n) \subset D$ *with* $\|x_n - x\| \to 0$, *we have* $\partial f(x_n) \subset V$ *for all sufficiently large* n.

Applying this result for $D = X$ and $F(x) = \int_0^{\|x\|} \varphi(t)dt$, and taking into account Asplund's result we get:

Theorem 6.24. *Let* $(X, \| \ \|)$ *be a Banach space. Any duality mapping* $J_\varphi : X \to 2^{X^*}$ *is norm-to-weak* upper semicontinuous.*

There are many consequences of Theorem 6.24. Some of them are gathered in the next theorem.

Theorem 6.25. *Assume that* $(X, \| \ \|)$ *is a smooth Banach space. Then one has:*

(a) *Any duality mapping* $J_\varphi : X \to X^*$ *is norm-to-weak* continuous.*

(b) *If, in addition,* X *is reflexive, then, any duality mapping is continuous from* X *with the norm topology into* X^* *with the weak topology on* X^*.

Proof:
(a) The result follows from Theorem 6.24, taking into account that, in case J_φ is single valued, the norm-to-weak* upper semicontinuity of J_φ is nothing but the norm-to-weak* continuity of $J_\varphi : X \to X^*$.

(b) It follows from (a), taking into account that the reflexivity of X implies that the weak* topology and the weak topology on X^* are the same.

Notice that, with a different proof, the result of (b) was already provided by Proposition 6.2.

6.5.2 *Duality mappings and partial differential equations: the p-Laplacian as a duality mapping*

In the last decades a wide literature has been devoted to the study of the so called p-Laplacian.

Under the hypotheses of Theorem 6.14 we define the operator

$$-\Delta_p : W_0^{1,p}(\Omega) \to \left(W_0^{1,p}(\Omega)\right)^* = W^{-1,p'}(\Omega)$$

as follows:

$$u \in W_0^{1,p}(\Omega) \longrightarrow -\Delta_p u = -\frac{\partial}{\partial x_i}\left(|\nabla u|^{p-2}\frac{\partial u}{\partial x_i}\right) \in W^{-1,p'}(\Omega)$$

or, equivalently,

$$\langle -\Delta_p u, h \rangle = \int_\Omega |\nabla u|^{p-2} \frac{\partial u}{\partial x_i} \frac{\partial h}{\partial x_i} dx = \int_\Omega |\nabla u|^{p-2} \nabla u \cdot \nabla h \, dx \qquad (6.54)$$

for all $h \in W_0^{1,p}(\Omega)$, the repeating index summation being used. (Here "$|\ |$" stands for the Euclidean norm in $\mathbb{R}^n$ and "$\cdot$" for the inner product in $\mathbb{R}^n$.)

This mapping is nothing but the duality mapping on $W_0^{1,p}(\Omega)$ corresponding to the gauge function $\varphi(t) = t^{p-1}$, $t \geq 0$. Indeed, from (6.38) we infer that any duality mapping on $W_0^{1,p}(\Omega)$, $1 < p < \infty$, is defined by:

$$J_\varphi 0_{W_0^{1,p}(\Omega)} = 0_{W^{-1,p'}(\Omega)},$$

$$J_\varphi u = \varphi\left(\|u\|_{0.p,\nabla}\right)\left(\text{grad} \|\ \|_{0.p,\nabla}\right)(u), \text{ if } u \neq 0_{W_0^{1,p}(\Omega)}, \qquad (6.55)$$

or, equivalently, according to Theorem 6.14,

$$\langle J_\varphi u, h \rangle = \frac{\varphi\left(\|u\|_{0.p,\nabla}\right)}{\|u\|_{0.p,\nabla}^{p-1}} \int_\Omega |\nabla u|^{p-2} \nabla u \cdot \nabla h \, dx \qquad (6.56)$$

for all $u \in W_0^{1,p}(\Omega) \setminus \left\{0_{W_0^{1,p}(\Omega)}\right\}$ and all $h \in W_0^{1,p}(\Omega)$.

In particular, denoting by $J_{(p-1)} : W_0^{1,p}(\Omega) \to W^{-1,p'}(\Omega)$ the duality mapping corresponding to the gauge function $\varphi(t) = t^{p-1}$, $t \geq 0$, we get

$$\langle J_{(p-1)} u, h \rangle = \int_\Omega |\nabla u|^{p-2} \nabla u \cdot \nabla h \, dx = \langle -\Delta_p u, h \rangle \text{ for all } u, h \in W_0^{1,p}(\Omega),$$

i.e., $J_{(p-1)} = -\Delta_p$.

This being the case, all the "nice" properties of duality mappings defined on uniformly convex spaces endowed with a Fréchet differentiable norm, may be converted into corresponding properties of $-\Delta_p$ as defined above.

Some of these properties are gathered in the following theorem.

Theorem 6.26. *As a mapping from $W_0^{1,p}(\Omega)$ into $W^{-1,p'}(\Omega)$, $-\Delta_p$, $1 < p < \infty$, is continuous, bounded, bijective and has a continuous and bounded inverse.*

Proof:

Since the norm $\|\ \|_{0.p,\nabla}$ is Fréchet differentiable and $-\Delta_p = J_{(p-1)} : W_0^{1,p}(\Omega) \to W^{-1,p'}(\Omega)$, the continuity of $-\Delta_p$ follows from Theorem 6.11, (a). Moreover, any duality mapping is bounded (even if it is a set-valued mapping). Indeed, if $\|x\| \leq C$ then, for any $x^* \in J_\varphi x$ one has $\|x^*\| \leq \varphi(C)$. Thus, $-\Delta_p$ is bounded.

Since $W_0^{1,p}(\Omega)$ is reflexive and uniformly convex, any duality mapping on $W_0^{1,p}(\Omega)$ is bijective (see Theorem 6.5).

Consequently the continuity and the boundedness of $(-\Delta_p)^{-1}$ are consequences of the following proposition.

Proposition 6.3. *If X is a reflexive, smooth and strictly convex Banach space which possesses the Kadeč-Klee property then any duality mapping $J_\varphi : X \to X^*$ is bijective and has a continuous and bounded inverse.*

Moreover,

$$J_\varphi^{-1} = \chi^{-1} J_{\varphi^{-1}}^* \tag{6.57}$$

where $J_{\varphi^{-1}}^* : X^* \to X^{**}$ is the duality mapping on X^* corresponding to the gauge function φ^{-1} and $\chi : X \to X^{**}$ is the canonical isomorphism defined by $\langle \chi(x), x^* \rangle = \langle x^*, x \rangle$ for all $x \in X$ and $x^* \in X^*$.

For the proof, [25, Corollary 2.3].

Here we only observe that, since X is reflexive, smooth and strictly convex so is X^* (by Klee's Theorem again). Thus, $J_{\varphi^{-1}}^*$ is well defined as duality mapping from X^* into X^{**}. Also, from (6.57) the boundedness of J_φ^{-1} follows.

From Theorem 6.26 and Proposition 6.3 we obtain:

Corollary 6.5. (a) *For any $F \in W^{-1,p'}(\Omega)$, there is a unique $u \in W_0^{1,p}(\Omega)$ which satisfies*

$$-\Delta_p u = F, \tag{6.58}$$

or, equivalently,

$$\int_\Omega |\nabla u|^{p-2} \nabla u \cdot \nabla v \, \mathrm{d}x = \langle F, v \rangle \tag{6.59}$$

for all $v \in W_0^{1,p}(\Omega)$.

The map $F \in W^{-1,p'}(\Omega) \longrightarrow u \in W_0^{1,p}(\Omega)$ is continuous and bounded.

(b) *An element $u \in W_0^{1,p}(\Omega)$ satisfies (6.58) or, equivalently, (6.59) if and only if u is a critical point of the functional*

$$v \in W_0^{1,p}(\Omega) \longrightarrow H(v) = \frac{1}{p} \|v\|_{0,p,\nabla}^p - \langle F, v \rangle. \tag{6.60}$$

(c) *In particular, for any $f \in L^{p'}(\Omega)$, there is a unique element which satisfies*

$$\int_\Omega |\nabla u|^{p-2} \nabla u \cdot \nabla v \, \mathrm{d}x = \int_\Omega f v \, \mathrm{d}x, \tag{6.61}$$

for all $v \in W_0^{1,p}(\Omega)$.

(d) *An element $u \in W_0^{1,p}(\Omega)$ satisfies (6.61) if and only if u is a critical point of the functional*

$$v \in W_0^{1,p}(\Omega) \longrightarrow L(v) = \frac{1}{p} \|v\|_{0,p,\nabla}^p - \int_\Omega f v \, \mathrm{d}x. \tag{6.62}$$

Proof:

The point (a) directly follows from Theorem 6.26 and Proposition 6.3.

(b) Since $\| \ \|_{0.p,\nabla}$ is Fréchet differentiable, it can be shown that L is C^1 and

$$(dL)(v) = -\Delta_p v - F.$$

The proof can be found in [24]. It follows that

$$(dL)(u) = 0 \text{ if and only if } -\Delta_p u = F.$$

(c) From Rellich-Kondrachov Theorem, $W_0^{1,p}(\Omega)$ is compactly imbedded in $L^p(\Omega)$. Let $i : W_0^{1,p}(\Omega) \to L^p(\Omega)$ be the compact injection of $W_0^{1,p}(\Omega)$ in $L^p(\Omega)$. The adjoint of i, $i^* : (L^p(\Omega))^* = L^{p'}(\Omega) \to \left(W_0^{1,p}(\Omega)\right)^* = W^{-1,p'}(\Omega)$ is also compact. Consequently we can identify any $f \in L^{p'}(\Omega)$ with $i^* f \in W^{-1,p'}(\Omega)$ where, by definition of i^*,

$$\langle i^* f, v \rangle_{W_0^{1,p}(\Omega),W^{-1,p'}(\Omega)} = \langle f, iv \rangle_{L^{p'}(\Omega),L^p(\Omega)}.$$

Now, for any $f \in L^{p'}(\Omega)$ consider the equation

$$-\Delta_p u = i^* f \text{ (equality in } W^{-1,p'}(\Omega)).$$

According to the result supplied by (a) and (b), applied for $F = i^* f$, there is a unique element u in $W_0^{1,p}(\Omega)$ which satisfies

$$-\Delta_p u = i^* f$$

or, equivalently

$$\int_\Omega |\nabla u|^{p-2} \nabla u \cdot \nabla v \ dx = \langle i^* f, v \rangle = \langle f, iv \rangle = \int_\Omega f(x) v(x) \, dx,$$

for all $v \in W_0^{1,p}(\Omega)$.

(d) The result directly follows from (b).

Remark 6.5. *Since any element $u \in W_0^{1,p}(\Omega)$ satisfies $u|_{\partial\Omega} = 0$ (in the sense of trace), an element $u \in W_0^{1,p}(\Omega)$ which satisfies*

$$-\Delta_p u = i^* f \text{ (equality in } W^{-1,p'}(\Omega))$$

for some $f \in L^{p'}(\Omega)$, $\frac{1}{p} + \frac{1}{p'} = 1$, can be viewed as a weak solution to the boundary value problem

$$-\Delta_p u = f \text{ in } \Omega \text{ and } u = 0 \text{ on } \partial\Omega. \tag{6.63}$$

Thus, point (c) of Corollary 6.5 can be read as a theorem of existence and uniqueness of the weak solution to the boundary problem (6.63) while point (d) gives us a variational characterisation of this unique weak solution as the unique critical point of the functional (6.62).

Remark 6.6. *Obviously, for $p = 2$, $-\Delta_p$ reduces to the classical Laplace operator,* $-\Delta : H_0^1(\Omega) \to H^{-1}(\Omega)$ *defined by*

$$\langle -\Delta u, v \rangle = \int_\Omega \nabla u \cdot \nabla v \, dx, \ u, v \in H_0^1(\Omega).$$

Consequently, by specifying the above results, we find some of the well-known results concerning the Laplace operator.

Remark 6.7. *Corollary 6.5 has paved the way for approaching a more complicated boundary value problem, namely,*

$$- \Delta_p u = f(x, u) \ \text{in} \ \Omega \ \text{and} \ u = 0 \ \text{on} \ \partial\Omega, \tag{6.64}$$

where $1 < p < \infty$, Ω is a domain in $\mathbb{R}^N$, $N \geq 2$ and $f : \Omega \times \mathbb{R} \to \mathbb{R}$, $(x, s) \in \Omega \times \mathbb{R} \longrightarrow f(x, s) \in \mathbb{R}$ is a Carathéodory function, i.e., for a.e. $x \in \Omega$, the map $s \in \mathbb{R} \longrightarrow f(x, s) \in \mathbb{R}$ is continuous and, for any $s \in \mathbb{R}$, the map $x \in \Omega \longrightarrow f(x, s) \in \mathbb{R}$ is (Lebesgue) measurable.

The starting point was the particular case corresponding to $p = 2$:

$$- \Delta u = f(x, u) \ \text{in} \ \Omega \ \text{and} \ u = 0 \ \text{on} \ \partial\Omega. \tag{6.65}$$

As it is known, adequate growth conditions (see, e.g. [17], [52], [35]) imposed on f guarantee that the Euler-Lagrange functional

$$\Phi_{(2)}(u) = \frac{1}{2} \|u\|^2_{H_0^1(\Omega)} - \int_\Omega F(x, u) \, dx \ \text{with} \ F(x, s) = \int_0^s f(x, \tau) \, d\tau \tag{6.66}$$

is well-defined and C^1 in $H_0^1(\Omega)$.

Furthermore, the critical points of $\Phi_{(2)}$ are then the H_0^1 solutions (i.e., weak solutions) of (6.65).

If supplementary conditions at $s = 0$ assure that $u \equiv 0$ is a critical point of $\Phi_{(2)}$, then the requirements of f to have nontrivial solutions become of interests.

The following condition was first considered by Ambrosetti and Rabinowitz in their well-known paper [3]:

There are numbers $\theta > 2$ and $s_0 > 0$ such that

$$0 < \theta F(x, s) \leq s f(x, s) \ \text{for} \ x \in \Omega \ \text{if} \ |s| \geq s_0. \tag{6.67}$$

Condition (6.67) plays a crucial role in ensuring that $\Phi_{(2)}$ satisfies the Palais-Smale condition and also $\Phi_{(2)}$ is bounded from below. (We recall that a C^1-functional Φ on a Banach space X satisfies the Palais-Smale condition if every sequence $(u_n) \subset X$ with $\Phi(u_n)$ bounded and $\Phi'(u_n) \to 0$, contains a convergent subsequence) So, a nontrivial critical point of $\Phi_{(2)}$ is obtained by using the Mountain Pass Theorem. Moreover, positive and negative nontrivial solutions of (6.65) are obtained, too.

Let's go back to the boundary value problem (6.64).

The main result which has been obtained in [24] reads as follows:

Theorem 6.27. *Let* $f : \Omega \times \mathbb{R} \to \mathbb{R}$ *be a Carathéodory function with primitive* $F(x,s) = \int_0^s f(x,\tau)\mathrm{d}\tau$. *Suppose the following conditions hold:*

(i) $\displaystyle \limsup_{s \to 0} \frac{f(x,s)}{|s|^{p-2}s} < \lambda_1$ *uniformly with* $x \in \Omega$;

(ii) *there is* $q \in (1, p^*)$ *such that*

$$|f(x,s)| \le c\left(1 + |s|^{q-1}\right) \text{ for all } x \in \Omega, \ s \in \mathbb{R};$$

(iii) *there are numbers* $\theta > p$, $s_0 > 0$ *such that*

$$0 < \theta F(x,s) \le sf(x,s) \text{ for a.e. } x \in \Omega \text{ if } |s| \ge s_0. \qquad (6.68)$$

Then problem (6.64) *admits nontrivial solutions* $u_- \le 0 \le u_+$.

Here, λ_1 is the first eigenvalue of $-\Delta_p$ on $W_0^{1,p}(\Omega)$;

$$\lambda_1 = \inf \left\{ \frac{\|v\|_{0,p,\nabla}^p}{\|v\|_{L^p(\Omega)}^p} : v \in W_0^{1,p}(\Omega) \text{ and } v \neq 0 \right\},$$

the infimum being achieved exactly when v is a multiple of a certain $v_1 > 0$, while

$$p^* = \begin{cases} \dfrac{Np}{N-p} & \text{if } p < N, \\ \infty & \text{if } p \ge N. \end{cases}$$

It is watchful to remark that condition (6.68) extends the Ambrosetti and Rabinowitz condition (6.67) corresponding to $p = 2$ to the general case $1 < p < \infty$. The proof of Theorem 6.27 is, again, based on the Mountain Pass Theorem of Ambrosetti and Rabinowitz. For details, see [24].

Besides the Mountain Pass Theorem, the Leray-Schauder topological degree for compact perturbations of the identity in a Banach space was also used to prove the existence of a solution to the boundary value problem (6.64).

More precisely, in [20], [24] the following theorem, which is known as the Leray-Schauder-Schäfer Theorem, is used:

Theorem 6.28. *Let* X *be a Banach space and let* $T : X \to X$ *be compact. Assume that there is an open ball* $\mathcal{B}(0_X, r)$ *such that*

$$\mathcal{S} = \{x \in X : x = tTx \text{ for some } t \in [0,1]\} \subset \mathcal{B}(0_X, r). \qquad (6.69)$$

Then

$$\mathrm{Fix}(T) = \{x \in X : x = Tx\}$$

is nonempty and contained in $\mathcal{B}(0_X, r)$.

Proof:

The proof is as follows. Consider the homotopy of compact transforms

$$H : [0,1] \times \overline{\mathcal{B}}(0_X, r) \to X, \ H(t,x) = tTx.$$

For any $t \in [0,1]$ consider the map

$$H_t : \overline{\mathcal{B}}(0_X, r) \to X, \ H_t(x) = H(t,x) \text{ for all } x \in \overline{\mathcal{B}}(0_X, r).$$

Clearly, H_t is compact and, by assumption (6.69),

$$x \neq H_t(x) \text{ for all } x \in \overline{\mathcal{B}}(0_X, r).$$

Consequently, the Leray-Schauder degree $d_{LS}(I - H_t, \mathcal{B}(0_X, r), 0)$ is well-defined and it does not depend on t. In particular

$$d_{LS}(I - H_1, \mathcal{B}(0_X, r), 0) = d_{LS}(I - H_0, \mathcal{B}(0_X, r), 0)$$

which rewrites as

$$d_{LS}(I - T, \mathcal{B}(0_X, r), 0) = d_{LS}(I, \mathcal{B}(0_X, r), 0) = 1.$$

Consequently, by the existence property of the degree, there exists $x \in \mathcal{B}(0_X, r)$ such that $(I - T)x = 0$ or, equivalently, $x = Tx$.

The idea of such an approach will first be brought to light in a simple functional framework and then applied to problem (6.64).

Let X be a Banach space, $J_\varphi : X \to X^*$ and $N : X \to X^*$. Consider the equation

$$J_\varphi x = Nx. \tag{6.70}$$

If J_φ is bijective then the equation (6.70) equivalently rewrites as

$$x = \left(J_\varphi^{-1} N\right) x. \tag{6.71}$$

If $T = J_\varphi^{-1} N : X \to X$ is compact (for example, if N is compact and J_φ^{-1} is continuous) then the whole machinery related to the existence of fixed points for compact operators in a Banach space can be put to work.

In particular, if there is an open ball $\mathcal{B}(0_X, r) \subset X$ such that

$$\left\{ x \in X; x = t\left(J_\varphi^{-1} N\right) x \text{ for some } t \in [0,1] \right\} \subset \mathcal{B}(0_X, r)$$

then, according to Leray-Schauder-Schäfer Theorem, $J_\varphi^{-1} N$ has a fixed point in $\mathcal{B}(0_X, r)$ or, equivalently, the equation (6.70) has a solution in the same open ball.

Next a more particular framework is considered. Assume that X is reflexive, smooth, strictly convex and possesses the Kadeč-Klee property. From Proposition 6.3 we infer that J_φ is a bijection of X onto X^* having a continuous and bounded inverse $J_\varphi^{-1} : X^* \to X$. Assume further that X is compactly imbedded into a Banach space Z. Let $i : X \to Z$ be the compact injection of X into Z, $i^* : Z^* \to X^*$ ($i^* z^* = z^* \circ i$ for all $z^* \in Z^*$) be the adjoint map of i and let $S : Z \to Z^*$ be demicontinuous ($z_n \to z \implies S z_n \rightharpoonup S z$). Then $(i^* \circ S \circ i) : X \to X^*$ is compact. Indeed, if (x_n) is a bounded sequence in X, $i(x_n)$ is relatively compact in Z. Passing to a subsequence we may assume that $(i x_n)$ converges to a $z_0 \in Z$: $i x_n \to z_0$. Since S is demicontinuous, it follows that $S(i x_n) \rightharpoonup S z_0$ and, since i^* is compact, $(i^* \circ S \circ i) x_n \to i^* (S z_0)$.

Under the above assumption, by solution of the equation

$$J_\varphi x = S x \qquad (6.72)$$

we understand an element $x \in X$ which satisfies

$$J_\varphi x = (i^* \circ S \circ i) x \text{ (equality in } X^*) \qquad (6.73)$$

or, equivalently, for all $h \in X$,

$$\langle J_\varphi x, h \rangle_{X,X^*} = \langle (i^* \circ S \circ i) x, h \rangle_{X,X^*} = \langle S(ix), ih \rangle_{Z,Z^*} = \langle Sx, h \rangle_{Z,Z^*}.$$

Next the above functional framework will be specified as follows. We take:

$$(X, \| \ \|) = \left(W_0^{1,p}(\Omega), \| \ \|_{0,p,\nabla} \right), 1 < p < \infty;$$

$$J_\varphi = J_{(p-1)} = -\Delta_p : W_0^{1,p}(\Omega) \to W^{-1,p'}(\Omega), \frac{1}{p} + \frac{1}{p'} = 1.$$

(Recall that $J_{(p-1)}$ designates the duality mapping corresponding to $\varphi(t) = t^{p-1}$, $t \geq 0$.)

Since $\left(W_0^{1,p}(\Omega), \| \ \|_{0,p,\nabla} \right)$ is uniformly convex, it possesses the Kadeč-Klee property and since the norm $\| \ \|_{0,p,\nabla}$ is Fréchet differentiable, $J_{(p-1)} = -\Delta_p$ is a continuous bounded bijection of $W_0^{1,p}(\Omega)$ onto $W^{-1,p'}(\Omega)$ having a continuous and bounded inverse $J_{(p-1)}^{-1} = (-\Delta_p)^{-1} : W^{-1,p'}(\Omega) \to W_0^{1,p}(\Omega)$.

Assume now that the Carathéodory function $f : \Omega \times \mathbb{R} \to \mathbb{R}$ satisfies

$$|f(x,s)| \leq c_1 |s|^{p/q} + c(x) \text{ for a.e. } x \in \Omega \text{ and all } s \in \mathbb{R},$$

with $c_1 = const. \geq 0$, $1 \leq p, q < \infty$ and $c \in L^q(\Omega)$.

Then, for any $u \in L^p(\Omega)$, the function (defined a.e. in Ω)

$$x \in \Omega \longrightarrow f(x, u(x)) \in \mathbb{R}$$

is well defined and it belongs to $L^q(\Omega)$.

Moreover, the so called Nemytskij (or superposition) operator

$$N_f : L^p(\Omega) \to L^q(\Omega), u \in L^p(\Omega) \to N_f u \in L^q(\Omega), (N_f u)(x) = f(x, u(x))$$

for a.e. $x \in \Omega$, is continuous bounded and satisfies

$$\|N_f u\|_{L^q(\Omega)} \leq c_1 \|u\|_{L^p(\Omega)}^{p/q} + \|c\|_{L^q(\Omega)} \text{ for all } u \in L^p(\Omega).$$

For the proof see, e.g., de Figueiredo [17], Kavian [35].

In particular, if the Carathéodory function f satisfies

$$|f(x, s)| \leq c_1 |s|^{p/p'} + c(x) \text{ for a.e. } x \in \Omega \text{ and all } s \in \mathbb{R}, \tag{6.74}$$

the Nemytskij operator generated by f is well-defined from $L^p(\Omega)$ into $L^{p'}(\Omega)$, $N_f : L^p(\Omega) \to L^{p'}(\Omega)$, continuous and bounded. Moreover,

$$\|N_f u\|_{L^{p'}(\Omega)} \leq c_1 \|u\|_{L^p(\Omega)}^{p/p'} + \|c\|_{L^{p'}(\Omega)}. \tag{6.75}$$

Finally, denote by $i : W_0^{1,p}(\Omega) \to L^p(\Omega)$ the compact injection of $\left(W_0^{1,p}(\Omega), \| \ \|_{0,p,\nabla} \right)$ into $\left(L^p(\Omega), \| \ \|_{L^p(\Omega)} \right)$ (Rellich-Kondrachov) and by $i^* : L^{p'}(\Omega) \to W^{-1,p'}(\Omega)$ its adjoint.

Assume that the Carathéodory function f appearing in (6.64) satisfies the growth condition (6.74). By solution in $W_0^{1,p}(\Omega)$ to the boundary value problem (6.64) we understand an element $u \in W_0^{1,p}(\Omega)$ which satisfies

$$J_{(p-1)} u \left(= -\Delta_p u \right) = (i^* \circ N_f \circ i) u. \tag{6.76}$$

The following diagram

$$W_0^{1,p}(\Omega) \ni u \xrightarrow[compact]{i} i(u) \in L^p(\Omega) \xrightarrow[continuous]{N_f} N_f(iu) \in L^{p'}(\Omega)$$

$$\xrightarrow[compact]{i^*} i^*(N_f(iu)) \in W^{-1,p'}(\Omega)$$

shows that $(i^* \circ N_f \circ i) : W_0^{1,p}(\Omega) \to W^{-1,p'}(\Omega)$ is compact. Since $J_{(p-1)}^{-1} : W^{-1,p'}(\Omega) \to W_0^{1,p}(\Omega)$ is continuous (and bounded), (6.76) rewrites as a fixed point problem

$$u = J_{(p-1)}^{-1} (i^* \circ N_f \circ i) u, \tag{6.77}$$

with

$$J_{(p-1)}^{-1} (i^* \circ N_f \circ i) : W_0^{1,p}(\Omega) \to W_0^{1,p}(\Omega) \tag{6.78}$$

a compact operator.

According to Leray-Schauder-Schäfer Theorem (Theorem 6.28) if there is an open ball $\mathcal{B}(0, r) \subset W_0^{1,p}(\Omega)$ such that

$$\left\{ u \in W_0^{1,p}(\Omega) ; u = t J_{(p-1)}^{-1} (i^* \circ N_f \circ i) u \text{ for some } t \in [0, 1] \right\} \subset \mathcal{B}(0, r)$$

then $J_{(p-1)}^{-1} (i^* \circ N_f \circ i)$ has a fixed point in $\mathcal{B}(0, r)$ or, equivalently, equation (6.77) has a solution in the same open ball.

Since for $t = 0$ the unique solution of the equation

$$u = t J_{(p-1)}^{-1} (i^* \circ N_f \circ i) u \tag{6.79}$$

is $u = 0$, let $u \in W_0^{1,p}(\Omega)$ satisfying (6.79) for some $t \in (0, 1]$.

Then, the following estimates hold:

$$\|u\|_{0.p,\nabla}^{p-1} \leq \left\| \frac{u}{t} \right\|_{0.p,\nabla}^{p-1} = \left\| J_{(p-1)} \left(\frac{u}{t} \right) \right\|_{W^{-1,p'}(\Omega)} = \|(i^* \circ N_f \circ i) u\|_{W^{-1,p'}(\Omega)}$$

$$\leq \|i^*\| \, \|N_f(iu)\|_{L^{p'}(\Omega)} \leq \|i^*\| \left(c_1 \, \|i(u)\|_{L^p(\Omega)}^{p-1} + \|c\|_{L^{p'}(\Omega)} \right)$$

$$\leq c_1 \, \|i\|^p \, \|u\|_{0,p,\nabla}^{p-1} + \|i\| \, \|c\|_{L^{p'}(\Omega)}$$

leading to $(1 - c_1 \|i\|^p) \, \|u\|_{0,p,\nabla}^{p-1} \leq \|i\| \, \|c\|_{L^{p'}(\Omega)}$.

Clearly, if $c_1 < \|i\|^{-p}$, this last inequality implies: there exists a constant $r > 0$ such that $\|u\| < r$.

Consequently, the Leray-Schauder-Schäfer Theorem applies.

We summarise the above considerations as a theorem.

Theorem 6.29. *If the Carathéodory function* $f : \Omega \times \mathbb{R} \to \mathbb{R}$ *satisfies the growth condition* (6.74) *with* $0 < c_1 < \|i\|^{-p}$ *(i being the compact injection of* $W_0^{1,p}(\Omega)$ *into* $L^p(\Omega)$*), the boundary value problem* (6.64) *has a solution in* $W_0^{1,p}(\Omega)$.

6.5.3 Duality mappings and the reflexivity of Banach spaces

6.5.3.1 James' Theorem on reflexivity in terms of duality mappings

A deep theorem of R. C. James ([31], [32], [33]) says that if X is nonreflexive, then there exists an element of X^* which does not attain its norm on the unit ball (see also [19]). What follows is a transcript of James' Theorem in terms of duality mappings.

Theorem 6.30. *Let* $(X, \|\cdot\|)$ *be a Banach space. The following statements are equivalent:*

(1) *X is reflexive;*

(2) *Any duality mapping* $J_\varphi : X \to 2^{X^*}$ *is surjective;*

(3) *The normalized duality mapping* $J : X \to 2^{X^*}$ *is surjective;*

(4) *Any* $x^* \in X^*$ *attains its norm on the unit ball.*

Proof:

$(1) \Rightarrow (2)$ Let $x^* \in X^*$ be given. We will show that there exists $y \in X$ such that $x^* \in J_\varphi y$. Since $J_\varphi 0_X = 0_{X^*}$, we assume that $x^* \neq 0_{X^*}$. By Hahn-Banach Theorem, there exists $x^{**} \in X^{**}$ such that $\|x^{**}\| = 1$ and $\langle x^{**}, x^* \rangle = \|x^*\|$. By reflexivity, there exists $x \in X$ such that:

$$\langle x^{**}, x^* \rangle = \langle x^*, x \rangle \text{ and } \|x\| = \|x^{**}\| = 1.$$

We claim that

$$x^* = J_\varphi y \text{ with } y = rx, \ \varphi(r) = \|x^*\|.$$

Indeed, it is obvious that

$$\|x^*\| = \varphi(r) = \varphi(\|y\|),$$

and

$$\langle x^*, y \rangle = r \langle x^*, x \rangle = r \|x^*\| = \|y\| \varphi(\|y\|).$$

$(2) \Rightarrow (3)$ Obvious.

$(3) \Rightarrow (4)$ Let $x^* \in X^* \setminus \{0_{X^*}\}$. According to (3), there exists $x \in X$ such that $x^* \in Jx$. By definition of J, one has

$$\langle x^*, x \rangle = \|x^*\| \|x\| \text{ and } \|x^*\| = \|x\|,$$

which implies

$$\left\langle x^*, \frac{x}{\|x\|} \right\rangle = \|x^*\|.$$

$(4) \Rightarrow (1)$ If not, then, from James' Theorem, there exists an element of X^* which does not attain its norm on the unit ball (in contradiction with (4)).

Corollary 6.6. *A Banach space X is reflexive if and only if any duality mapping on X is surjective.*

6.5.3.2   *Laursen's Theorem on reflexivity in terms of duality mappings*

One of the most popular criterion for reflexivity of a Banach space is the weak compactness of the unit ball $\overline{B}(0,1) = \{x \in X \mid \|x\| \leq 1\}$.

In [38] Laursen has given an extension of this criterion. Namely, he constructed a topology on a normed vector space X which is in general weaker than the weak topology and he showed that the space is reflexive if and only if the unit ball is compact in this weaker topology. The construction is essentially based on the existence of the normalized duality mapping on any normed space.

We follow [38] for a short description.

If X is a vector space we denote by X^+ the space of all linear functionals on X. If $F \subset X^+$ is a linear subspace with the property that $f(x) = 0$ for all f in F then $x = 0$, we say that F is total over X. Suppose that X is a vector space and that F is a total subspace over X. Following [27] we define the F-topology of X (or the weak topology in X induced by F) as the topology with base of a point $x_0 \in X$ consisting of all sets of the form

$$V(x_0, A, \varepsilon) = \{x \in X \mid |f(x) - f(x_0)| < \varepsilon \text{ for all } f \in A\}$$

where A is a finite subset of F and $\varepsilon > 0$.

Now, let X be a normed vector space and let X^* be its dual space. Let $W : X \to X^*$ be a mapping satisfying the following conditions:

(i) $\|W(x)\| = \|x\|$,

(ii) $\langle W(x), x \rangle = \|x\|^2$ for all $x \in X$.

The image of X under W, $W(X)$ is a total set over X, i.e., if $x \in X$ is such that

$$\langle W(u), x \rangle = 0 \text{ for all } u \in X \tag{6.80}$$

then $x = 0$. Indeed, it follows from (6.80) that, in particular, $\langle W(x), x \rangle = 0$ which, according with (ii), implies $x = 0$. Consequently, the linear span of $W(X)$, $F = Sp(W(X))$ is a subspace of X^* which is total over X. Thus the $Sp(W(X))$-topology of X induced by $Sp(W(X))$ makes sense. According to what is said above, a base of a point $x_0 \in X$ will consist of all sets of the form

$$V(x_0, A, \varepsilon) = \{x \in X \mid |f(x) - f(x_0)| < \varepsilon \text{ for all } f \in A\}$$

where A is a finite subset of $Sp(W(X))$ and $\varepsilon > 0$.

Clearly, this topology is Hausdorff and it is weaker than the weak topology $\sigma(X, X^*)$ over X.

Remark that if $W : X \to X^*$ satisfies (i) and (ii) then, for any $x \in X$, $W(x) \in Jx$, i.e. W is a selection of J. Conversely, any selection of J, i.e. any mapping $W : X \to X^*$ with $W(x) \in Jx$ for all $x \in X$, satisfies (i) and (ii). Thus, a mapping $W : X \to X^*$ satisfies (i) and (ii) if and only if W is a selection of the normalized duality mapping $J : X \to 2^{X^*}$. Since $Jx \neq \emptyset$ for any $x \in X$, we conclude that mappings $W : X \to X^*$ satisfying (i) and (ii) exist.

Now, the main result in [38] can be stated as follows:

Theorem 6.31. *Let X be a Banach space. Then X is reflexive if and only if there exists a selection $W : X \to X^*$ of the normalized duality mapping on X such that the unit ball B of X is compact in the weak topology induced by $Sp\,(W\,(X))$.*

Remark 6.8. *If X is a smooth Banach space or, equivalently, the norm of X is Gâteaux differentiable, then $J : X \to X^*$ is single valued. If this is the case then J has a unique selection, namely $W = J$, and the weak topology induced by $Sp\,(W\,(X)) = Sp\,(J\,(X))$ equals the weak topology $\sigma\,(X, X^*)$. If X is not a smooth Banach space, then, generally, Jx, $x \in X$, doesn't reduce to a point and, consequently, we have no uniqueness for W. Every such a W-mapping induces a corresponding W-topology on X. Since all such W-topologies are weaker than the weak topology and since reflexivity implies weak compactness of B, it follows that if B is compact in one W-topology, it is compact in them all.*

For a detailed proof see [38].

6.5.4 Duality mappings and the subreflexivity: Bishop-Phelps' Theorem in terms of duality mappings

Theorem 6.32. *Let X be a Banach space. The following statements are equivalent:*

    (1) $\mathcal{A} = \{x^* \in X^*; \exists x \text{ with } \|x\| = 1 \text{ such that } \langle x^*, x \rangle = \|x^*\|\}$ is dense in X^*.

    (2) For any duality mapping $J_\varphi : X \to 2^{X^*}$, $J_\varphi\,(X)$ is dense in X^*.

    (3) For the normalized duality mapping $J : X \to 2^{X^*}$, $J\,(X)$ is dense in X^*.

Proof:
(1)$\Rightarrow$(2) Let $x^* \in X^*$. According to (1) there exist sequences $(x_n^*) \subset X^*$, $(x_n) \subset X$ with $\|x_n\| = 1$ and $\langle x_n^*, x_n \rangle = \|x_n^*\|$, such that $x_n^* \to x^*$. It suffices to observe that for any such x_n^* and x_n, one has $x_n^* \in J_\varphi\,(y_n)$, with $y_n = r_n x_n$, $\varphi\,(r_n) = \|x_n^*\|$. Indeed, simple computations give us:

$$\|x_n^*\| = \varphi\,(r_n) = \varphi\,(\|y_n\|),$$

and

$$\langle x_n^*, y_n \rangle = r_n \langle x_n^*, x_n \rangle = r_n \|x_n^*\| = \|y_n\|\, \varphi\,(\|y_n\|)$$

showing that $x_n^* \in J_\varphi\,(X)$, thus $J_\varphi\,(X)$ is dense in X^*.

(2)⇒(3) Obvious.

(3)⇒(1) It suffices to show that $J(X) \subset \mathcal{A}$. Let $x^* \in J(X)$. There exists some $x \in X$ such that $x^* \in Jx$, that is $\langle x^*, x \rangle = \|x^*\|^2$ and $\|x^*\| = \|x\|$, which implies $\left\langle x^*, \dfrac{x}{\|x\|} \right\rangle = \|x\| = \|x^*\|$. Thus $x^* \in \mathcal{A}$.

We conclude that the subreflexivity of any Banach space is equivalent with the density in X^* of $J_\varphi(X)$ for any gauge function φ.

For more details concerning the deep theorem of Bishop and Phelps see [6], [34] and the fascinating history written by R. R. Phelps [50]. See also [19, Chapter One].

6.5.5 Duality mappings and the Kuratowsky measure of non-compactness

Recall that, given any bounded subset B of a Banach space X, the Kuratowski measure of noncompactness of B, $\alpha(B)$, is defined as the infimum of those $\varepsilon > 0$ such that B can be covered with a finite number of subsets of B having diameter less or equal to ε. For the properties of α see M. Furi, M. Martelli and A. Vignoli [29], J. M. Ayerbe Toledano, T. Dominguez Benavides and G. López Acedo [2]. We only recall here the following two properties which are needed for the purpose of this paper: for any bounded set $B \subset X$, $\alpha(B) = 0$ if and only if $\overline{B}$ is compact and $\alpha(B) = \alpha(\overline{B})$. We also recall Nussbaum's nice result concerning the Kuratowski measure of noncompactness of the sphere in an infinite dimensional Banach space X: for any $r > 0$, denote by $S_{X,r} = \{x \in X \mid \|x\| = r\}$. Then $\alpha(S_{X,r}) = 2r$. For the proof, cf. R. D. Nussbaum [46] (see also M. Furi and A. Vignoli [28]).

Let X and Y be Banach spaces and $F : X \to Y$ be a continuous and bounded operator. By definition, the Kuratowski measure of non-compactness of F is

$$\alpha(F) = \inf\{k \geq 0 \mid \alpha[F(B)] \leq k \cdot \alpha(B), B \subset X \text{ bounded}\}.$$

If $\dim X = \infty$, $\alpha(F)$ may be equivalently defined as

$$\alpha(F) = \sup\left\{\frac{\alpha[F(B)]}{\alpha(B)} \mid B \subset X \text{ bounded}, \alpha(B) > 0\right\}. \tag{6.81}$$

By definition of $\alpha(F)$, it easily follows that $\alpha(F) = 0$ if and only if F is compact. For many other properties of $\alpha(F)$, cf. M. Furi, M. Martelli and A. Vignoli [29], J. M. Ayerbe Toledano, T. Dominguez Benavides and G. López Acedo [2].

Theorem 6.33. ([21]) *Assume that $(X, \|\cdot\|)$ is a Banach space with Fréchet differentiable norm. Then one has:*

(a) *Any duality mapping $J_\varphi : X \to X^*$ is norm-to-norm continuous and bounded;*

(b) $\alpha(J_\varphi) = 0$ *if and only if* $\dim X < \infty$;

(c)

$$\alpha(J_\varphi) \geq \sup\left\{\frac{\varphi(r)}{r} \mid r > 0\right\} \quad if \dim X = \infty. \tag{6.82}$$

For the proof we need the following lemma:

Lemma 6.2. *Let $(X, \|\cdot\|)$ be a real Banach space with Gâteaux differentiable norm. Then one has: for any gauge function φ and any $r > 0$, $J_\varphi(S_{X,r})$ is dense in $S_{X^*, \varphi(r)}$.*

Proof:
Clearly, J_φ is defined by (6.38) and acts from $S_{X,r}$ into $S_{X^*,\varphi(r)}$.

Let $x^* \in S_{X^*,\varphi(r)}$. According to Theorem 6.32, there is a sequence $(x_n) \subset X$ such that

$$Jx_n = \|x_n\| (\operatorname{grad} \|\cdot\|)(x_n) \to x^*. \tag{6.83}$$

We deduce from this that $\|x_n\| \to \|x^*\| = \varphi(r)$ such that from (6.83) we infer that

$$\varphi(r) \operatorname{grad} \|\cdot\|(x_n) \to x^*. \tag{6.84}$$

Setting $y_n = rx_n/\|x_n\|$, (6.84) reads as $\varphi(\|y_n\|)(\operatorname{grad} \|\cdot\|)(y_n) \to x^*$, that is $J_\varphi y_n \to x^*$ with $y_n \in S_{X,r}$.

Proof:
[Proof of Theorem *6.33*](a) See Theorem 6.11.

(b) Assume that $\alpha(J_\varphi) = 0$. Then J_φ is compact. Accordingly, $\overline{J_\varphi(S_{X,r})}$ is compact. But, according to lemma 6.2, $\overline{J_\varphi(S_{X,r})} = S_{X^*,\varphi(r)}$ and the compactness of $S_{X^*,\varphi(r)}$ implies that X is finite dimensional.

Conversely, if $\dim X < \infty$, any continuous and bounded operator from X into X^* is compact. In particular, $J_\varphi : X \to X^*$ is compact thus, $\alpha(J_\varphi) = 0$.

(c) It follows from (b) that, if X is an infinite dimensional Banach space with a Fréchet differentiable norm then $J_\varphi : X \to X^*$ is norm-to-norm continuous and bounded but never compact. That is why, under the above hypotheses, studying the measure of noncompactness of J_φ makes sense.

Since $\dim X = \infty$, $\alpha(J_\varphi)$ is given by (see (6.81))

$$\alpha(J_\varphi) = \sup\left\{\frac{\alpha[J_\varphi(B)]}{\alpha(B)} \mid B \subset X \text{ bounded}, \alpha(B) > 0\right\}.$$

Take $B = S_{X,r}$, for any $r > 0$. The above quoted properties of α, lemma 6.2 and Nussbaum's result allow us to write

$$\frac{\alpha[J_\varphi(S_{X,r})]}{\alpha(S_{X,r})} = \frac{\alpha\left[\overline{J_\varphi(S_{X,r})}\right]}{\alpha(S_{X,r})} = \frac{\alpha(S_{X^*,\varphi(r)})}{\alpha(S_{X,r})} = \frac{\varphi(r)}{r}.$$

Consequently

$$\left\{\frac{\varphi(r)}{r} \mid r > 0\right\} \subset \left\{\frac{\alpha[J_\varphi(B)]}{\alpha(B)} \mid B \subset X \text{ bounded}, \alpha(B) > 0\right\}$$

and, from this, estimate (6.82) follows.

Application: the Kuratowski measure of noncompactness for p-Laplacian

Since $-\Delta_p : \left(W_0^{1,p}(\Omega), \|\ \|_{0,p,\nabla}\right) \to W^{-1,p'}(\Omega)$ is the duality mapping on $W_0^{1,p}(\Omega)$ corresponding to $\varphi(t) = t^{p-1}$, $t \geq 0$, and the norm $\|\ \|_{0,p,\nabla}$ is Fréchet differentiable, according to (6.82) we will have:

$$\alpha(-\Delta_p) \geq \sup\left\{r^{p-2} \mid r > 0\right\}. \tag{6.85}$$

It follows that, for $p \in (1,2) \cup (2,\infty)$, $\alpha(-\Delta_p) = \infty$.

For $p = 2$, it follows from (6.56) that

$$-\Delta_2 : W_0^{1,2}(\Omega) = H_0^1(\Omega) \to \left(H_0^1(\Omega)\right)^* = H^{-1}(\Omega)$$

is defined by

$$-\Delta_2 u = -\frac{\partial}{\partial x_i}\left(\frac{\partial u}{\partial x_i}\right) \text{ for any } u \in H_0^1(\Omega)$$

or, equivalently

$$\langle -\Delta_2 u, v\rangle_{H_0^1(\Omega),H^{-1}(\Omega)} = (u,v)_{H_0^1(\Omega)}, \text{ for all } u,v \in H_0^1(\Omega),$$

where $\langle \cdot, \cdot\rangle_{H_0^1(\Omega),H^{-1}(\Omega)}$ stands for the duality pairing between $H_0^1(\Omega)$ and its dual $H^{-1}(\Omega)$ and $(\cdot,\cdot)_{H_0^1(\Omega)}$ designates the inner product on $H_0^1(\Omega)$.

In other words, $-\Delta_2 = -\Delta$ viewed as the canonical isomorphism between $H_0^1(\Omega)$ and its dual $H^{-1}(\Omega)$ given by Riesz Theorem. Consequently, we have (see M. Furi, M. Martelli and A. Vignoli [29]) $\alpha(-\Delta_2) = \alpha(-\Delta) \leq \|-\Delta\| = 1$. On the other hand, the estimation (6.85) gives us $\alpha(-\Delta_2) \geq 1$. Thus $\alpha(-\Delta_2) = 1$ and the proof is complete.

6.5.6   Duality mappings and the geometry of Banach spaces

6.5.6.1   Petryshyn's result: characterisation of strictly convex Banach spaces in terms of duality mappings

Theorem 6.34. *A necessary and sufficient condition for a Banach space* X *to be strictly convex is that the multivalued duality mapping* $J : X \to 2^{X^*}$ *(the normalized duality mapping) be strictly monotone.*

For a detailed proof see [47].

6.5.6.2   Characterisation of strictly convex Banach spaces in terms of Lumer's semi-inner product

Let X be a real vector space.

By definition ([39]), a Lumer semi-inner product on X is a mapping $[\ ,\ ] : X \times X \to \mathbb{R}$ having the properties:

    (i) $[x + y, z] = [x, z] + [y, z]$,

    (ii) $[\lambda x, y] = \lambda [x, y]$,

    (iii) $[x, x] > 0$ if $x \neq 0_X$,

    (iv) $[x, y] \leq [x, x]^{1/2} [y, y]^{1/2}$,

    (v) $[x, \lambda y] = \lambda [x, y]$,

for all $x, y, z \in X$ and $\lambda \in \mathbb{R}$.

If $(X, \| \ \|)$ is a normed space and $[\ ,\ ]$ is a Lumer semi-inner product on X, we say that $[\ ,\ ]$ is consistent with the norm of X if $\|x\| = [x, x]^{1/2}$ for all $x \in X$.

Theorem 6.35. *([51]) Let* $(X, \| \ \|)$ *be a normed space. Any Lumer semi-inner product on* X *which is consistent with the norm of* X *has the form*

$$[x, y] = \left\langle \tilde{J}y, x \right\rangle, \ x, y \in X,$$

where $\tilde{J}$ *is a selection of the normalized duality mapping* $J : X \to 2^{X^*}$ *(i.e.,* $\tilde{J} : X \to X^*$ *and* $\tilde{J}x \in Jx$ *for all* $x \in X$*).*

Proposition 6.4. *Let* $(X, \| \ \|)$ *be a real normed space and let* $[\ ,\ ] : X \times X \to \mathbb{R}$ *be a Lumer semi-inner product on* X *consistent with the norm of* X. *The following statements are equivalent:*

    (i) $(X, \| \ \|)$ *is strictly convex;*

    (ii) *For any two elements* $x, y \in X \setminus \{0_X\}$, *the equality* $[x, y] = \|x\| \|y\|$ *implies the existence of a real* $\lambda > 0$ *such that* $x = \lambda y$.

Proof:

(i)⇒(ii) Let $x \neq 0_X$ and $y \neq 0_X$ be such that $[x, y] = \|x\| \, \|y\|$. Since $[\,,\,]$ is consistent with the norm of X, there is a selection $\tilde{J} : X \to X^*$ of the normalized duality mapping $J : X \to 2^{X^*}$, such that $[x, y] = \left\langle \tilde{J}y, x \right\rangle$ (Theorem 6.35). Thus we get $\left\langle \tilde{J}y, x \right\rangle = \|x\| \, \|y\|$ and, from this, it follows that

$$\left\langle \tilde{J}y, \frac{x}{\|x\|} \right\rangle = \|y\| = \left\| \tilde{J}y \right\|.$$

On the other hand, by definition of $\tilde{J}$,

$$\left\langle \tilde{J}y, \frac{y}{\|y\|} \right\rangle = \|y\| = \left\| \tilde{J}y \right\|.$$

As X is assumed to be strictly convex, $\tilde{J}y$ cannot reach its norm at two different points of the unit ball. It follows that $\dfrac{x}{\|x\|} = \dfrac{y}{\|y\|}$ i.e. $x = \lambda y$ with $\lambda = \dfrac{\|x\|}{\|y\|} > 0$.

(ii)⇒(i) We shall show that, if assumption (ii) holds, then for any $x \neq 0_X$ and $y \neq 0_X$ satisfying $\|x + y\| = \|x\| + \|y\|$, there exists a real $\lambda > 0$ such that $x = \lambda y$. Accordingly, X is strictly convex.

Indeed, we first show that condition

$$\|x + y\| = \|x\| + \|y\| \text{ with } x \neq 0_X, \, y \neq 0_X,$$

implies

$$[x, x + y] = \|x\| \, \|x + y\| \text{ and } [y, x + y] = \|y\| \, \|x + y\|. \tag{6.86}$$

Assume the contrary. Since

$$[x, x + y] \leq \|x\| \, \|x + y\| \text{ and } [y, x + y] \leq \|y\| \, \|x + y\|, \tag{6.87}$$

assuming the contrary is to assume that at least one of the above inequalities is strict, say,

$$[x, x + y] < \|x\| \, \|x + y\|. \tag{6.88}$$

From (6.87) and (6.88) it follows (by addition)

$$[x + y, x + y] < (\|x\| + \|y\|) \, \|x + y\| = \|x + y\|^2,$$

which is a contradiction.

It remains that (6.86) hold. From (6.86) and assumption (ii) together, there are $t > 0$ and $s > 0$ such that

$$x = t \, (x + y) \text{ and } y = s \, (x + y). \tag{6.89}$$

Clearly, it follows from (6.89) that $t \neq 1$, $s \neq 1$, and $t + s = 1$. Thus, in fact, $0 < t < 1$ and $0 < s < 1$. Finally $x = \dfrac{t}{1 - t} y$ which completes the proof.

Dedication. In memory of Professor Solomon Marcus.

References

[1]   Adams, R. A., *Sobolev spaces*, Academic Press, New York, San Francisco, London, 1975.

[2]   Ayerbe Toledano, J. M., Dominguez Benavides, T., and López Acedo, G., *Measures of Noncompactness in Metric Fixed Point Theory*, Birkhäuser Verlag, 1997.

[3]   Ambrosetti, A. and Rabinowitz, P.H., Dual variational methods in critical points theory and applications, *J. Funct. Anal.*, **14** (1973), 349–381.

[4]   Asplund, E., Positivity of duality mappings, *Bull. Amer. Math. Soc.*, **73** (1967), 200–203.

[5]   Beurling, A. and Livingston, A. E., A theorem on duality mapping in Banach spaces, *Ark. Math.*, **4**, 5 (1962), 405–411.

[6]   Bishop, E., Phelps, R. R., A proof that every Banach space is subreflexive, *Bull. Amer. Math. Soc.*, **67** (1961), 97–98.

[7]   Bishop, E., Phelps, R. R., The support functionals of a convex set, *Proc. Symp. Pure Math.*, **7** (1962), A.M.S., 27–35.

[8]   Brezis, H., *Functional Analysis, Sobolev Spaces and Partial Differential Equations*, Springer, 2011.

[9]   Browder, F. E., *Les problèmes non-linéaires*, Les Presses de l'Université de Montréal, 1964.

[10] Browder, F. E., On a theorem of Beurling and Livingston, *Canad. J. Math.*, **17** (1965), 367–372.

[11] Browder, F. E., Multivalued monotone nonlinear mappings and duality mappings in Banach spaces, *Trans. Amer. Math. Soc.*, **118** (1965), 338–351.

[12] Browder, F. E., Nonlinear operators and nonlinear equations of evolution in Banach spaces, *Proc. Symp. Nonlinear Functional Anal. Amer. Math. Soc.*, vol. 2 (1970).

[13] Ciarlet, Ph. G., *Linear and Nonlinear Functional Analysis with Applications*, SIAM, 2013.

[14] Ciarlet, Ph. G., Dincă, G., and Matei, P., Fréchet differentiability of the norm in a Sobolev space with a variable exponent, *Analysis and Applications*, **11**, 4 (2013), 1350012 (31 pages).

[15] Cioranescu, I., *Geometry of Banach spaces, Duality mappings and Nonlinear Problems*, Kluwer Academic Publisher, 1990.

[16] De Figueiredo, D. G., *Topics in Nonlinear Functional Analysis*, Lect. Notes Math., No. **48**, University of Maryland, 1967.

[17] De Figueiredo, D. G., *Lectures on the Ekeland Variational Principle with Applications and Detours*, Tata Institute of Fundamental Research, Springer Verlag, 1989.

[18] Diening, L., Harjulehto, P., Hästö, P., and Ružička, M., *Lebesgue and Sobolev spaces with variable exponent*, Lect. Notes Math., vol. 2017, Springer-Verlag, 2011.

[19] Diestel, J., *Geometry of Banach Spaces – Selected Topics*, Lect. Notes Math., **485**, Springer Verlag, Berlin, 1975.

[20] Dincă, G., Jebelean, P., Une méthode de point fixe pour le p-Laplacien, *C. R. Acad. Sci. Paris*, **234** (1997), 165–168.

[21] Dincă, G., On the Kuratowski measure of noncompactness for duality mappings, *Topological Methods in Nonlinear Analysis*, **40** (2012), 181–187.

[22] Dincă, G., Dense single extension points in Hahn-Banach theorem, *Libertas Mathematica* (new series), **32**, 2 (2012), 155–160.

[23] Dincă, G., Goeleven, D., and Pasca, D., Duality mappings and the existence of periodic solutions for non-autonomous second order systems, *Portugaliae Mathematica*, **63**, 1 (2005), 47–68.

[24] Dincă, G., Jebelean, P., and Mawhin, J., Variational and topological methods for Dirichlet's problems with the p-Laplacian, *Portugal. Math.*, **58**, 3 (2001), 339–378.

[25] Dincă, G., Rochdi, M., On the structure of the solution set for a class of nonlinear equations involving a duality mapping, *Topological Methods in Nonlinear Analysis*, **31**, 1 (2008), 29–49.

[26] Dubinsky, Yu. A., Quasilinear elliptic and parabolic equations of an arbitrary order, *Uspehi Mat. Nauk.*, **23** (1968), 45–90.

[27] Dunford, N., Schwartz, J. T., *Linear operators* I, New York, 1957.

[28] Furi, M., Vignoli, A., On a property of the unit sphere in a linear normed space, *Bull. Acad. Pol. Sci.* **18** (1970), 333–334.

[29] Furi, M., Martelli M. and Vignoli, A., Contributions to the spectral theory of nonlinear operators in Banach spaces, *Ann. Mat. Pura Appl.* **118** (1978), 229–294.

[30] Jahn, J., *Introduction to the Theory of Nonlinear Optimization* (Second Revised Edition), Springer-Verlag, 1996.

[31] James, R. C., A non-reflexive Banach space isometric with its second conjugate space, *Proc. Nat. Acad. Sci.*, USA, **37** (1951), 174–177.

[32] James, R. C., Characterization of reflexivity, *Studia Mathematica*, **23** (1964), 205–216.

[33] James, R. C., Reflexivity and the sup of linear functionals, *Israel J. Math.* **13** (1972), 289–301.

[34] Kadeč, M. I., Conditions for the differentiability of the norm in a Banach space, *Uspehi Mat. Nauk*, XX, **3**(123), 1965, 183–187 (in Russian).

[35] Kavian, O., *Introduction à la théorie des points critiques*, Springer-Verlag France, Paris, 1993.

[36] Kato, T., Nonlinear semigroups and evolution equations, *J. Math. Soc. Japan*, **19** (1967), 508–520.

[37] Klee, V., Some new results on smoothness and rotundity in normed linear spaces, *Math. Annalen*, 139 (1959), 51–63.

[38] Laursen, K. B., A characterization of reflexivity of Banach spaces, *Math. Scand.*, 16 (1965), 169–174.

[39] Lumer, G., Semi-inner product spaces, *Trans. Amer. Math. Soc.*, **100** (1961), 29–43.

[40] Mawhin, J. and Willem, M., *Critical Point Theory and Hamiltonian Systems*, Springer-Verlag, Berlin/New York, 1989.

[41] Milman, D. P., On some criteria for the regularity of spaces of type (B), *Doklady Akademii Nauk SSSR*, **20** (1938), 243–246.

[42] Minty, G. J., Monotone (nonlinear) operators in Hilbert space, *Duke Mathematical Journal*, **29** (1962), 341–346.

[43] Minty, G. J., On a monotonicity method for the solution of nonlinear equations in Banach spaces, *Proc. Nat. Acad. Sci. USA*, **50** (1963), 1038–1041.

[44] Nečas, J., *Les Méthodes Directes en Théorie des Equations Elliptiques*, Masson, 1967.

[45] Nirenberg, L., *Topics in Nonlinear Functional Analysis*, Lecture Notes, Courant Institute, New York University, NY, 1974 (Second edition: American Mathematical Society, Providence, RI, 1994).

[46] Nussbaum, R. D., The fixed point index for local condensing maps, *Ann. Mat. Pura Appl.* **89** (1971), 217–258.

[47] Petryshyn, W. V., A characterization of strict convexity of Banach spaces and other uses of duality mappings, *J. Funct. Anal.*, **6**, 2 (1970), 282–292.

[48] Pettis, B. J., A proof that every uniformly convex space is reflexive, *Duke Mathematical Journal*, 5 (1939), 249–253.

[49] Phelps, R. R., *Convex Functions, Monotone Operators and Differentiability*, 2nd edition, Springer-Verlag, 1989.

[50] Phelps, R. R., The Bishop-Phelps Theorem, in "Ten Mathematical Essays on Approximation in Analysis and Topology", J. Ferrera, J. López-Gomez and F. R. Ruiz del Portal, Editors, Elsevier, 2005.

[51] Rosca, I., Semi-produit scalaires et répresentations du type Riesz pour les fonctionnelles linéaires et bornées sur les espaces normés, *C. R. Acad. Sci. Paris*, **283** (19), 1976, 79–81.

[52] Struwe, M., *Variational Methods; Applications to Nonlinear Partial Differential Equations and Hamiltonian Systems*, Springer-Verlag, 1990.

[53] Vajnberg, M. M., *Variational Methods for the Study of Nonlinear Operators*, Holden-Day, San Francisco, 1964.

[54] Zarantonello, E. H., Dense single-valuedness of monotone operators, *Israel J. Math.*, **15** (1973), 158–166.

Chapter 7

Primitive Ideal Spaces of Postliminal AF Algebras

Aldo J. Lazar
School of Mathematical Sciences
Tel Aviv University
Tel Aviv 69978, Israel
aldo@post.tau.ac.il

Abstract. A proof is given for the characterisation of the primitive ideal spaces of AF algebras due to O. Bratteli and G. A. Elliott [5, Theorem 6].

7.1 Introduction

The topological spaces that serve as primitive ideal spaces of C^*-algebras were characterised in [6]. Previously only the primitive ideal spaces of AF algebras were characterised. A first characterisation was given by O. Bratteli in [4]. Then a more elegant characterisation due to O. Bratteli and G. A. Elliott appeared in [5]: a topological space T is homeomorphic to the primitive ideal of an AF algebra if and only if T is a spectral space and has a countable basis of compact open subsets. By a spectral space one means a T_0 space in which a non void closed subset that is not the union of two proper subsets is the closure of a singleton. A different proof of this result was given in [7, Corollary 5.2].

The above mentioned paper of Bratteli and Elliott also contained a characterisation of the primitive ideal spaces of the postliminal AF algebras [5, Theorem 6]. However, the characterisation given there was incomplete and counterexamples were easy to find. The authors of [5] become aware of the flaw in the statement immediately after the publication and the reprints they distributed contained a hand written corrected version of the result.

Until now no proof has appeared of the correct characterisation and the purpose of this paper is to fill this lacuna.

One says that a topological space T is almost Hausdorff if every closed subspace of T contains a dense relatively open Hausdorff subset. All the terms related to AF algebras, their diagrams and ideal subdiagrams can be found in [3] and [8]. We denote the algebra of all compact operators on a separable Hilbert space by $\mathbb{K}$.

7.2   Results

The following lemma may be of some independent interest.

Lemma 7.1. *Let T be a spectral topological space that has a countable basis of compact open sets, G an open dense subset of T, and $F := T \setminus G$. Suppose that there are AF algebras $\mathbb{B}$, $\mathbb{C}$ and homeomorphisms h_G, h_F of G, F onto $\mathrm{Prim}(\mathbb{B})$, respectively, $\mathrm{Prim}(\mathbb{C})$. Then there exists an AF algebra $\mathcal{A}$ that contains a closed two-sided ideal $\mathcal{I}$ stably isomorphic with B and such that the quotient $A/\mathcal{I}$ is stably isomorphic with C. Moreover, there is a homeomorphism h of T onto $\mathrm{Prim}(\mathcal{A})$ such that, with the obvious identifications given by the isomorphisms mentioned above, $h \mid G = h_G$ and $h \mid F = h_F$.*

Proof:
Let $\{O_n\}_{n \in \mathbb{N}}$ be a basis of T consisting of compact open sets and $\mathbb{M} := \{n \in \mathbb{N} \mid O_n \cap F \neq \emptyset\} = \{n_k\}_{k \in \mathbb{N}}$ where $n_k < n_{k+1}$, $k \in \mathbb{N}$. We choose a diagram $D^{\mathbb{B}} = \{(m, i) \mid m \in \mathbb{N}, \, 1 \leq i \leq r(m)\}$ for $\mathbb{B}$ with the given edges between the elements (called vertices in the sequel) of $D^{\mathbb{B}}$ and their multiplicities and the dimensions assigned to the vertices. Similarly, we choose a diagram for $\mathbb{C}$ with the set of vertices $D^{\mathbb{C}} = \{(m, i) \mid m \in \mathbb{N}, \, r(m) < i \leq s(m)\}$. We let $\mathcal{J}_n^{\mathbb{B}}$ be the ideal of $\mathbb{B}$ corresponding to the open subset $h_G(O_n \cap G)$ of $\mathrm{Prim}(\mathbb{B})$ and $\mathcal{J}_{n_k}^{\mathbb{C}}$ be the ideal of $\mathbb{C}$ that satisfies $\mathrm{Prim}(\mathcal{J}_{n_k}^{\mathbb{C}}) = h_F(O_{n_k} \cap F)$. We denote by $D_n^{\mathbb{B}}$ the set of vertices of the subdiagram of $\mathcal{J}_n^{\mathbb{B}}$ and by $D_{n_k}^{\mathbb{C}}$ the set of vertices in the subdiagram of $\mathcal{J}_{n_k}^{\mathbb{C}}$.

We now begin to construct the diagram of $\mathcal{A}$. Its set of vertices is $D := D^{\mathbb{B}} \cup D^{\mathbb{C}} = \{(m, i) \mid m \in \mathbb{N}, \, 1 \leq i \leq s(m)\}$. Next we temporarily assign to each vertex of D the dimension it had in $D^{\mathbb{B}}$ or in $D^{\mathbb{C}}$, as may be the case. Now we copy in D the edges from $D^{\mathbb{B}}$ and $D^{\mathbb{C}}$ with their multiplicities. We shall add some new vertices which will have no ancestors and new edges to get the full diagram of $\mathcal{A}$ as it will be explained below. The dimension assigned to each new vertex will be 1 and the multiplicity of each new edge will also be 1. The dimension assigned to a vertex to which new edges are coming will be increased by the minimum necessary: the sum of the dimensions of its new ancestors. The dimensions of its descendants will be increased accordingly.

Set $m_0 := 0$. Let $k \in \mathbb{N}$ and suppose that the sequence of natural numbers $\{m_1 < \ldots m_{k-1}\}$ has already been defined. Let m_k be the first natural number greater than m_{k-1} such that on the rows $m_k + 1$ of $D^{\mathbb{B}}$ and of $D^{\mathbb{C}}$ there are elements of $D^{\mathbb{B}}_{n_k}$, respectively, $D^{\mathbb{C}}_{n_k}$. We add on a new vertex to the m_k row of $D^{\mathbb{C}}$ and join it with a vertex of $D^{\mathbb{C}}_{n_k}$ in the $m_k + 1$ row and with all the vertices of $D^{\mathbb{B}}_{n_k}$ in the $m_k + 1$ row. Next, whenever in a row p, $p > m_k + 1$, there is an element of $D^{\mathbb{B}}_{n_k}$ which has no ancestor in the $m_k + 1$ row of $D^{\mathbb{B}}_{n_k}$ we add on a new vertex to the $p - 1$ row of $D^{\mathbb{C}}$ and join it with a vertex of $D^{\mathbb{C}}_{n_k}$ in the p row and with all the vertices of $D^{\mathbb{B}}_{n_k}$ in the p row. In this way only finitely many (possibly none) new vertices are affixed to each row of $D^{\mathbb{C}}$. We shall denote the union of $D^{\mathbb{C}}$ with the set of all the new vertices by $D^{\tilde{\mathcal{C}}}$. We obtained a diagram of an AF algebra $\mathcal{A}$ with the set of vertices $D^{\mathcal{A}} = D^{\mathbb{B}} \cup D^{\tilde{\mathcal{C}}}$, with the erstwhile edges and the new edges and with the dimensions affixed to the vertices as indicated in the previous paragraph. Clearly $D^{\mathbb{B}}$ with the edges joining these vertices and the new dimensions is the diagram of a closed two sided ideal $\mathcal{I}$ of $\mathcal{A}$ and from here on we shall use the new notation $D^{\mathcal{I}}$ instead of $D^{\mathbb{B}}$. Similarly, we shall replace the notation $D^{\mathbb{B}}_n$ by $D^{\mathcal{I}}_n$. There is an obvious one-to-one correspondence between the two sided closed ideals of $\mathbb{B}$ and those of $\mathcal{I}$ that induces a homeomorphism from $\mathrm{Prim}(\mathbb{B})$ to $\mathrm{Prim}(\mathcal{I})$. We shall use this homeomorphism to identify $\mathrm{Prim}(\mathbb{B})$ with $\mathrm{Prim}(\mathcal{I})$ and from now on h_G will be considered as having $\mathrm{Prim}(\mathcal{I})$ as its range. Moreover, since the diagrams of $\mathbb{B}$ and $\mathcal{I}$ differ only by the dimensions assigned to the vertices, it is clear that $\mathbb{B}$ and $\mathcal{I}$ have isomorphic ordered K_0 groups. Thus these C^*-algebras are stably isomorphic by Elliott's theorem, see [1, Corollary 7.3.3]. Now, set $\tilde{\mathcal{C}} := \mathcal{A}/\mathcal{I}$; as in the case of $\mathbb{B}$ and $\mathcal{I}$, the existence of a natural homeomorphism between $\mathrm{Prim}(\mathbb{C})$ and $\mathrm{Prim}(\tilde{\mathcal{C}})$ allows us to look at $\mathrm{Prim}(\tilde{\mathcal{C}})$ as the range of h_F. Since all the vertices that we added on to $D^{\tilde{\mathcal{C}}}$ have all their immediate $D^{\tilde{\mathcal{C}}}$ descendants contained in $D^{\mathbb{C}}$, it is easily seen that $\mathbb{C}$ and $\tilde{\mathcal{C}}$ have isomorphic ordered K_0 groups thus we can use Elliott's theorem again to conclude that $\mathbb{C}$ and $\tilde{\mathcal{C}}$ are stably isomorphic.

It remains to show that there exists a homeomorphism from T to $\mathrm{Prim}(\mathcal{A})$ with the needed properties. We define the map $h : T \to \mathrm{Prim}(\mathcal{A})$ by $h \mid G = h_G$ and $h \mid F = h_F$. Clearly h is one to one and onto $\mathrm{Prim}(\mathcal{A})$ and we intend to show that it is open and continuous. The set of vertices $D_n^{\mathcal{I}}$ with the edges joining them is the subdiagram of an ideal of $\mathcal{A}$. When $n \notin \mathbb{M}$ we shall call this ideal $\mathcal{I}_n$. It is contained in $\mathcal{I}$ and its primitive ideal space is $h(O_n) = h_F(O_n)$. Let $k \in \mathbb{N}$; we look now at the union D_{n_k} of the set D'_{n_k} consisting of all the vertices in $D_{n_k}^{\mathbb{C}}$ situated in a row from $m_k + 1$ on with $D_{n_k}^{\mathcal{I}}$ and with the set of all the vertices of $D^{\tilde{\mathcal{C}}}$ whose all descendants on some row belong to $D'_{n_k} \cup D_{n_k}^{\mathcal{I}}$. It is plain that D_{n_k} is the set of vertices of a subdiagram corresponding to an ideal of $\mathcal{A}$ that shall be named $\mathcal{I}_{n_k}$. Since every connected sequence in $D^{\mathcal{A}}$ belongs from a certain vertex on either to $D^{\mathcal{I}}$ or to $D^{\mathbb{C}}$ it is clear that $h(O_{n_k}) = h_G(O_{n_k} \cap G) \cup h_F(O_{n_k} \cap F) = \mathrm{Prim}(I_{n_k})$. Thus $h(O_n)$ is an open subset of $\mathrm{Prim}(\mathcal{A})$ for every $n \in \mathbb{N}$; hence h is an open map. Now let U be an open subset of $\mathrm{Prim}(\mathcal{A})$ and denote by $\mathcal{J}_U$ the ideal of $\mathcal{A}$ corresponding to it. We have $h^{-1}(U) = h_G^{-1}(U \cap \mathrm{Prim}(\mathcal{I})) \cup h_F^{-1}(U \cap \mathrm{Prim}(\tilde{\mathcal{C}}))$. If $U \cap \mathrm{Prim}(\tilde{\mathcal{C}}) = \emptyset$ then clearly $h^{-1}(U)$ is an open subset of T so we have to consider only the case $U \cap \mathrm{Prim}(\tilde{\mathcal{C}}) \neq \emptyset$. Let $Q \in U \cap \mathrm{Prim}(\tilde{\mathcal{C}})$. The map h_F is continuous thus there is $k \in \mathbb{N}$ such that $Q \in h_F(O_{n_k} \cap F) \subset U \cap \mathrm{Prim}(\tilde{\mathcal{C}})$. Hence each vertex in $D_{n_k} \cap D^{\mathbb{C}}$ belongs to the subdiagram of J_U. It follows from this and the construction of the diagram of $\mathcal{A}$ that every vertex of D_{n_k} belongs to the subdiagram of $\mathcal{J}_U$. We infer that $h^{-1}(Q) \in O_{n_k} \subset h^{-1}(U)$ and we conclude that $h^{-1}(U)$ is an open subset of T. This establishes the continuity of h and the proof is complete.

The conclusion of the lemma remains valid without assuming that G is dense. In this case we let $D^{\mathcal{J}}$ be the subdiagram of $D^{\mathbb{C}}$ corresponding to $\mathrm{Int}(F)$. To the definition of m_k one should add the requirement that in the row $m_k + 1$ of $D^{\mathbb{C}}$ there is an element of $D_{n_k}^{\mathbb{C}}$ not in $D^{\mathcal{J}}$. The new vertex of the m_k row is joined with this vertex of the $m_k + 1$ row of $D_{n_k}^{\mathbb{C}}$. The changes in the proof that h is a homeomorphism are obvious.

Remark 7.1. (i) If $\mathbb{B}$ and $\mathbb{C}$ are stable then $\mathcal{I}$ is isomorphic to $\mathbb{B}$ and $\tilde{\mathcal{C}}$ is isomorphic to $\mathbb{C}$. Moreover, in this case $\mathcal{A}$ is stable by a result of Blackadar [2, Theorem 4.10 and Remark]: an AF algebra is stable if and only if it has no nonzero finite traces. Indeed, it is obvious that $\mathcal{A}$ has no nonzero finite traces if its ideal $\mathcal{I}$ and the quotient $\mathcal{A}/\mathcal{I}$ do not have such a trace.

(ii) If $\mathbb{B}$ and $\mathbb{C}$ are postliminal then $\mathcal{A}$ is postliminal too.

The following is (part of) [9, Lemma 6.3].

Lemma 7.2. *A locally compact topological space T is almost Hausdorff if and only if there are an ordinal γ and a family of open subsets $\{U_\alpha \mid 0 \leq \alpha \leq \gamma\}$ of T such that*

(i) $U_0 = \emptyset$ and $U_\gamma = T$;

(ii) $U_\alpha \subset U_\beta$ whenever $0 \le \alpha < \beta \le \gamma$;

(iii) $U_{\alpha+1} \setminus U_\alpha$ is a dense Hausdorff subset of $T \setminus U_\alpha$ if $\alpha < \gamma$;

(iv) if β is a limit ordinal then $U_\beta = \cup_{\alpha<\beta}U_\alpha$.

Now we get to the amended Theorem of [5, p. 79].

Theorem 7.1. *Let T be an almost Hausdorff spectral space that has a countable basis of compact open subsets. Then there exists a postliminal AF algebra such that its primitive ideal space is homeomorphic to T.*

Proof:

Let γ and $\{U_\alpha \mid 0 \le \alpha \le \gamma\}$ be as given by Lemma 7.2. We are going to establish by transfinite induction the existence of a family $\{\mathcal{A}_\alpha \mid 1 \le \alpha \le \gamma\}$ of stable postliminal AF algebras such that for each α as above there exists a homeomorphism h_α of U_α onto $\mathrm{Prim}(\mathcal{A}_\alpha)$. Moreover, if $1 \le \alpha < \beta \le \gamma$ then $\mathcal{A}_\alpha$ is an ideal of $\mathcal{A}_\beta$ and $h_\beta \mid U_\alpha = h_\alpha$. Once this is done it is clear that the completion $\mathcal{A}$ of $\cup\{\mathcal{A}_\alpha \mid 1 \le \alpha \le \gamma\}$ will satisfy the conclusion.

Let $\mathcal{A}_1 := \mathcal{C}_0(U_1) \otimes \mathbb{K}$. Suppose now that for $1 \le \beta < \gamma$ the C^*-algebras $\mathcal{A}_\alpha$ and the homeomorphisms h_α, $1 \le \alpha \le \beta$ have been constructed as needed. By using Lemma 7.1, some obvious identifications and Remarks 7.1 (i) and (ii) with $\mathcal{C}_0(U_{\beta+1} \setminus U_\beta) \otimes \mathbb{K}$ playing the role of $\mathcal{C}$ from the statement of the lemma we obtain the C^*-algebra $\mathcal{A}_{\beta+1}$ and the homeomorphism $h_{\beta+1}$ with the right properties.

Suppose now β is a limit ordinal, $\beta \le \gamma$, $\mathcal{A}_\alpha$, h_α, $1 \le \alpha < \beta$ have the required properties. Let $\{\alpha_n\}$ be an increasing sequence of ordinals converging to β; then the completion $\mathcal{A}_\beta$ of $\cup_n\mathcal{A}_{\alpha_n}$ and the obviously defined h_β have the needed properties.

Dedication. To the memory of my esteemed teacher Solomon Marcus.

References

[1] B. Blackadar, *K-Theory for Operator Algebras*, Springer-Verlag, 1986.

[2] B. Blackadar, Traces on simple AF C^*-algebras, *J. of Functional Analysis*, **38** (1980), 156–168.

[3] O. Bratteli, Inductive limits of finite dimensional C^*-algebras, *Trans. Amer. Math. Soc.* **171** (1972), 195–234.

[4] O. Bratteli, Structure spaces of approximately finite-dimensional C^*-algebras, *J. of Functional Analysis* **16** (1974), 192–204.

[5] O. Bratteli and G. A. Elliott, Structure spaces of approximately finite-dimensional C^*-algebras, II, *J. of Functional Analysis* **30** (1978), 74–82.

[6] H. Harnisch and E. Kirchberg, *The inverse problem for primitive ideal spaces*, SBF478 preprint, nr. 399, University of Münster, Münster 2005.

[7] K. H. Hofmann and F. J. Thayer, *Approximately finite-dimensional C^*-algebras*, Dissertationes Math. (Rozprawy Mat.) **174** (1980), 64 pp.

[8] A. J. Lazar and D. C. Taylor, Approximately finite dimensional C^*-algebras and Bratteli diagrams, *Trans. Amer. Math. Soc.* **259** (1980), 599–619.

[9] D. P. Williams, *Crossed Products of C^*-Algebras*, Amer. Math. Soc., Providence RI, 2007.

Chapter 8

An Application of Proof Mining to the Proximal Point Algorithm in CAT(0) Spaces

Laurenţiu Leuştean[a,b] and Andrei Sipoş[a,b]

[a]Faculty of Mathematics and Computer Science, University of Bucharest,
Academiei 14, 010014 Bucharest, Romania

[b]Simion Stoilow Institute of Mathematics of the Romanian Academy,
P. O. Box 1-764, 014700 Bucharest, Romania

laurentiu.leustean@unibuc.ro, Andrei.Sipos@imar.ro

Dedicated to the memory of Professor Solomon Marcus (1925–2016)

Abstract. We compute, using techniques originally introduced by Kohlenbach, the first author and Nicolae, uniform rates of metastability for the proximal point algorithm in the context of CAT(0) spaces (as first considered by Bačák), specifically for the case where the ambient space is totally bounded. This result is part of the program of proof mining, which aims to apply methods of mathematical logic with the purpose of extracting quantitative information out of ordinary mathematical proofs, which may not be necessarily constructive.

8.1 Introduction

The proximal point algorithm is a fundamental tool of convex optimization, going back to Martinet [19], Rockafellar [20] and Brézis and Lions [3]. Since its inception, the schema turned out to be highly versatile, covering in its various developments, *inter alia*, the problems of finding zeros of monotone operators, minima of convex functions and fixed points of nonexpansive mappings. For a general introduction to the field in the context of Hilbert spaces, see the book of Bauschke and Combettes [2].

A recent breakthrough was achieved by Bačák [1], who proved the weak convergence in complete CAT(0) spaces (that is, Δ-convergence) of the

153

variant of the algorithm used to find minima of convex, lower semicontinuous (lsc) proper functions. Let us detail the statement of his result. If X is a complete CAT(0) space and $f : X \to (-\infty, +\infty]$ is a convex, lsc proper function that has minimizers, then, following Jost [8], we may define its resolvent by the relation

$$J_f(x) := \operatorname{argmin}_{y \in X} \left[f(y) + \frac{1}{2} d^2(x, y) \right].$$

For such an f, a starting point $x \in X$, and a sequence of weights $(\gamma_n)_{n \in \mathbb{N}}$, the proximal point algorithm $(x_n)_{n \in \mathbb{N}}$ is defined by setting:

$$x_0 := x, \quad x_{n+1} := J_{\gamma_n f} x_n \text{ for any } n \in \mathbb{N}.$$

Bačák's result then states that, under the condition that $\sum_{n=0}^{\infty} \gamma_n = \infty$, the sequence (x_n) converges weakly to a minimizer of f. As a consequence, one gets (see [1, Remark 1.7])

Theorem 8.1. *In the addition to the above hypotheses, assume, furthermore, that X is a complete locally compact CAT(0) space. Then (x_n) converges strongly to a minimizer of f.*

The proof of Theorem 8.1 is what we are going to build upon, roughly, in our quantitative analysis from the viewpoint of proof mining.

Proof mining is a subfield of applied logic that seeks to use proof interpretations, like Gödel's Dialectica or functional interpretation [6], originally developed with the purpose of giving consistency arguments for systems of arithmetic, in order to extract quantitative information out of proofs in ordinary mathematics. Under the name of "proof unwinding", it was first proposed as a viable research program by G. Kreisel in the 1950s and after several decades of sporadic advances (one of the most significant being H. Luckhardt's 1989 analysis [18] of the proof of Roth's theorem on diophantine approximations) it was given maturity in the 1990s and the 2000s by U. Kohlenbach and his collaborators. The project has culminated into the general logical metatheorems developed by Kohlenbach [9] and by Gerhardy and Kohlenbach [5] for proofs in metric, (uniformly convex) normed and inner product spaces, as well as geodesic spaces like W-hyperbolic spaces and CAT(0) spaces. These logical metatheorems were extended to other classes of fundamental spaces in nonlinear and functional analysis, optimization, geometric group theory and geodesic geometry: Gromov hyperbolic spaces, $\mathbb{R}$-trees and a class of uniformly convex geodesic spaces [16], completions of metric and normed spaces [10], totally bounded metric spaces [10, 13], uniformly smooth normed spaces [12], Banach lattices and $C(K)$ spaces [7], L^p-spaces [7, 21] and CAT(κ) spaces [15]. These logical metatheorems guarantee that from proofs of $\forall\exists$-sentences (satisfying some conditions) in formal systems associated to such abstract spaces X, one can extract effective uniform bounds on existentially quantified variables. Kohlenbach's monograph from 2008 [10] covers the major results in the field until then, while a survey of recent developments is [11].

The canonical example of an existentially quantified variable in ordinary mathematics comes from the definition of the limit of a sequence in a metric space (X, d). If (x_n) is a sequence in X and $x \in X$, then $\lim_{n\to\infty} x_n = x$ if and only if

$$\forall k \in \mathbb{N} \, \exists N \in \mathbb{N} \, \forall n \geq N \left(d(x_n, x) \leq \frac{1}{k+1} \right).$$

A witness for this existentially quantified N, also called *rate of convergence* for the sequence, as it will be defined in more detail further below, would consist of a formula giving it in terms of k. Unfortunately, as the sentence above has three alternating quantifiers in a row (i.e. $\forall\exists\forall$), the techniques of proof mining preclude the extraction of such a computable rate if the proof is non-constructive in the sense of using at least once the law of excluded middle (one can show that the existence of a general procedure for these cases would contradict the impossibility of the halting problem). Four avenues have generally been tried so far in proof mining, if the convergence of a sequence was under discussion. The first one is the extraction of the full rate of convergence in the rare case that the proof is fully or at least partially constructive. The second one is to settle for a weaker property, like the limit inferior, which may have a tractable $\forall\exists$ form (and if the sequence is nonincreasing, the extracted modulus of liminf would also be a rate of convergence). The third one is to use some uniqueness properties of the limit in order to extract the rate of convergence from a distantly related property like the rate of asymptotic regularity. Finally, the fourth way is what we are going to focus on here. It consists of considering instead of convergence the Cauchy property of the sequence

$$\forall k \in \mathbb{N} \, \exists N \in \mathbb{N} \, \forall p \in \mathbb{N} \left(d(x_N, x_{N+p}) \leq \frac{1}{k+1} \right)$$

and replacing it with an equivalent formulation (known in logic as its Herbrand normal form or its Kreisel no-counterexample interpretation), called *metastability* by Tao [22, 23]. The following sentence expresses the metastability of the sequence above:

$$\forall k \in \mathbb{N} \, \forall g : \mathbb{N} \to \mathbb{N} \, \exists N \in \mathbb{N} \, \forall i, j \in [N, N + g(N)] \; \left(d(x_i, x_j) \le \frac{1}{k+1} \right).$$

It is immediately seen that this sentence is of a reduced $\forall \exists$ logical complexity. It is, however, a simple exercise, to check that it is classically (but not intuitionistically) equivalent to the assertion that the sequence under discussion is Cauchy. Therefore, one can now say that the fourth way is focused on obtaining a *rate of metastability* for the sequence, i.e. a mapping $\Phi : \mathbb{N} \times \mathbb{N}^{\mathbb{N}} \to \mathbb{N}$ satisfying, for all $k \in \mathbb{N}$ and all $g : \mathbb{N} \to \mathbb{N}$,

$$\exists N \le \Phi(k, g) \, \forall i, j \in [N, N + g(N)] \; \left(d(x_i, x_j) \le \frac{1}{k+1} \right). \tag{8.1}$$

In a recent paper, Kohlenbach, the first author and Nicolae [13] have studied a general line of argument used in convergence proofs in nonlinear analysis and convex optimization. Specifically, it is often the case that an iterative sequence is proven to be convergent to a point in a certain set F (e.g. the set of fixed points of an operator using which the sequence was constructed) if it sits inside a compact space, it is *Fejér monotone* with respect to F (that is, for all $q \in F$ and all $n \in \mathbb{N}$, $d(x_{n+1}, q) \le d(x_n, q)$) and it has "approximate F-points", i.e. points which are, in a sense, near F. The main result in [13] is that all this can be made effective. For that to work, however, the three hypotheses must also be transformed into a quantitative form. A "modulus of total boundedness" witnesses the space being compact. For the other two properties, one must formulate what exactly does it mean for a point to be "near" F. This is done in terms of an approximation $F = \bigcap_{k \in \mathbb{N}} AF_k$, which helps formulate both the "modulus of uniform Fejér monotonicity" and the "approximate F-point bound". The choice of an approximation to F, as well as the computation of these moduli, has been done in [13, 14, 17] for some classical iterations associated to important classes of mappings and operators.

In this paper we apply the techniques developed in [13] to obtain a quantitative version of Theorem 8.1, providing an effective uniform rate of metastability for the proximal point algorithm in totally bounded CAT(0) spaces. The next section will give some preliminaries on the proximal point algorithm, while the last section of the paper is dedicated to the proof of our main quantitative result, Theorem 8.2.

We finish this Introduction with a recall of definitions from [13] and quantitative notions that will be used throughout the paper. We point out, first, that $\mathbb{N} = \{0, 1, 2, \ldots\}$ and that we denote $[m, n] = \{m, m+1, \ldots, n\}$ for any $m, n \in \mathbb{N}$ with $m \leq n$.

Let (X, d) be a metric space. For any mapping $T : X \to X$ we denote by $Fix(T)$ the set of fixed points of T.

A *modulus of total boundedness* for X is a function $\alpha : \mathbb{N} \to \mathbb{N}$ such that for any $k \in \mathbb{N}$ and any sequence (x_n) in X there exist $i < j$ in $[0, \alpha(k)]$ such that

$$d(x_i, x_j) \leq \frac{1}{k+1}.$$

This notion was first used in [4] to analyze, using proof mining methods, the Furstenberg-Weiss proof of the Multiple Birkhoff Recurrence Theorem. One can easily see that X is totally bounded if and only if it has a modulus of total boundedness.

Let $F \subseteq X$. We say that a family $(AF_k)_{k \in \mathbb{N}}$ of subsets of X is an *approximation* to F if

$$F = \bigcap_{k \in \mathbb{N}} AF_k \quad \text{and} \quad AF_{k+1} \subseteq AF_k \text{ for all } k \in \mathbb{N}.$$

Elements of AF_k are also called k-approximate F-points.

Definition 8.1. [13] Let $F \subseteq X$ be a set with an approximation (AF_k).

(i) F is *uniformly closed* with respect to (AF_k) with moduli $\delta_F, \omega_F : \mathbb{N} \to \mathbb{N}$ if for all $k \in \mathbb{N}$ and all $p, q \in X$ we have

$$q \in AF_{\delta_F(k)} \text{ and } d(p, q) \leq \frac{1}{\omega_F(k) + 1} \quad \text{imply} \quad p \in AF_k.$$

(ii) (x_n) is *uniformly Fejér monotone* with respect to (AF_k) with modulus χ if for all $n, m, r \in \mathbb{N}$, all $p \in AF_{\chi(n,m,r)}$ and all $l \leq m$ we have

$$d(x_{n+l}, p) < d(x_n, p) + \frac{1}{r+1}.$$

(iii) (x_n) has *approximate F-points* with respect to (AF_k) with modulus Φ (which is taken to be nondecreasing) if for all $k \in \mathbb{N}$ there is an $N \leq \Phi(k)$ such that $x_N \in AF_k$.

We refer to [13, Sections 3 and 4] for details and intuitions behind the above definitions. We remark that one can get nondecreasing moduli using the following transformation. For any $f : \mathbb{N} \to \mathbb{N}$, one defines $f^M : \mathbb{N} \to \mathbb{N}$ by $f^M(n) := \max_{i \leq n} f(i)$. Then f^M is nondecreasing and for any n, we have $f(n) \leq f^M(n)$.

We now give some notions that are customary in quantitatively expressing some basic properties of real-valued sequences. Let $(a_n)_{n \in \mathbb{N}}$ be a sequence of nonnegative real numbers. If (a_n) converges to 0, then a *rate of convergence* for (a_n) is a mapping $\beta : \mathbb{N} \to \mathbb{N}$ such that for all $k \in \mathbb{N}$,

$$\forall n \geq \beta(k) \ \left(a_n \leq \frac{1}{k+1} \right).$$

If the series $\sum\limits_{n=0}^{\infty} a_n$ diverges, then a function $\theta : \mathbb{N} \to \mathbb{N}$ is called a *rate of divergence* of the series if for all $P \in \mathbb{N}$ we have

$$\sum_{n=0}^{\theta(P)} a_n \geq P.$$

A *modulus of liminf* for (a_n) is a mapping $\Delta : \mathbb{N} \times \mathbb{N} \to \mathbb{N}$, satisfying, for all $k, L \in \mathbb{N}$,

$$\exists N \in [L, \Delta(k, L)] \ \left(a_N \leq \frac{1}{k+1} \right).$$

Such a modulus exists if and only if $\liminf\limits_{n \to \infty} a_n = 0$.

More generally, let $(b_n)_{n \in \mathbb{N}}$ be a sequence of real numbers and $b \in \mathbb{R}$. If (b_n) converges to b, then a *a rate of convergence* of (b_n) is a mapping $\beta : \mathbb{N} \to \mathbb{N}$ such that for all $k \in \mathbb{N}$,

$$\forall n \geq \beta(k) \ \left(|b_n - b| \leq \frac{1}{k+1} \right). \tag{8.2}$$

Thus, a rate of convergence of (b_n) coincides with a rate of convergence of the sequence $(|b_n - b|)$ of nonnegative reals.

8.2 Preliminaries on the proximal point algorithm

In the sequel, X is a CAT(0) space and $f : X \to (-\infty, +\infty]$ is a convex, lower semicontinuous (lsc) proper function. Let us recall that a minimizer of f is a point $x \in X$ such that $f(x) = \inf_{y \in X} f(y)$. We denote the set of minimizers of f by $Argmin(f)$ and we assume that $Argmin(f)$ is nonempty.

The *proximal point mapping* or the *(Moreau-Yosida) resolvent*, as first introduced for CAT(0) spaces by Jost [8], is a tool for finding minimizers of such functions. For $\gamma > 0$, the *resolvent* (or the *proximal mapping*) of f of order γ is the map $J_f^\gamma : X \to X$, defined, for any $x \in X$, by the following relation

$$J_f^\gamma(x) := \mathrm{argmin}_{y \in X} \left[\gamma f(y) + \frac{1}{2} d^2(x, y) \right].$$

This is the definition from [1], as the factor of 2 does not appear in the original paper of Jost, but this is, obviously, insignificant. By [8, Lemma 2], the operator J_f^γ is well-defined. We shall denote J_f^1 simply by J_f. Then, for all $\gamma > 0$ and for all $x \in X$,

$$J_{\gamma f}(x) = J_f^\gamma(x) = \mathrm{argmin}_{y \in X}\left[\gamma f(y) + \frac{1}{2}d^2(x,y)\right]$$

$$= \mathrm{argmin}_{y \in X}\left[f(y) + \frac{1}{2\gamma}d^2(x,y)\right].$$

The following property was also proved in [8].

Proposition 8.1 ([8, Lemma 4]). *For any $\gamma > 0$, $J_{\gamma f}$ is nonexpansive, that is, for all $x, y \in X$,*

$$d(J_{\gamma f}(x), J_{\gamma f}(y)) \leq d(x,y).$$

We note that the definition of the proximal point mapping is motivated by the following proposition.

Proposition 8.2. *Let $x \in X$. Then x is a minimizer of f if and only if x is a fixed point of J_f.*

Proof:
Suppose first that x is a minimizer of f. It follows that, for all y,

$$f(x) + \frac{1}{2}d^2(x,x) = f(x) \leq f(y) \leq f(y) + \frac{1}{2}d^2(x,y),$$

therefore x is also the argmin of the right hand side w.r.t. y — that is, $x = J_f(x)$.

Suppose now that $J_f(x) = x$. Then, for all $y \in X$, as before,

$$f(x) \leq f(y) + \frac{1}{2}d^2(x,y).$$

Let $w \in X$. Using the fact that f is convex, we get, for any $t \in (0,1)$,

$$f(x) \leq f((1-t)x + tw) + \frac{1}{2}d^2(x, (1-t)x + tw)$$

$$\leq (1-t)f(x) + tf(w) + \frac{1}{2}d^2(x, (1-t)x + tw)$$

$$= (1-t)f(x) + tf(w) + \frac{1}{2}t^2d^2(x,w).$$

Subtracting $(1-t)f(x)$ and dividing by t, we obtain that

$$f(x) \leq f(w) + \frac{1}{2}td^2(x,w),$$

and by letting $t \to 0$, it follows that $f(x) \leq f(w)$. Since w was chosen arbitrarily, we get that x is a minimizer of f.

Since, trivially, $Argmin(\gamma f) = Argmin(f)$, we get that

Corollary 8.1. *For any $\gamma > 0$, $Fix(J_{\gamma f}) = Fix(J_f) = Argmin(f)$.*

We may now proceed to study the algorithm itself. Let $(\gamma_n)_{n \in \mathbb{N}}$ be a sequence in $(0, \infty)$. The *proximal point algorithm* $(x_n)_{n \in \mathbb{N}}$ starting with $x \in X$ is defined as follows:

$$x_0 := x, \qquad x_{n+1} := J_{\gamma_n f} x_n \text{ for all } n \in \mathbb{N}.$$

Let us give some useful properties of the sequence (x_n).

Lemma 8.1. *For all $n, m \in \mathbb{N}$ and all $p \in X$,*

$$d(x_{n+1}, p) \le d(x_n, p) + d(p, J_{\gamma_n f} p), \tag{8.3}$$

$$d(x_{n+m}, p) \le d(x_n, p) + \sum_{i=n}^{i=n+m-1} d(p, J_{\gamma_i f} p). \tag{8.4}$$

Proof:
We have

$$d(x_{n+1}, p) = d(J_{\gamma_n f} x_n, p) \le d(J_{\gamma_n f} x_n, J_{\gamma_n f} p) + d(J_{\gamma_n f} p, p)$$
$$\le d(x_n, p) + d(p, J_{\gamma_n f} p).$$

(8.4) follows immediately by induction on m.

The following lemma contains results from [1].

Lemma 8.2.

(i) *The sequence $(f(x_n))$ is nonincreasing.*
(ii) *For all $n \in \mathbb{N}$ and all $p \in Argmin(f)$,*

$$2\gamma_n(f(x_{n+1}) - \min(f)) \le d^2(x_n, p) - d^2(x_{n+1}, p) - d^2(x_n, x_{n+1}) \tag{8.5}$$

$$d^2(x_n, x_{n+1}) \le d^2(x_n, p) - d^2(x_{n+1}, p) \tag{8.6}$$

$$f(x_{n+1}) - \min(f) \le \frac{d^2(x, p)}{2 \sum_{i=0}^{n} \gamma_i}. \tag{8.7}$$

Proof:

(i) This is used without proof in [1], and hence we shall justify it. Let $n \in \mathbb{N}$. By the definition of $J_{\gamma_n f}$ and considering that $x_{n+1} = J_{\gamma_n f} x_n$, we have:

$$\gamma_n f(x_{n+1}) + \frac{1}{2} d^2(x_n, x_{n+1}) \le \gamma_n f(x_n) + \frac{1}{2} d^2(x_n, x_n) = \gamma_n f(x_n),$$

and so, $\gamma_n f(x_{n+1}) \le \gamma_n f(x_n)$, hence $f(x_{n+1}) \le f(x_n)$.

(ii) With the assumption made in [1] that $\min(f) = 0$, (8.5) is the last inequality in the proof of (7) from [1], while (8.7) is obtained from the inequality before (8) in [1]. Note also that λ_k in [1] corresponds to our γ_{k-1}. (8.6) follows immediately from (8.5).

We finish this section with two effective results on the behaviour of the proximal point algorithm, results that will be also used in the next section to get our main quantitative theorem.

Lemma 8.3. *Let $b \in \mathbb{R}$ be such that $d(x, p) \leq b$ for some $p \in Argmin(f)$.*

(i) $\liminf_{n\to\infty} d(x_n, x_{n+1}) = 0$ *with modulus of liminf*

$$\Delta_b(k, L) := \lceil b^2(k+1)^2 \rceil + L - 1. \tag{8.8}$$

(ii) Assume that $\sum_{n=0}^{\infty} \gamma_n = \infty$ with rate of divergence θ. Then $\lim_{n\to\infty} f(x_n) = \min(f)$, with a (nondecreasing) rate of convergence

$$\beta_{b,\theta}(k) := \theta^M(\lceil b^2(k+1)/2 \rceil) + 1. \tag{8.9}$$

Proof:

(i) By (8.6), we get that for all $j \geq k$,

$$\sum_{n=j}^{k} d^2(x_n, x_{n+1}) \leq \sum_{n=0}^{k} d^2(x_n, x_{n+1}) \leq \sum_{n=0}^{k} (d^2(x_n, p) - d^2(x_{n+1}, p))$$

$$\leq d^2(x, p) \leq b^2.$$

Suppose that $d(x_n, x_{n+1}) > \frac{1}{k+1}$ for all $n \in [L, \Delta_b(k, L)]$. Then

$$(\Delta_b(k, L) - L + 1)\frac{1}{(k+1)^2} < \sum_{n=L}^{\Delta_b(k,L)} d^2(x_n, x_{n+1}) \leq b^2,$$

from which we get $\Delta_b(k, L) < b^2(k+1)^2 + L - 1$, a contradiction.

(ii) Since $f(x_n) \geq \min(f)$ for all $n \in \mathbb{N}$ and, by Lemma 8.2.(i), $(f(x_n))$ is nonincreasing, all we have to show is that

$$f(x_{\beta_{b,\theta}(k)}) - \min(f) \leq \frac{1}{k+1}.$$

Assume that this is not true. Then, using (8.7) and the fact that θ is a rate of divergence, we get that

$$\frac{1}{k+1} < f(x_{\beta_{b,\theta}(k)}) - \min(f) \leq \frac{b^2}{2\sum_{i=0}^{\theta^M(\lceil b^2(k+1)/2 \rceil)} \lambda_i}$$

$$\leq \frac{b^2}{2\sum_{i=0}^{\theta(\lceil b^2(k+1)/2 \rceil)} \lambda_i} \leq \frac{b^2}{2\lceil b^2(k+1)/2 \rceil} \leq \frac{1}{k+1},$$

a contradiction.

8.3   Quantitative results on the proximal point algorithm

We will now proceed to derive the moduli that are needed in order to apply
the results of [13].

As in the previous section, $f : X \to (-\infty, +\infty]$ is a convex, lsc proper
function, and we set $F := Argmin(f) \neq \emptyset$. For every $k \in \mathbb{N}$, let us define

$$AF_k := \left\{ x \in X \mid \text{for all } i \leq k, \, d(x, J_{\gamma_i f}x) \leq \frac{1}{k+1} \right\}. \tag{8.10}$$

Proposition 8.3. (AF_k) *is an approximation to* F.

Proof:
Since, obviously, (AF_k) is a nonincreasing sequence, it remains to prove
that $F = \bigcap_{k \in \mathbb{N}} AF_k$.

"$\subseteq$" Let $x \in F$ and $k \in \mathbb{N}$ be arbitrary. Then, for all $i \leq k$, by Corollary
8.1, we have $F = Fix(J_{\gamma_i f})$, hence, in particular, $d(x, J_{\gamma_i f}x) \leq \frac{1}{k+1}$. Thus,
$x \in AF_k$.

"$\supseteq$" Let $x \in \bigcap_{k \in \mathbb{N}} AF_k$. It follows, in particular, that for any $k \in \mathbb{N}$,

$$d(x, J_{\gamma_0 f}x) \leq \frac{1}{k+1}.$$

As a consequence, we get that $x \in Fix(J_{\gamma_0 f}) = F$, again by Corollary 8.1.

This approximation will turn out to be convenient for the results we are
aiming for.

Proposition 8.4. *With respect to the above approximation,* F *is uniformly
closed with moduli*

$$\delta_F(k) := 2k + 1, \quad \omega_F(k) := 4k + 3. \tag{8.11}$$

Proof:
Let $k \in \mathbb{N}$ and $p, q \in X$ be such that $q \in AF_{2k+1}$ and $d(p, q) \leq \frac{1}{4k+4}$. We
need to show that $p \in AF_k$, i.e. that for all $i \leq k$, $d(p, J_{\gamma_i f}p) \leq \frac{1}{k+1}$. Let
$i \leq k$ be arbitrary. We get that

$$d(p, J_{\gamma_i f}p) \leq d(p, q) + d(q, J_{\gamma_i f}q) + d(J_{\gamma_i f}q, J_{\gamma_i f}p) \leq 2d(p, q) + d(q, J_{\gamma_i f}q)$$
$$\leq \frac{2}{4k+4} + \frac{1}{2k+2} = \frac{1}{k+1},$$

where we have used at the second inequality the fact that $J_{\gamma_i f}$ is nonexpansive.

Lemma 8.4. *The sequence (x_n) is uniformly Fejér monotone w.r.t. (AF_k) with modulus*

$$\chi(n, m, r) := \max\{n + m - 1, m(r + 1)\}. \tag{8.12}$$

Proof:

Let $n, m, r \in \mathbb{N}$, $p \in AF_{\chi(n,m,r)}$ and $l \leq m$. We get that

$$d(x_{n+l}, p) \leq d(x_n, p) + \sum_{i=n}^{i=n+l-1} d(p, J_{\gamma_i f}p) \quad \text{by (8.4)}$$

$$\leq d(x_n, p) + \sum_{i=n}^{i=n+m-1} d(p, J_{\gamma_i f}p)$$

$$\leq d(x_n, p) + \frac{m}{\chi(n, m, r) + 1}$$

$$< d(x_n, p) + \frac{1}{r + 1},$$

where at the second-to-last inequality we used that $\chi(n, m, r) \geq n + m - 1$, so $d(p, J_{\gamma_i f}p) \leq \frac{1}{\chi(n,m,r)+1}$ for all $i = n, \ldots, n + m - 1$, and at the last one, that $\chi(n, m, r) \geq m(r + 1)$.

Proposition 8.5. *Let $b \in \mathbb{R}$ be such that $d(x, p) \leq b$ for some $p \in F$ and assume that $\sum_{n=0}^{\infty} \gamma_n = \infty$ with rate of divergence θ. Suppose, moreover, that $M : \mathbb{N} \to (0, \infty)$ is such that $M(k) \geq \max_{0 \leq i \leq k} \gamma_i$ for all $k \in \mathbb{N}$. Then (x_n) has approximate F-points w.r.t. (AF_k) with a (nondecreasing) modulus*

$$\Phi_{b,\theta,M}(k) := \lceil b^2(k + 1)^2 \rceil + \beta_{b,\theta}(\lceil 2(k + 1)^2 M(k) \rceil - 1), \tag{8.13}$$

where $\beta_{b,\theta}$ is defined by (8.9).

Proof:

Let $k \in \mathbb{N}$ be arbitrary. Denote, for simplicity,

$$c := \beta_{b,\theta}(\lceil 2(k + 1)^2 M(k) \rceil - 1).$$

Applying Lemma 8.3.(i), we obtain that there is an $N \in [c, \Delta_b(k, c)]$ such that

$$d(x_N, x_{N+1}) \leq \frac{1}{k + 1},$$

where Δ_b is given by (8.8). We remark, first, that

$$N \leq \Delta_b(k, c) = \lceil b^2(k + 1)^2 \rceil + c - 1 < \lceil b^2(k + 1)^2 \rceil + c = \Phi_{b,\theta,M}(k).$$

Since $N \geq c$ and $\beta_{b,\theta}$ is a rate of convergence of $(f(x_n))$ towards $\min(f)$ (by Lemma 8.3.(ii)), we get that

$$f(x_N) \leq \min(f) + \frac{1}{\lceil 2(k+1)^2 M(k) \rceil}.$$

On the other hand, for all $i \leq k$, we have, by the definition of $J_{\gamma_i f}$, that

$$\gamma_i f(J_{\gamma_i f} x_N) + \frac{1}{2} d^2(x_N, J_{\gamma_i f} x_N) \leq \gamma_i f(x_N) + \frac{1}{2} d^2(x_N, x_N) = \gamma_i f(x_N).$$

As $f(J_{\gamma_i f} x_N) \geq \min(f)$, it follows that, for all $i \leq k$,

$$d^2(x_N, J_{\gamma_i f} x_N) \leq 2\gamma_i (f(x_N) - f(J_{\gamma_i f} x_N)) \leq 2\gamma_i (f(x_N) - \min(f))$$

$$\leq 2M(k) \frac{1}{\lceil 2(k+1)^2 M(k) \rceil} \leq \frac{1}{(k+1)^2}.$$

Thus, we have proved that for all $k \in \mathbb{N}$ there is an $N \leq \Phi_{b,\theta,M}(k)$ such that for all $i \leq k$,

$$d(x_N, J_{\gamma_i f} x_N) \leq \frac{1}{k+1}.$$

That's what was required.

Now that all the necessary moduli have been computed, we may apply [13, Theorems 5.1 and 5.3] to get our main result, which finitarily expresses the strong convergence of the proximal point algorithm to a minimizer of f.

Theorem 8.2. *Let $b > 0$, $\alpha, \theta : \mathbb{N} \to \mathbb{N}$ and $M : \mathbb{N} \to (0, \infty)$. Define $\Psi_{b,\theta,M,\alpha}$, $\Omega_{b,\theta,M,\alpha} : \mathbb{N} \times \mathbb{N}^{\mathbb{N}} \to \mathbb{N}$ as in Table 8.1. Then for all*

- *(i) totally bounded CAT(0) spaces with modulus of total boundedness α;*
- *(ii) convex lsc proper mappings $f : X \to (-\infty, \infty]$ with $Argmin(f) \neq \emptyset$;*
- *(iii) $x \in X$ such that $d(x, p) \leq b$ for some minimizer p of f;*
- *(iv) sequences (γ_n) in $(0, \infty)$ such that $\sum_{n=0}^{\infty} \gamma_n = \infty$ with rate of divergence θ and $M(k) \geq \max_{0 \leq i \leq k} \gamma_i$ for all $k \in \mathbb{N}$;*

we have

- *(i) $\Psi_{b,\theta,M,\alpha}$ is a rate of metastability for the proximal point algorithm (x_n) starting with x, i.e. for all $k \in \mathbb{N}$ and all $g : \mathbb{N} \to \mathbb{N}$ there is an $N \leq \Psi_{b,\theta,M,\alpha}(k, g)$ such that for all $i, j \in [N, N + g(N)]$,*

$$d(x_i, x_j) \leq \frac{1}{k+1}.$$

Table 8.1 Definitions of $\Psi_{b,\theta,M,\alpha}$ and $\Omega_{b,\theta,M,\alpha}$.

$\Psi_{b,\theta,M,\alpha}(k,g) := (\Psi_0)_{b,\theta,M}(\alpha(4k+3),k,g)$

$(\Psi_0)_{b,\theta,M}(0,k,g) := 0$

$(\Psi_0)_{b,\theta,M}(n+1,k,g) := \Phi_{b,\theta,M}\left(\chi_g^M((\Psi_0)_{b,\theta,M}(n,k,g),4k+3)\right)$

$\chi_g^M(n,r) = \max_{i\leq n}\max\{i+g(i)-1,g(i)(r+1)\}$

$\Omega_{b,\theta,M,\alpha}(k,g) := (\Omega_0)_{b,\theta,M}(\alpha(8k+7),k,g)$

$(\Omega_0)_{b,\theta,M}(0,k,g) := 0$

$(\Omega_0)_{b,\theta,M}(n+1,k,g) := \Phi_{b,\theta,M}\left(\tilde{\chi}_g^M((\Omega_0)_{b,\theta,M}(n,k,g),8k+8)\right)$

$\tilde{\chi}_g^M(n,r) = \max\{2k+1,\max_{i\leq n}\max\{i+g(i)-1,g(i)(r+1)\}\}$

with $\Phi_{b,\theta,M}$ given by (8.13)

(ii) *For all $k \in \mathbb{N}$ and all $g : \mathbb{N} \to \mathbb{N}$ there is an $N \leq \Omega_{b,\theta,M,\alpha}(k,g)$ such that for all $i,j \in [N, N+g(N)]$,*

$$d(x_i, x_j) \leq \frac{1}{k+1}$$

and for all $i \in [N, N+g(N)]$ and all $d \leq k$,

$$d(x_i, J_{\gamma_d f} x_i) \leq \frac{1}{k+1}.$$

Proof:

Apply [13, Theorem 5.1] to get (i) and [13, Theorem 5.3] to obtain (ii). Remark that in our case, using the notation from [13], $\alpha_G = \beta_H = id_{\mathbb{R}_+}$, hence $P = \alpha(4k+3)$ and, furthermore,

$$\chi_g^M(n,r) = \max_{i\leq n}\chi_g(i,r) = \max_{i\leq n}\chi(i,g(i),r)$$

$$= \max_{i\leq n}\max\{i+g(i)-1,g(i)(r+1)\}, \text{ by } (8.12)$$

$$k_0 = \max\left\{k,\left\lceil\frac{\omega_F(k)-1}{2}\right\rceil\right\} = 2k+1, \text{ by } (8.11)$$

$$(\chi_{k,\delta_F})_g^M(n,r) = \max\{2k+1,\max_{i\leq n}\max\{i+g(i)-1,g(i)(r+1)\}\}.$$

We denote, for simplicity, χ_{k,δ_F} by $\tilde{\chi}$.

The above theorem can be considered a "true" finitization (in the sense of Tao) of Theorem 8.1, since

(i) it involves only a finite segment of the proximal point algorithm (x_n);

(ii) the existence of a rate of metastability $\Psi_{b,\theta,M,\alpha}$ is, as previously stated, classically equivalent to Cauchyness;

(iii) the existence of the second rate $\Omega_{b,\theta,M,\alpha}$ guarantees, for complete CAT(0) spaces, that the limit of the sequence is an element of $F = Argmin(f)$ (see [13, Remark 5.5]);

(iv) the modulus of total boundedness only needs to apply to the ball of radius b considered in the proof, therefore we have derived strong convergence for locally compact CAT(0) spaces, as pointed out in [13, Remark 5.4].

Furthermore, both rates $\Psi_{b,\theta,M,\alpha}$ and $\Omega_{b,\theta,M,\alpha}$ are computable and are, moreover, expressed using primitive recursive functionals.

References

[1] M. Bačák, The proximal point algorithm in metric spaces, Israel J. Math. 194 (2013), 689–701.

[2] H. Bauschke, P. Combettes, *Convex Analysis and Monotone Operator Theory in Hilbert Spaces*, Springer, 2010.

[3] H. Brézis, P. Lions, Produits infinis de résolvantes, Israel J. Math. 29 (1978), 329–345.

[4] P. Gerhardy, Proof mining in topological dynamics, Notre Dame J. Form. Log. 49 (2008), 431–446.

[5] P. Gerhardy, U. Kohlenbach, General logical metatheorems for functional analysis, Trans. Amer. Math. Soc. 360 (2008), 2615–2660.

[6] K. Gödel, Über eine bisher noch nicht benützte Erweiterung des finiten Standpunktes, Dialectica 12 (1958), 280–287.

[7] D. Günzel, U. Kohlenbach, Logical metatheorems for abstract spaces axiomatized in positive bounded logic, Adv. Math. 290 (2016), 503–551.

[8] J. Jost, Convex functionals and generalized harmonic maps into spaces of non positive curvature, Comment. Math. Helv. 70 (1995), 659–673.

[9] U. Kohlenbach, Some logical metatheorems with applications in functional analysis, Trans. Amer. Math. Soc. 357 (2005), 89–128.

[10] U. Kohlenbach, *Applied proof theory: Proof interpretations and their use in mathematics*, Springer Monographs in Mathematics, Springer, 2008.

[11] U. Kohlenbach, Recent progress in proof mining in nonlinear analysis, to appear in IFCoLog Journal of Logic and its Applications. Special issue with invited articles by recipients of a Gödel Centenary Research Prize Fellowship.

[12] U. Kohlenbach, L. Leuştean, On the computational content of convergence proofs via Banach limits, Philos. Trans. R. Soc. Lond. Ser. A Math. Phys. Eng. Sci. A 370 (2012), 3449–3463.

[13] U. Kohlenbach, L. Leuştean, A. Nicolae, Quantitative results on Fejér monotone sequences, arXiv:1412.5563 [math.LO], 2015, to appear in Commun. in Contemp. Math.

[14] U. Kohlenbach, G. López-Acedo, A. Nicolae, Quantitative asymptotic regularity for the composition of two mappings, Optimization 66 (2017), 1291–1299.

[15] U. Kohlenbach, A. Nicolae, A proof-theoretic bound extraction theorem for CAT(κ) spaces, Studia Logica 105 (2017), 611–624.

[16] L. Leuştean, Proof mining in $\mathbb{R}$-trees and hyperbolic spaces, Electron. Notes Theor. Comput. Sci (Proceedings of WoLLIC 2006) 165 (2006), 95–106.

[17] L. Leuştean, V. Radu, A. Sipoş, Quantitative results on the Ishikawa iteration of Lipschitz pseudo-contractions, J. Nonlinear Convex Anal. 17 (2016), 2277–2292.

[18] H. Luckhardt, Herbrand-Analysen zweier Beweise des Satzes von Roth: Polynomiale Anzahlschranken, J. Symbolic Logic 54 (1989), 234–263.

[19] B. Martinet, Régularisation d'inéquations variationnelles par approximations successives, Rev. Française Informat. Recherche Opérationnelle 4 (1970), 154–158.

[20] T. Rockafellar, Monotone operators and the proximal point algorithm, SIAM J. Control Optim. 14 (1976), 877–898.

[21] A. Sipoş, Proof mining in L^p spaces, arXiv:1609.02080 [math.LO], 2016, submitted.

[22] T. Tao, Soft analysis, hard analysis, and the finite convergence principle, Essay posted May 23, 2007, appeared in: T. Tao, *Structure and Randomness: Pages from Year One of a Mathematical Blog*, Amer. Math. Soc., 2008.

[23] T. Tao, Norm convergence of multiple ergodic averages for commuting transformations, Ergodic Theory Dynam. Systems 28 (2008), 657–688.

Chapter 9

Generic Well-posedness of the Fixed Point Problem for Monotone Nonexpansive Mappings

Simeon Reich and Alexander J. Zaslavski

Department of Mathematics

The Technion – Israel Institute of Technology

32000 Haifa, Israel

sreich@tx.technion.ac.il, ajzasl@tx.technion.ac.il

Abstract. We consider monotone nonexpansive self-mappings of a bounded, closed and convex subset of a Banach space. Using the Baire category approach, we show that for most such mappings the fixed point problem is well posed.

9.1 Introduction and preliminaries

It is well known that the notion of well-posedness is of great importance in many areas of mathematics and its applications. In this paper we study generic well-posedness of the fixed point problem for monotone nonexpansive mappings. In this connection we recall that since Banach's classical theorem [2], fixed point theory has been, and continues to be, an important part of nonlinear operator theory [3, 8–11, 13, 14, 18, 19, 21]. For example, several results regarding the existence of fixed points for general nonexpansive mappings in special Banach spaces were presented in [8, 9] and an existence result for contractive mappings was obtained in [12]. A number of existence and convergence results in the generic sense were obtained for general classes of nonlinear mappings by using the Baire category approach [4–6, 15–17, 19, 20, 22–24]. For instance, in some of these results, given a certain space of mappings equipped with a complete metric, it is shown that this space contains a subset, which is a countable intersection of open and everywhere dense sets, such that for each one of its elements, the corresponding fixed point problem has a unique solution and moreover, is well posed. In particular, this is true for the class of nonexpansive self-mappings of a bounded, convex and closed set in a Banach space [4,22]. In the present paper, by using the Baire category approach, we show generic well-posedness of the fixed point problem for monotone nonexpansive mappings — a class of nonlinear mappings which is the subject of a rapidly growing area of research [1,7].

Let $(X, \|\cdot\|)$ be a Banach space partially ordered by a closed and convex cone $X_+ \subset X$ satisfying

$$X_+ \cap (-X_+) = \{0\}.$$

Note that for $x, y \in X$,

$$x \le y \text{ if and only if } y - x \in X_+.$$

Assume that

$$\|x\| \le \|y\| \text{ for all } x, y \in X_+ \text{ satisfying } x \le y. \tag{1.1}$$

Let K be a nonempty bounded, closed and convex subset of X. Set

$$d(K) := \sup\{\|x - y\| : x, y \in K\}.$$

Denote by $\mathcal{A}$ the set of all continuous mappings $T : K \to K$ such that

$$T(x) \le T(y) \text{ for all } x, y \in K \text{ satisfying } x \le y \tag{1.2}$$

and

$$\|T(x) - T(y)\| \le \|x - y\| \tag{1.3}$$

for all $x, y \in K$ satisfying $x \le y$. The elements of the set $\mathcal{A}$ are called *monotone nonexpansive mappings*.

For each $T_1, T_2 \in \mathcal{A}$, set

$$d(T_1, T_2) := \sup\{\|T_1(x) - T_2(x)\| : x \in K\}. \tag{1.4}$$

It is clear that $(\mathcal{A}, d)$ is a complete metric space. Denote by $\mathcal{A}_u$ the set of all $A \in \mathcal{A}$ which are uniformly continuous. It is not difficult to see that $\mathcal{A}_u$ is a closed subset of the metric space $(\mathcal{A}, d)$. In the sequel we consider the space $\mathcal{A}_u$ equipped with the metric d.

Consider $A \in \mathcal{A}$. We say that the fixed point problem (FPP) is *well posed* for A if there exists a unique point $x_A \in K$ such that

$$A(x_A) = x_A$$

and the following property holds:

(WP) for each $\varepsilon > 0$, there exists a natural number n_ε such that for each $x \in K$,

$$\|x_A - A^{n_\varepsilon}(x)\| \leq \varepsilon.$$

In this paper we prove the following results.

Theorem 9.1. *Assume that the FPP is well posed for a mapping $A \in \mathcal{A}_u$ and that $x_A \in K$ is the unique fixed point of A, that is, $A(x_A) = x_A$. Let $\varepsilon > 0$. Then there exist a natural number $\tilde{n}$ and a number $\delta > 0$ such that for each sequence $\{x_i\}_{i=0}^\infty \subset K$ which satisfies*

$$\|x_{i+1} - A(x_i)\| \leq \delta, \ i = 0, 1, \ldots,$$

the inequality

$$\|x_i - x_A\| \leq \varepsilon$$

holds for all integers $i \geq \tilde{n}$.

Theorem 9.2. *Let $x_K \in K$ satisfy*

$$x_K \leq x \text{ for all } x \in K. \tag{1.5}$$

Then there exists a set $\mathcal{F} \subset \mathcal{A}_u$, which is a countable intersection of open and everywhere dense subsets of the complete metric space $(\mathcal{A}_u, d)$, such that the FPP is well posed for every $A \in \mathcal{F}$.

These theorems are established in Section 9.2 and Section 9.3, respectively. In addition, Theorem 9.3, which complements Theorem 9.2, is stated and proved in Section 9.4.

9.2 Proof of Theorem 9.1

By property (WP), there exists a natural number $\tilde{n}$ such that the following property holds:

(i) for each $x \in K$, we have

$$\|x_A - A^{\tilde{n}}(x)\| \leq \varepsilon/4.$$

Set

$$\varepsilon_{\tilde{n}} := \varepsilon/4. \tag{2.1}$$

Since the mapping A is uniformly continuous, we can construct by induction a finite sequence of positive numbers $\{\varepsilon_i\}_{i=0}^{\tilde{n}}$ such that for each integer $i \in \{1, \ldots, \tilde{n}\}$, we have

$$\varepsilon_{i-1} < \varepsilon_i/4 \tag{2.2}$$

and

$$\|A(x) - A(y)\| \le \varepsilon_i/4 \qquad (2.3)$$

for all $x, y \in K$ satisfying $\|x - y\| \le \varepsilon_{i-1}$.

Set

$$\delta := \varepsilon_0. \qquad (2.4)$$

Let $\{x_i\}_{i=0}^{\tilde{n}} \subset K$ satisfy for all $i = 0, \ldots, \tilde{n} - 1$,

$$\|x_{i+1} - A(x_i)\| \le \delta. \qquad (2.5)$$

In order to complete the proof, it suffices to show that

$$\|x_{\tilde{n}} - x_A\| \le \varepsilon. \qquad (2.6)$$

By (2.2), (2.4) and (2.5),

$$\|x_1 - A(x_0)\| \le \delta = \varepsilon_0 < \varepsilon_1. \qquad (2.7)$$

We now show by induction that for all $i = 1, \ldots, \tilde{n}$,

$$\|x_i - A^i(x_0)\| \le \varepsilon_i. \qquad (2.8)$$

In view of (2.7), inequality (2.8) does hold for $i = 1$.

Now assume that $i < \tilde{n}$ is a natural number for which (2.8) holds. It then follows from (2.3) and (2.8) that

$$\|A(x_i) - A^{i+1}(x_0)\| = \|A(x_i) - A(A^i(x_0))\| \le \varepsilon_{i+1}/4. \qquad (2.9)$$

By (2.2), (2.4), (2.5) and (2.9), we have

$$\|x_{i+1} - A^{i+1}(x_0)\| \le \|x_{i+1} - A(x_i)\| + \|A(x_i) - A^{i+1}(x_0)\| \le \delta + \varepsilon_{i+1}/4 \le \varepsilon_{i+1}.$$

Thus (2.8) indeed holds for all $i = 1, \ldots, \tilde{n}$, and, in particular, in view of (2.1),

$$\|x_{\tilde{n}} - A^{\tilde{n}}(x_0)\| \le \varepsilon_{\tilde{n}} = \varepsilon/4. \qquad (2.10)$$

Property (i) implies that

$$\|x_A - A^{\tilde{n}}(x_0)\| \le \varepsilon/4. \qquad (2.11)$$

Now by (2.10) and (2.11), we have

$$\|x_{\tilde{n}} - x_A\| \le \|x_{\tilde{n}} - A^{\tilde{n}}(x_0)\| + \|A^{\tilde{n}}(x_0) - x_A\| < \varepsilon.$$

This completes the proof of Theorem 9.1.

9.3 Proof of Theorem 9.2

We first note that Theorem 9.1 implies the following result.

Proposition 9.1. *Assume that the FPP for a mapping $A \in \mathcal{A}_u$ is well posed and that $x_A \in K$ is the unique fixed point of A, that is, $A(x_A) = x_A$. Let $\varepsilon > 0$. Then there exist a natural number $\tilde{n}$ and a neighborhood $\mathcal{U}$ of A in $\mathcal{A}$ such that for each $B \in \mathcal{U}$, each point $x \in K$ and each integer $i \geq \tilde{n}$,*

$$\|B^i(x) - x_A\| \leq \varepsilon.$$

Now let $A \in \mathcal{A}_u$ and $\gamma \in (0, 1)$. Define

$$A_\gamma(x) := (1 - \gamma)A(x) + \gamma x_K, \ x \in K. \tag{3.1}$$

It is clear that A_γ is a uniformly continuous self-mapping of K and if $x, y \in K$ satisfy $x \leq y$, then

$$A_\gamma(x) \leq A_\gamma(y). \tag{3.2}$$

Let $x, y \in K$ satisfy $x \leq y$. By (1.3) and (3.1),

$$\|A_\gamma(x) - A_\gamma(y)\|$$

$$= \|(1 - \gamma)A(x) + \gamma x_K - (1 - \gamma)A(y) - \gamma x_K\|$$

$$= (1 - \gamma)\|A(x) - A(y)\| \leq (1 - \gamma)\|x - y\|. \tag{3.3}$$

In view of (3.1), we have

$$d(A, A_\gamma)$$

$$= \sup\{\|A(x) - A_\gamma(x)\| : x \in K\}$$

$$= \sup\{\|A(x) - (1 - \gamma)A(x) - \gamma x_K\| : x \in K\} \leq \gamma d(K). \tag{3.4}$$

It now follows from (3.4) that the set

$$\{A_\gamma : A \in \mathcal{A}_u, \ \gamma \in (0, 1)\}$$

is everywhere dense in the metric space $(\mathcal{A}_u, d)$.

For any $A \in \mathcal{A}$, denote by A^0 the identity operator $I : K \to K$, that is, $I(x) = x$ for all $x \in K$.

Lemma 9.1. *Let $A \in \mathcal{A}_u$ and $\gamma \in (0, 1)$. Then the FPP for A_γ is well posed.*

Proof:

By (1.5), (3.2) and (3.3), for all points $x \in K$ and all integers $n \geq 0$, we have

$$(A_\gamma)^n(x_K) \leq (A_\gamma)^n(x) \tag{3.5}$$

and

$$\|(A_\gamma)^{n+1}(x) - (A_\gamma)^{n+1}(x_K)\| \leq (1 - \gamma)\|(A_\gamma)^n(x) - (A_\gamma)^n(x_K)\|. \tag{3.6}$$

This implies that for all points $x \in K$ and all integers $n \geq 0$,

$$\|(A_\gamma)^n(x) - (A_\gamma)^n(x_K)\| \leq (1 - \gamma)^n\|x - x_K\| \leq (1 - \gamma)^n d(K). \tag{3.7}$$

Let $\varepsilon \in (0, 1)$. There exists a natural number n_0 such that

$$4(1 - \gamma)^{n_0} d(K) < \varepsilon.$$

By (3.7) and the above relation,

$$\|(A_\gamma)^{n_0}(x_K) - (A_\gamma)^{n_0}(x)\| < \varepsilon/4 \text{ for all } x \in K. \tag{3.8}$$

This implies that for all natural numbers $n_1, n_2 \geq n_0$,

$$\|(A_\gamma)^{n_1}(x_K) - (A_\gamma)^{n_2}(x_K)\| < \varepsilon/2.$$

Since ε is any element of the interval $(0, 1)$, we conclude that $\{(A_\gamma)^n(x_K)\}_{n=1}^\infty$ is a Cauchy sequence and there exists

$$x_* = \lim_{n \to \infty} (A_\gamma)^n(x_K). \tag{3.9}$$

It is clear that

$$A_\gamma(x_*) = x_*. \tag{3.10}$$

In view of (3.8) and (3.10),

$$\|(A_\gamma)^{n_0}(x_K) - x_*\| \leq \varepsilon/4. \tag{3.11}$$

By (3.8) and (3.11), for all $x \in K$,

$$\|x_* - (A_\gamma)^{n_0}(x)\| \leq \|x_* - (A_\gamma)^{n_0}(x_K)\| + \|(A_\gamma)^{n_0}(x_K) - (A_\gamma)^{n_0}(x)\| \leq \varepsilon/2.$$

This completes the proof of Lemma 9.1.

Completion of the proof of Theorem 9.2

Let $A \in \mathcal{A}_u$, $\gamma \in (0, 1)$ and let n be a natural number. By Lemma 9.1, there exists a unique point $x_{A,\gamma} \in K$ such that

$$A_\gamma(x_{A,\gamma}) = x_{A,\gamma} \tag{3.12}$$

and the FPP for A_γ is well posed. By Proposition 9.1, there exist an open neighbourhood $\mathcal{U}(A, \gamma, n)$ of A_γ in $\mathcal{A}_u$ and a natural number $k(A, \gamma, n)$ such that:

For each $B \in \mathcal{U}(A, \gamma, n)$, each $x \in K$ and each integer $i \geq k(A, \gamma, n)$,

$$\|B^i(x) - x_{A,\gamma}\| \leq (2n)^{-1}. \tag{3.13}$$

Set

$$\mathcal{F} := \cap_{p=1}^{\infty} \cup \{\mathcal{U}(A, \gamma, n) : A \in \mathcal{A}_u, \gamma \in (0, 1), n \geq p \text{ is an integer}\}. \tag{3.14}$$

It is clear that $\mathcal{F}$ is a countable intersection of open and everywhere dense subsets of the metric space $(\mathcal{A}_u, d)$.

Let

$$B \in \mathcal{F} \text{ and } \varepsilon > 0. \tag{3.15}$$

Choose a natural number p such that

$$2p^{-1} < \varepsilon. \tag{3.16}$$

By (3.14) and (3.15), there exist

$$A \in \mathcal{A}_u, \gamma \in (0, 1) \text{ and an integer } n \geq p$$

such that it now follows from (3.13), (3.16) and (3.17) that for each $x \in K$ and each integer $i \geq k(A, \gamma, n)$,

$$\|B^i(x) - x_{A,\gamma}\| \leq (2n)^{-1} \leq (2p)^{-1} < \varepsilon/4. \tag{3.18}$$

This implies that for each pair of integers $i_1, i_2 \geq k(A, \gamma, n)$,

$$\|B^{i_1}(x) - B^{i_2}(x)\| \leq \varepsilon/2 \text{ for each } x \in K.$$

Therefore for each $x \in K$, $\{B^i(x)\}_{i=1}^{\infty}$ is a Cauchy sequence and there exists

$$\lim_{i \to \infty} B^i(x),$$

and in view of (3.18), we have

$$\|\lim_{i \to \infty} B^i(x) - x_{A,\gamma}\| \leq \varepsilon/4. \tag{3.19}$$

By (3.19), for each $x, y \in K$,

$$\|\lim_{i \to \infty} B^i(x) - \lim_{i \to \infty} B^i(y)\| \leq \varepsilon/2.$$

Since ε is an arbitrary positive number, we conclude that there exists a point $x_B \in K$ such that

$$x_B = \lim_{i \to \infty} B^i(x) \text{ for all } x \in K. \tag{3.20}$$

It is clear that

$$B(x_B) = x_B. \tag{3.21}$$

In view of (3.19) and (3.20),

$$\|x_B - x_{A,\gamma}\| \leq \varepsilon/4. \tag{3.22}$$

By (3.18) and (3.22), for each point $x \in K$ and each integer $i \geq k(A, \gamma, n)$,

$$\|B^i(x) - x_B\| \leq \|B^i(x) - x_{A,\gamma}\| + \|x_{A,\gamma} - x_B\| \leq \varepsilon.$$

This completes the proof of Theorem 9.2.

9.4 A complementary theorem

Let the point $y_K \in K$ satisfy

$$x \leq y_K \text{ for all } x \in K. \tag{4.1}$$

In this section we prove the following result, which complements Theorem 9.2.

Theorem 9.3. *Let the point $y_K \in K$ satisfy (4.1). Then there exists a set $\mathcal{F} \subset \mathcal{A}_u$, which is a countable intersection of open and everywhere dense subsets of the complete metric space $(\mathcal{A}_u, d)$, such that the FPP is well posed for every $A \in \mathcal{F}$.*

We first note that Theorem 9.1 implies the following result.

Proposition 9.2. *Assume that the FPP is well posed for a mapping $A \in \mathcal{A}_u$ and that $x_A \in K$ is the unique fixed point of A, that is, $A(x_A) = x_A$. Let $\varepsilon > 0$. Then there exist a natural number $\tilde{n}$ and a neighborhood $\mathcal{U}$ of A in $\mathcal{A}$ such that for each $B \in \mathcal{U}$, each point $x \in K$ and each integer $i \geq \tilde{n}$, we have*

$$\|B^i(x) - x_A\| \leq \varepsilon.$$

Next, let $A \in \mathcal{A}_u$ and $\gamma \in (0, 1)$. Define

$$A_\gamma(x) := (1 - \gamma)A(x) + \gamma y_K, \ x \in K. \tag{4.2}$$

It is clear that $A_\gamma \in \mathcal{A}_u$. Arguing as in Section 9.3, we can show that for all $x, y \in K$ which satisfy $x \leq y$, we have

$$\|A_\gamma(x) - A_\gamma(y)\| \leq (1 - \gamma)\|x - y\| \tag{4.3}$$

and

$$d(A, A_\gamma)$$

$$= \sup\{\|A(x) - A_\gamma(x)\| : x \in K\}$$

$$= \sup\{\|A(x) - (1 - \gamma)A(x) - \gamma y_K\| : x \in K\} \leq \gamma d(K). \tag{4.4}$$

It follows from (4.4) that the set

$$\{A_\gamma : A \in \mathcal{A}_u, \ \gamma \in (0, 1)\}$$

is everywhere dense in the metric space $(\mathcal{A}_u, d)$.

Lemma 9.2. *Let $A \in \mathcal{A}_u$ and $\gamma \in (0, 1)$. Then the FPP is well posed for A_γ.*

Proof:

By (4.1) and (4.3), for all points $x \in K$ and all integers $n \geq 0$, we have

$$(A_\gamma)^n(x) \leq (A_\gamma)^n(y_K)$$

and

$$\|(A_\gamma)^{n+1}(x) - (A_\gamma)^{n+1}(y_K)\| \leq (1 - \gamma)\|(A_\gamma)^n(x) - (A_\gamma)^n(y_K)\|.$$

This implies that for all points $x \in K$ and all integers $n \geq 0$,

$$\|(A_\gamma)^n(x) - (A_\gamma)^n(y_K)\| \leq (1 - \gamma)^n\|x - y_K\| \leq (1 - \gamma)^n d(K). \qquad (4.5)$$

Arguing as in the proof of Lemma 9.1, we can show that $\{(A_\gamma)^n(y_K)\}_{n=1}^\infty$ is a Cauchy sequence and there exists

$$y_* = \lim_{n \to \infty} (A_\gamma)^n(y_K). \qquad (4.6)$$

It is clear that

$$A_\gamma(y_*) = y_*. \qquad (4.7)$$

By (4.5) and (4.7), for all points $x \in K$ and all integers $n \geq 1$,

$$\|y_* - (A_\gamma)^n(x)\| = \|(A_\gamma)^n(y_*) - (A_\gamma)^n(x)\|$$

$$\leq \|(A_\gamma)^n(x) - (A_\gamma)^n(y_K)\| + \|(A_\gamma)^n(y_K) - (A_\gamma)^n(y_*)\|$$

$$\leq 2(1 - \gamma)^n d(K).$$

This completes the proof of Lemma 9.2.

Arguing as in the proof of Theorem 9.2, we can now complete the proof of Theorem 9.3.

Acknowledgments. The first author was partially supported by the Israel Science Foundation (Grant No. 389/12), by the Fund for the Promotion of Research at the Technion and by the Technion General Research Fund.

References

[1] M. R. Alfuraidan and M. A. Khamsi, *A fixed point theorem for monotone asymptotically nonexpansive mappings*, Proc. Amer. Math. Soc., to appear.

[2] S. Banach, *Sur les opérations dans les ensembles abstraits et leur application aux équations intégrales*, Fund. Math. **3** (1922), 133–181.

[3] A. Betiuk-Pilarska and T. Domínguez Benavides, *Fixed points for nonexpansive mappings and generalized nonexpansive mappings on Banach lattices*, Pure Appl. Func. Anal. **1** (2016), 343–359.

[4] F. S. de Blasi and J. Myjak, *Sur la convergence des approximations successives pour les contractions non linéaires dans un espace de Banach*, C. R. Acad. Sci. Paris **283** (1976), 185–187.

[5] F. S. de Blasi and J. Myjak, *Sur la porosité de l'ensemble des contractions sans point fixe*, C. R. Acad. Sci. Paris **308** (1989), 51–54.

[6] F. S. de Blasi, J. Myjak, S. Reich and A. J. Zaslavski, *Generic existence and approximation of fixed points for nonexpansive set-valued maps*, Set-Valued Var. Anal. **17** (2009), 97–112.

[7] R. Espínola and A. Wiśnicki, *The Knaster-Tarski theorem versus monotone nonexpansive mappings*, preprint.

[8] K. Goebel and W. A. Kirk, *Topics in Metric Fixed Point Theory*, Cambridge University Press, Cambridge, 1990.

[9] K. Goebel and S. Reich, *Uniform Convexity, Hyperbolic Geometry, and Nonexpansive Mappings*, Marcel Dekker, New York and Basel, 1984.

[10] W. A. Kirk, *Contraction mappings and extensions*, Handbook of Metric Fixed Point Theory, Kluwer, Dordrecht, 2001, 1–34.

[11] R. Kubota, W. Takahashi and Y. Takeuchi, *Extensions of Browder's demiclosedness principle and Reich's lemma and their applications*, Pure Appl. Func. Anal. **1** (2016), 63–84.

[12] E. Rakotch, *A note on contractive mappings*, Proc. Amer. Math. Soc. **13** (1962), 459–465.

[13] S. Reich, *The alternating algorithm of von Neumann in the Hilbert ball*, Dynamic Systems Appl. **2** (1993), 21–25.

[14] S. Reich and I. Shafrir, *Nonexpansive iterations in hyperbolic spaces*, Nonlinear Anal. **15** (1990), 537–558.

[15] S. Reich and A. J. Zaslavski, *Convergence of generic infinite products of affine operators*, Abst. Appl. Anal. **4**(1999), 1–19.

[16] S. Reich and A. J. Zaslavski, *Convergence of generic infinite products of order-preserving mappings*, Positivity **3** (1999), 1–21.

[17] S. Reich and A. J. Zaslavski, *Convergence of Krasnoselskii-Mann iterations of nonexpansive operators*, Math. Comput. Modelling **32** (2000), 1423–1431.

[18] S. Reich and A. J. Zaslavski, *Well-posedness of fixed point problems*, Far East J. Math. Sci., Special Volume (Functional Analysis and Its Applications), Part III (2001), 393–401.

[19] S. Reich and A. J. Zaslavski, *Generic aspects of metric fixed point theory*, Handbook of Metric Fixed Point Theory, Kluwer, Dordrecht, 2001, 557–575.

[20] S. Reich and A. J. Zaslavski, *A note on well-posed null and fixed point problems*, Fixed Point Theory Appl. **2005** (2005), 207–211.

[21] S. Reich and A. J. Zaslavski, *Approximate fixed points of nonexpansive mappings in unbounded sets*, J. Fixed Point Theory Appl. **13** (2013), 627–632.

[22] S. Reich and A. J. Zaslavski, *Genericity in Nonlinear Analysis*, Developments in Mathematics, vol. 34, Springer, New York, 2014.

[23] S. Reich and A. J. Zaslavski, *Approximate fixed points of nonexpansive set-valued mappings in unbounded sets*, J. Nonlinear Convex Anal. **16** (2015), 1707–1716.

[24] X. Wang, *Most maximally monotone operators have a unique zero and a super-regular resolvent*, Nonlinear Analysis **87** (2013), 69–82.

PART 3

Linguistics, Computer Science and Physics

Chapter 10

Analytical Linguistics and Formal Grammars: Contributions of Solomon Marcus and Their Further Developments

Mark Burgin

University of California at Los Angeles

Los Angeles, CA 90095 USA

mburgin@math.ucla.edu

10.1 Introduction

It is possible to discern three types of linguistics:

(1) classical or descriptive linguistics, which is represented, for example, by the works of such famous linguists as Ferdinand de Saussure and Louis Hjelmslev;

(2) computational linguistics; and

(3) mathematical linguistics, which is represented, for example, by the famous linguist Noam Chomsky and mathematician Solomon Marcus.

In turn, mathematical linguistics can be divided into structural, generative and quantitative (in particular, statistical) forms.

The outstanding Roumanian mathematician Solomon Marcus is one of the founders of the first two directions of mathematical linguistics, to which he made essential contributions. Remarkably, he developed the direction called algebraic linguistics, or set-theoretical linguistics, which is an important part of analytical linguistics as well as of structural linguistics. This direction is called algebraic linguistics because it employs a variety of algebraic operations with linguistic structures. It is also called set-theoretical linguistics because it is based on such basic set-theoretical structures as partitions. Marcus published several books and dozens of papers on this subject. His Roumanian book *Lingvistica matematică*[1] (Bucureşti, 1963)

---

[1] *Mathematical Linguistics.*

was one of the first books in mathematical linguistics. His other book *Algebraic Linguistics: Analytical Models* (Academic Press, 1967) was translated into many languages.

In what follows we will analyse the contributions of Solomon Marcus to mathematical linguistics and some of their further developments. The theory of named sets provides various efficient tools for mathematical linguistics and the foundation of structural linguistics, [4, 5, 7]. We will use it to give a concise exposition of Marcus' algebraic or structural direction in mathematical linguistics.

10.2 Named sets

A named set, also called a fundamental triad, has the following structure (form):

$$X \xrightarrow{\quad f \quad} N.$$

In detail, a named set is a triad $\mathbf{X} = (X, f, N)$, in which X and N are two objects and f is a correspondence (e.g., a binary relation) between X and N. Here X is called the support of $\mathbf{X}$, N is called the component of names (reflector) or set of names of $\mathbf{X}$, and f is called the naming correspondence (reflection) of $\mathbf{X}$. Note that f is not necessarily a mapping or a function.

The standard example is a basic named set (fundamental triad) in which X consists of people, N consists of their names and f is the correspondence between people and their names. Another example is a basic named set in which X consists of things, N consists of their names and f is the correspondence between things and their names [15].

A named set is called set-theoretical if X and N are sets while f is a binary relation between sets X and N. Note that there are many named sets that are not set-theoretical. For instance, an algorithmic named set $\mathbf{A} = (X, A, Y)$ consists of an algorithm A, the set X of inputs and the set Y of outputs.

Named sets play a prominent role in linguistics in general [36, 37] and in analytical linguistics in particular. Productions in generative grammars and triads X/RY and X/LY from categorical grammars [1, 39] are elementary set-theoretical named sets.

Many mathematical systems are particular cases of named sets or fundamental triads. The most important of such systems are fuzzy sets [40], multisets [17], graphs and hypergraphs [2], topological and fiber bundles [16]. Moreover, any ordinary set is, as a matter of fact, a single named set, i.e. a named set in which all elements have the same name [5, 7]. It is interesting that the use of single named sets instead of ordinary sets allows solutions of some problems in science, e.g. Gregg's paradox in biology [3].

Languages provide many other examples of named sets, which are especially important in the direction developed by Solomon Marcus and his followers. As [23] writes, there are two fundamental types of models in mathematical linguistics: generative and analytic. All generative models of languages, such as regular, context-free, recursive, recursively enumerable and inductively computable languages, are generated by some type of automata or formal grammars: regular languages are generated by finite automata and regular grammars, context-free languages are generated by pushdown automata and context-free grammars, recursive languages are generated by everywhere defined Turing machines, recursively enumerable languages are generated by Turing machines and unrestricted or phrase structure grammars, and inductively computable languages are generated by inductive Turing machines of the first order. All kinds of automata are intrinsically connected to named sets. The same is true for different kinds of generative and inference grammars.

10.3 Analytical models in algebraic linguistics

The role of named sets in analytical models is even more explicit because analytical models in algebraic linguistics directly use partitions, as well as binary and other set-theoretical relations, which are, in essence, set-theoretical named sets [9, 10, 18, 20, 22, 23]. For instance, an analytic grammar of a language L gives descriptions of the relations between the words of the language L and between substrings of such words with respect to their position in these words [23]. Analytical models supply an effective approach to the investigation of semantics of natural languages based on the construction of set-theoretic models when the set of words or phrases in the original language is divided into certain equivalence classes. Such partitions are basic concepts of algebraic linguistics as it is demonstrated in Marcus' book *Algebraic Linguistics: Analytical Models*.

Let us consider the vocabulary of a language, that is, a finite set of words. In the theory of formal languages, the vocabulary (alphabet) Γ of a formal language is an arbitrary finite set of elements which are called words (symbols or letters). When T is the set of all finite strings of elements from Γ, then any subset L of T is called a formal language over the vocabulary (alphabet) Γ. All natural and artificial languages are special kinds of formal languages satisfying additional conditions. Elements from L are called texts when Γ is the vocabulary of L, and words when Γ is the alphabet of L.

Definition 1. If P is a partition of the vocabulary Γ of a language L, then the triad (Γ, P, L) is called a language with a paradigmatic structure. Each set of the partition P is called a P-cell, and $P(w)$ denotes the P-cell containing the word w from Γ. For two distinct words u and v, we have either $P(u) = P(v)$ or $P(u)$ and $P(v)$ are disjoint (that is, their intersection is the empty set). As we know, any partition is defined by an equivalence relation, which in turn, is a set-theoretical named set.

The linguistic analysis in machine translation requires a richer structure for language representation. In this case, a language is represented by the system

$$(\Gamma, P, L, K, g),$$

where K is the named set $K = (D, d, G)$, in which D is the class of subsets of L called grammatical categories, G consists of the names of grammatical categories and d is the relation which connects grammatical categories with their names, while g is the function that associates words with the set of all grammatical categories that contain these words.

Definition 2. The structure (Γ, P, L, K, g) is called a language with paradigmatic and categorical structures.

We see that the extended model of a language involves two more named sets: the partition K of the language L and the function g.

Based on the previous research, Marcus developed an extensive system of operations with and relations between linguistic structures and studied their properties. He explicated important classes of languages, such as adequate languages and homogeneous languages, developed mathematical models of parts of speech, syntactic types and grammatical gender. This modelling provided tools for rigorous studies of various linguistic phenomena.

An important example of relation used in analytical algebraic linguistics is domination.

Definition 3. For $x, y \in \Gamma$, the word x dominates the word $y (x \to y)$ with respect to the language L if for each pair of strings p and q such that the string pxq belongs to L, the string pyq also belongs to L.

As domination is a reflexive and transitive relation, the system of sets $S(x) = \{y; x \to y \text{ and } y \to x\}$ determines a partition of Γ into disjoint sets.

The partition $E(x) = \{x\}$ is called the unit partition of T. Partitions S and E are most useful in the study of languages.

Domination is useful for modelling parts of speech. As [23] writes, the notion part of speech is fundamental to linguistics and many authors have tried to give a rigorous description of it. The difficulties in this area arise from the very complex character of this notion, which is a mixture of semantic, morphologic, and syntactic factors. The proportion in which each of these factors occurs in the structure of the parts of speech depends on the language considered.

It is possible to interpret the components of a language with a paradigmatic structure (Γ, P, L) in the following way:

- Γ plays the role of the vocabulary of a natural language **L**,
- the elements of the partition P are the sets $P(x)$, where x is a word from the language L and each $P(x)$ consists of all inflected forms of x,
- L is the set of all well-formed sentences in the language **L**.

However, according to [23], such an interpretation does not correspond to the real situation in a natural language, since the condition that P is a partition of Γ is violated because one word, for example, structure, can belong to different parts of speech.

Studies of single-valued partitions were motivated by the fact that in-depth semantic structures of natural languages are very complex, so that the construction of models faithfully representing these structures involves considerable difficulties. As we can see, the customary linguistic interpretation of a vocabulary partition is the decomposition of the set of words in paradigms, where a paradigm of a word is the set of all its flectional forms [20]. In contrast, paradigms in natural languages do not form a partition of the vocabulary because there are distinct paradigms that are not disjoint. While the single-valued partitions and other set-theoretical structures only describe small fragments of natural languages, a more complete description of these languages requires set-theoretic models using multivalued partitions, which are basically named sets. The exploration and use of multivalued partitions in mathematical linguistics began in [9,10] which continued the studies of Marcus and other linguists in this area.

Definition 4. A multivalued partition of a vocabulary (alphabet) A of a language L is a binary relation P between the alphabet A (language L) and some set F, i.e. $P \subset A \times F(P \subset L \times F)$. The set F is called the set of attributes of the partition P.

It is also natural to consider multivalued partitions of a language L as a binary relation P between the language L and some set F, i.e. $P \subset L \times F$, while any binary relation is a set-theoretical named set [7].

Definition 5. If P is a multivalued partition of the vocabulary Γ of a language L, then the triad (Γ, P, L) is called a language with a multivalued paradigmatic structure.

Multivalued partitions have been used to solve certain problems for which only partial results could be obtained by conventional algebraic models of languages [9]. For instance, multivalued partitions can be used to derive descriptions of various depth structures in natural languages.

Note that derivation of partitions in languages, which plays an important role in algebraic linguistics, is the sequential composition of the corresponding named sets [9, 10, 23].

The investigation of the properties of linguistic multivalued partitions is also useful for the design of efficient information retrieval systems because named set constructions are usually employed in designing of such systems, as databases, knowledge bases and Internet browsers, and languages [10, 38].

10.4   Contextual grammars

In addition to algebraic linguistics, Solomon Marcus effectively contributed to generative linguistics, introducing and investigating a useful class of grammars, which are called *contextual grammars, or contextual Marcus grammars* [25, 26, 34].

Definition 6. A *contextual grammar* G is a triad (A, B, C), where A is a set of symbols called the alphabet of the grammar G, C is a set of pairs of words in the alphabet A called the contextual component of the grammar G and B is a set of words in the alphabet A called the base of the grammar G. Contextual grammars generate contextual languages.

Definition 7. A language L in the alphabet A is generated by a contextual grammar $G = (A, B, C)$ if it is the least language that satisfies the following conditions:

(a) $B \in L$,
(b) If $x \in L$ and $(u, v) \in C$, then $uxv \in L$.

Definition 8. A language L is called *contextual* if it is generated by a contextual grammar.

Marcus obtained many interesting properties of contextual languages specifying their relations to other types of languages studied before. In particular, he proved the following results [25, 26].

Proposition 1. *Every finite language is contextual.*

Proposition 2. *Every contextual language is context-free.*

Proposition 3. *There are contextual languages that are not regular.*

In general, one can prove the following relation between contextual grammars and conventional generative grammars, which generate languages using productions.

Theorem 1. *For any contextual grammar, there is a generative grammar that generates the same language.*

Indeed, taking a contextual grammar $G = (A, B, C)$, we can use a set V of variables, for which a one-to-one correspondence $g : V \to B$ exists, and define three forms of productions rules R: productions $x \to uxv$, for all $x \in V$ and all $(u, v) \in C$, productions $S \to x$, for all $x \in V$ and productions $x \to g(x)$ for all $x \in V$. Then the generative grammar G_g with the terminal alphabet A, variables alphabet V, the set of rules R and the start symbol S generates the same language as the contextual grammar G. The proof can be done by induction on the length of words.

Studies of contextual grammars and languages became very active and researchers did not only find new properties of contextual grammars (cf., for example, [35]), but also introduced and studied different generalisations of contextual grammars (cf., for example, [32, 33]). In addition, contextual grammars also found useful applications in computational linguistics (cf., for example, [31]). The most detailed exposition of the theory of contextual Marcus grammars is presented in the book [34].

Interesting problems related to contextual grammars emerged in the context of grammars with prohibition [6, 8], which are also called correction grammars [12–14].

Definition 9. A grammar G with prohibition (correction grammar) consists of two generative grammars: a grammar P_G with positive rules and a grammar N_G with negative rules.

First, these grammars generate two languages $L(P_G)$ and $L(N_G)$ and then they are combined in the language of G.

Definition 10. The language of the grammar $G = (P_G, N_G)$ with prohibition is $L(G) = L(PG) \setminus L(NG)$.

Positive rules are used for generating (accepting) words from the language, while negative rules are used for exclusion of incorrect forms. When there are no negative rules, we obtain conventional generative grammars and their languages. Constructing languages by means of grammars with prohibition is more relevant to the technique used by people for natural language text generation than conventional generative grammars. Indeed, first, general rules for generating words and texts are used. Then exclusions from these general rules are applied when some of the generated words are excluded as incorrect and changed into correct versions. Generating languages by means of grammars with prohibition is also adequate to learning processes as it is demonstrated in [8].

In addition, it is proved that grammars with prohibition have essentially higher computational power and expressive capabilities in comparison with conventional generative grammars [6]. In particular, they can generate languages that are not recursively enumerable.

Each pair of classes $\mathbf{G}_1$ and $\mathbf{G}_2$ of conventional generative grammars allows building four classes of grammars with prohibition:

$(\mathbf{G}_1, \mathbf{G}_2) = \{(G_1, G_2) \mid G_1 \in \mathbf{G}_1, G_2 \in \mathbf{G}_2\}$,
$(\mathbf{G}_2, \mathbf{G}_1) = \{(G_2, G_1) \mid G_1 \in \mathbf{G}_1, G_2 \in \mathbf{G}_2\}$,
$(\mathbf{G}_1, \mathbf{G}_1) = \{(G_1, G_2) \mid G_1, G_2 \in \mathbf{G}_1\}$,
$(\mathbf{G}_2, \mathbf{G}_2) = \{(G_1, G_2) \mid G_1, G_2 \in \mathbf{G}_2\}$.

An important problem is to explore how languages of grammars with prohibition depend on classes $\mathbf{G}_1$ and $\mathbf{G}_2$ of conventional generative grammars. In [8] this analysis was done for grammars from the Chomsky hierarchy.

This brings us to the problem of studying grammars with prohibition when positive and/or negative part of the grammar with prohibition is a contextual Marcus grammar, a generalised contextual Marcus grammar, or a hybrid grammar.

References

[1] Bar-Hillel, Y., Gaifman, H. and Shamir, E. On categorial and phrase structure grammars, *The Bulletin of the Research Council of Israel*, 9F (1960), 1–16.

[2] Berge, C. *Graphs and Hypergraphs*, North Holland, Amsterdam/New York, 1973.

[3] Burgin, M. On Greg's paradox in taxonomy, *Abstracts presented to the American Mathematical Society*, v. 4, No. 3, (1983), 303.

[4] Burgin M. Theory of named sets as a foundational basis for mathematics, in *Structures in Mathematical Theories*, San Sebastian, 1990, 417–420.

[5] Burgin, M. *Unified Foundations of Mathematics*, Preprint Mathematics LO/0403186, 2004, 39 pp.; https://arxiv.org/abs/math/0403186.

[6] Burgin, M. Grammars with prohibition and human-computer interaction,

in *Proceedings of the Business and Industry Simulation Symposium, Society for Modeling and Simulation*, San Diego, California, 2005, 143–147.

[7] Burgin, M. *Theory of Named Sets*, Mathematics Research Developments, Nova Science, New York, 2011.

[8] Burgin, M. *Basic Classes of Grammars with Prohibition*, Preprint in Computer Science, cs.FL/CL. 1302.5181, 2013, 15 pp.

[9] Burgin, M. and Burgina, E. Partitions in languages and parallel computations, *Programming and Computer Software*, v. 8, No. 3, (1982), 112–120.

[10] Burgin, M. and Burgina, E. Information retrieval and multi-valued partitions in languages, *Cybernetics and System Analysis*, No. 1 (1982), 30–42.

[11] Burgin, M. and Burgina, E. Computational complexity of processes defined by parallel partitions, *VI All-Union Conference on Mathematical Logic*, Tbilisi, 1982. (in Russian)

[12] Carlucci, L., Case, J. and Jain, S. Learning correction grammars, *J. Symb. Logic*, v. 74 (2009), 489–516.

[13] Case, J. and Jain, S. Rice and Rice-Shapiro theorems for transfinite Correction grammars, *Mathematical Logic Quarterly*, October (2011), 1–13.

[14] Case, J. and Royer, J. Program size complexity of correction grammars in the Ershov hierarchy, in pursuit of the universal, in *Proceedings of the 12th Conference of Computability in Europe (CiE 2016)*, Lecture Notes in Computer Science, v. 7921 (2016), 240–250.

[15] Dalla Chiara, M. L. and di Francia, T. G. Individuals, kinds and names in physics, in *Bridging the Gap: Philosophy, Mathematics, Physics*, Kluwer Ac. Publ., 1993, 261–283.

[16] Husemöller, D. *Fibre Bundles*, Springer Verlag, Berlin, 1994.

[17] Knuth, D. *The Art of Computer Programming, v.2: Seminumerical Algorithms*, Addison-Wesley, Reading, Mass., 1997.

[18] Kulagina, O. S. (1958) One method of defining grammatical concepts on the basis of set theory, *Probl. Kibern.*, No. 1 (1958), 203–214. (in Russian)

[19] Marcus, S. Structures linguistiques et structures topologiques, *Rev. de Math. Pures et Appl.* vol. 6, 3, (1961), 501–506.

[20] Marcus, S. (1962). Sur un modele logique de la categorie grammaticale elementaire, I, *Rev.de Math. Pures et Appl.*, v. 7, No. 1, (1962), 91–107.

[21] Marcus, S. *Lingvistica Matematica. Modele Matematice in Lingvistica*, Ed. Didactica si Pedagogica. Bucuresti, 1963, 220p. (in Romanian)

[22] Marcus, S. Typologie des langues et modeles logiques, *Acta Math. Acad. Sci. Hung.*, v. 14, No. 3-4 (1963), 269–283.

[23] Marcus, S. *Algebraic Linguistics: Analytical Models*, Academic Press, New York/London, 1967.

[24] Marcus, S. *Introduction mathématique a la linguistique structurale*, Dunod, Paris, 1967.

[25] Marcus, S. (1969) Deux types nouveaux de grammaires generatives, *Cahiers de Linguistique Thèorique et Appliquée*, v. 6, (1969), 69–74.

[26] Marcus, S. Contextual grammars, *Rev. Roum. de Math. Pures et Appl.*, v. 14, nr. 10, (1969), 1473–1482.

[27] Marcus, S. *Words and Languages Everywhere*, Polimetrica, Milano, 2007.

[28] Marcus, S. and Vasiliu, E. Mathematique et phonologie. Theorie des graphes et consonantisme de la langue roumaine, I. *Rev. de Math. Pures et Appl.*, v. 5, nr. 2 (1960), 319–340.

[29] Marcus, S. and Vasiliu, E. Mathématique et phonologie. Theorie des graphes et consonantisme de la langue roumaine, II. *Rev. de Math. Pures et Appl.*, v. 5, nr. 3-4 (1960), 681–703.

[30] Marcus, S. and Vasiliu, Description, a l'aide de la theorie des ensembles, de certains phenomenes morphologiques, *Rev. de Math. Pures et Appl.*, v. 6, nr. 4 (1961), 735–744.

[31] Marcus, S., Păun, G. and Martin-Vide, C. Contextual grammars as generative models of natural languages, *Computational Linguistics* 24(2) (1998), 245–274.

[32] Martin-Vide, C., Mateescu, A. and Păun, G. Hybrid grammars: the Chomsky-Marcus case, *Bulletin of the EATCS*, v. 64 (1998), 159–165.

[33] Păun, G. On semicontextual grammars, *Bulletin Mathématique de la Société des Sciences Mathématiques de la République Socialiste de Roumanie, Nouvelle Série*, v. 28 (76), No. 1 (1984), 63–68.

[34] Păun, G. *Marcus Contextual Grammars*, Kluwer, Boston/Dordrecht/London, 1997.

[35] Păun, G., Rozenberg, G. and Salomaa, A. Marcus contextual grammars: modularity and leftmost derivation, in *Mathematical aspects of natural and formal languages*, World Scientific Publishing Co., Inc. River Edge, NJ, 1994, 375–392.

[36] Rudenko, D.I. Common name as a phenomenon of a natural language, *Izvestiya of the Academy of Sciences of the USSR, Ser. Literature and Language*, v. 45, No. 1, (1986), 7–9. (in Russian)

[37] Rudenko, D.I. Names of natural classes, proper names and names of nominal classes in semantics of a natural language, *Izvestiya of the Academy of Sciences of the USSR, Ser. Literature and Language*, v. 46, No. 1, (1987), 9–11. (in Russian)

[38] Tomioka, S. (2007) Information structure as information-based partition, *Interdisciplinary Studies on Information Structure*, v. 6 (2007), 97–107.

[39] Wood, M. M. *Categorial Grammars*, Routledge, London, 1993.

[40] Zadeh, L. Fuzzy sets, *Information and Control*, v. 8, No. 3 (1965), 338–353.

Chapter 11

A Contagious Creativity[1]

Gheorghe Păun

Romanian Academy

Calea Victoriei 125, Bucharest, Romania

gpaun@us.es, curteadelaarges@gmail.com

11.1 Preliminaries

The title above recalls the title of a special issue of *Fundamenta Informaticae* (vol. 64), edited in 2005, by Cristian Calude (Auckland, New Zealand), Grzegorz Rozenberg (Leiden, The Netherlands) and myself, in honour of Professor Solomon Marcus on the occasion of his 85th birthday anniversary. It was a quadruple volume, a rather rare case — if not unique — in the history of the journal, of about 500 pages.

This syntagma describes very accurately the activity and the personality of professor Solomon Marcus, his very special position in the Romanian mathematics, in the Romanian science and culture in general. I have somewhere called him *the man with five or six top careers*: mathematical analysis (with international level achievements, in terms of the number of papers and citations, including handbooks for students in mathematics, published in several consecutive editions), mathematical linguistics (he was one of the founders of the domain, having monographs published by Dunod and Academic Press already at the middle of the sixties), formal language theory, theoretical computer science in general (I will come back to this topic), mathematical poetics, semiotics, history and philosophy of science, bio-informatics, education, cultural journalism. A bibliography of

---

[1]This is a slightly modified English version of the introduction to the two-volume book *Solomon Marcus: Selected Papers — Computer Science*, edited by Gh. Păun, Spandugino Publishing House, Bucharest, Romania, in press.

unusual dimension and variety, a continuous participation/involvement in everything around, somewhat in the tradition of Moisil.[2]

A Renaissance-like personality, so naturally multi- and inter-disciplinary that the term which better fits to him is *trans-disciplinarity*.

A *contagious* personality, the scholar — more adequate, the culture personality — being intimately associated with the creator and leader of scientific groups/schools, always of an exemplary and efficient altruism.

However, not these issues will be the topics to discuss in these pages. Details of this kind can be found in the forewords of the many anniversary volumes dedicated to him, in particular, in the book titled *Meetings with Solomon Marcus* published by Spandugino Publishing House (2011, second edition). The goal of these pages is to briefly introduce to the reader the contributions of Solomon Marcus to computer science. Briefly, because also this direction of his activity is of a large size: several books authored or edited, about 100 research papers published along more than five decades, in journals, collective volumes or conference proceedings. The list of papers is provided in the end of this presentation.

11.2   Two significant papers

The first formal language theory (the terminology will become "standard" in the beginning of the seventies, especially after the publication of the book *Formal Languages*, by Arto Salomaa, Academic Press, 1973) of Solomon Marcus was published in 1963, in *Compte rendus de l'Academie des Science Paris* (his first papers in mathematical linguistics were published in 1960), while the last paper of computer science was published in 2013, in the proceedings of a bio-informatics conference (*Conference on Membrane Computing*, Budapest, 2012) — it is possible that unfinished manuscripts remained unpublished, maybe with his collaborators.

The two mentioned papers are rather significant, each alone and both together, as a couple, for the whole computer science research activity of professor Solomon Marcus.

The first paper is already symptomatic for his inclination-passion-expertise in exploring and building bridges among different, at a superficial sight disjoint, areas. Finite automata, arithmetical progressions, finite state grammars (later, named regular grammars). The automata theory and the number theory, grammars and automata (the "parallelism" between the two

---

[2]Grigore C. Moisil, 1906–1973, a Romanian mathematician with important contributions to mechanics, algebra, logics, the founder of Romanian computer science.

approaches, the generative and the analytic one, the grammatical approach and the one based on automata, is nowadays a common fact in language theory, but it was not so at the beginning of the sixties). In the last part of the 1963 paper, one also discusses the significance of the formal language theory results in terms of natural languages.

In the other end of the bibliography, we find a paper written in collaboration with Sorin Istrail, born in Iassy and having a top level career in computer science (bio-informatics) in the United States. The paper was presented at the 2012 edition of the Conference on Membrane Computing held in Budapest. Actually, the attention paid to bio-informatics goes back to the beginning of the seventies, when a large paper was published, in 1974, in *Cahiers de Linguistique Théorique et Appliquée*.

11.3 A paper published too early

The title of this 1974 paper is *Linguistic structures and generative devices in molecular genetics*.

It was a comprehensive paper, on the one hand, synthesising previous approaches and results, on the other hand, opening new research vistas, a paper probably published ahead of its time, because its impact was not as important as deserved. It was the time when the researchers were still looking for mathematical tools useful in addressing questions in the genetic area, of modelling DNA and its biochemistry. Speculations about using DNA molecules as a support for computations were publicly made only in the next years (Michael Conrad, Richard Feynmann, Charles H. Bennet), while the first computing model based on an operation specific to DNA recombination was introduced only in 1987, by Thomas Head. After 1994, when Leonard Adleman reported the first DNA computing experiment, this research area has spectacularly grown, under the name of *DNA Computing* (since then, a yearly international conference with this topic is organised).

The paper from 1974 was not discussing about *computing*, about using DNA for the use of computer science, but, the other way round, about the relevance of mathematical, computer science, semiotic tools in the study of DNA and of related processes. However, it is worth emphasising the attention paid by Marcus, in this first paper and after that in many others, to a proposal made, in 1965, by the Polish mathematician Zdzislaw Pawlak (famous for introducing, around 1990, the so-called *rough sets*), of generating proteins starting from amino acids, in a specific representation, by means of certain *picture grammars* (a domain developed later, that is why S. Marcus considered Z. Pawlak a precursor of picture grammars).

A similar fate, that is, an audience less important than deserved, had also a book published by Solomon Marcus in 1964, *Gramatici și automate finite — Finite State Grammars and Automata* (The Publishing House of the Romanian Academy, Bucharest). It was one of the first monographs in the world in automata and formal language theory but it has remained in Romanian language, hence it was not sufficiently known in the international community.

In a strong contrast with this book, the mathematical linguistics books of Marcus, translated in several languages (French, English, Russian, Italian, Czech, Spanish), have known a very high international audience — but we will not discuss them here.

Similarly, in contrast with the paper from 1974 mentioned above it is placed a paper from 1969, where Solomon Marcus introduced the *contextual grammars*, called now *Marcus contextual grammars*. A powerful branch of formal language theory was open by this paper, so that we will come back to this topic with details.

11.4   A working classification

Of course, it is difficult to classify the computer science papers of professor Solomon Marcus, simply because of their inter/multi-disciplinarity. In the list from the end of these pages, we have clustered the papers in four large categories: formal language theory, applications of formal language theory, bio-informatics, and recursive functions.

In the first class there are papers dealing with various different topics: finite state grammars and automata, contextual grammars, the history of formal language theory, combinatorics on words and on infinite sequences (periodicity and quasi-periodicity, unavoidable patterns, density of words of a given length), mathematical analysis notions extended to languages (among the most fruitful proposals, we mention the Darboux property formulated for hierarchies of languages, the notions of symmetry and convexity, of attractor) and so on.

It is worth mentioning the permanent effort of establishing links among the algebraic/analytical approach to language (the "classic" mathematical linguistics, developed in the Russian, Czech, German, American, Romanian linguistics schools, where Solomon Marcus was a protagonist and a connecting scholar) and the generative approaches, mainly based on the Chomsky grammars, the visible attraction towards "functional" tools, such as iterated morphisms and the iterated "reading" of sequences of symbols, the systematic attempt to pass from the continuous mathematics to discrete mathematics. Actually, the title of a paper from 1999 is rather explicit and significant in this respect: *From real analysis to discrete mathematics and back*, with immediate details already in the title: *Symmetry, convexity, almost periodicity, and strange attractors*. In the beginning of this paper we find: "Despite its importance, the relation between continuous and discrete mathematics is a rather neglected topic. (...) Working in real analysis in the fifties and in the sixties and then in discrete mathematics (the mathematical theory of languages), I became interested to look for the discrete analog of some facts belonging to continuous mathematics."

Another "invariant" of "Marcus style" is the formulation of open problems, of new research directions. On the one hand, this originates in his immense mathematical, linguistic and computer science knowledge, but this is also related to his personality — *always wondering*, as he used to say. Another explanation is related to his mathematical background, which, again similar to the Moisil style, makes irrelevant the distinction between applicative and pure mathematics, there are only interesting and of high quality mathematics — and their opposites. Any research idea deserves our attention, especially the interesting, unexpected ones, with a particular attraction for the frontier questions, establishing links between different domains.

Many of the questions formulated by Solomon Marcus were addressed by his disciples, collaborators, by researchers in mathematics and computer science from Romania and from other countries. Some problems were, partially or totally, solved — many of them are still waiting for research efforts.

11.5 Marcus contextual grammars

Solomon Marcus has papers which open new research directions in formal language theory, the most important one being the paper where he has introduced the *contextual grammars*. It has been published in 1969 in *Revue Roumaine de Mathématiques Pures et Appliquées*, but it had been presented one year before, in an international linguistics conference held in Stockholm, Sweden.

The paper itself has ten pages, while a Google Academic search of it returned (on September 3, 2017) 321 web pages, with 275 citations of the version presented at the Stockholm conference. There probably were published more than 400 papers on contextual grammars, and one or two dozens of PhD and master theses were presented; there are two monographs on contextual grammars, one published by the Publishing House of the Romanian Academy, Bucharest, 1982 (in Romanian), and one by Kluwer Publishing, The Netherlands, in 1997 (*Marcus Contextual Grammars*), both of them authored by Gh. Păun. In the second volume of the massive *Handbook of Formal Languages*, Springer-Verlag, 1997 (3 volumes), edited by Grzegorz Rozenberg and Arto Salomaa, there are two chapters dedicated to this topic, one by Solomon Marcus, *Contextual grammars and natural languages*, which discusses motivations of and developments in this area, and a technical chapter, *Contextual grammars and formal languages*, by Andrzej Ehrenfeucht, Gh. Păun, and Grzegorz Rozenberg.

The basic idea is simple, with the origins in the algebraic linguistics: with respect to a natural language L (over an alphabet V), with every word w over V one associates a set of contexts $\langle u, v \rangle$ over V which *accept w* with respect to L (that is, $uwv \in L$). Can we use this phenomenon, of *selecting words by contexts* (one can also conversely state it), in order to describe a language? The answer is initially given in the form of *simple contextual grammars*, triples of the form $G = (V, A, C)$, where V is an alphabet, A is a finite language over V (its elements are called *axioms*), and C is a finite set of *contexts* over V. Such a grammar generates a language $L(G)$ which contains (1) all axioms in A and (2) all strings obtained from axioms by adjoining contexts to them. More formally, $L(G)$ contains all strings of the form $u_n \ldots u_1 x v_1 \ldots v_n$, where $x \in A$ and $\langle u_i, v_i \rangle \in C$ for all $1 \le i \le n$, with $n \ge 0$; for $n = 0$ the string is an axiom from A.

This is a simple model, not having a very large generative capacity. Moreover, it does not take into consideration the string-contexts selectivity mentioned above. However, in the end of the paper, Marcus also proposes the *contextual grammars with choice*, of the form $G = (V, A, C, \varphi)$, where $\varphi : V^* \to 2^C$ is the *selection mapping* (of contexts by the strings). This time, a string is in $L(G)$ if and only if it is of the form $u_n \ldots u_1 x v_1 \ldots v_n$ as above, but with $\langle u_1, v_1 \rangle \in \varphi(x)$ and $\langle u_i, v_i \rangle \in \varphi(u_{i-1} \ldots u_1 x v_1 \ldots u_{i-1})$ for all $i = 2, \ldots, n$.

A large research program starts from here, following the usual questions of formal language theory: variants (extensions and restrictions), characterisations, generative power, comparisons of the obtained families among them and with the known families of languages, especially with those in the Chomsky hierarchy, a reference hierarchy in formal language theory, closure and decidability properties, parsing complexity, equivalent automata, etc.

An important detail, which makes so attractive the Marcus contextual grammars is the fact that they are not using, like the Chomsky grammars, *nonterminal symbols*, categorial auxiliary symbols, they are *intrinsic grammars*; each string derived belongs to the generated language. (Of course, there were introduced also versions of contextual grammars which use auxiliary symbols which are removed in the end of derivations, but they are not central to this research area.)

Still, there is an embarrassing restriction in the initial model, the possibility to adjoin contexts only in the ends of the current string. A real breakthrough was proposed in the end of the seventies, when the Vietnamese Nguyen Xuan My came to Romania in order to start a PhD program with professor Solomon Marcus. In a joint paper Nguyen–Păun, we have introduced the *inner contextual grammars*, where the contexts can be added in any place inside the current string, under the control of the selection mapping. In this way, the generative capacity is significantly increased, the flexibility (hence the adequacy) of the model is accordingly augmented, hence one can hope that the new model can cover certain special constructions in natural languages (such as the multiple agreement, the crossed agreements, the reduplication) which the context-free Chomsky grammars, hence the regular grammars, too, cannot model.

Another important advance in this area was made at the beginning of the nineties when Grzegorz Rozenberg, Arto Salomaa, Andrzej Ehrenfeucht became interested in contextual grammars. Details can be found in the Kluwer monograph mentioned before and in the two chapters from the *Handbook of Formal Languages*.

The progresses were rather rapid. Certain classes of contextual grammars were proved to be relevant for the modelling of typical constructions in natural languages, classes of contextual grammars were introduced which are *mildly context sensitive* (parsable in polynomial time and containing strings whose lengths are not making large jumps — sometimes one asks only that the language is semilinear), in the sense requested by linguists (A.K. Joshi and others). In this way, the impressive bibliography we mentioned above has been accumulated. And this bibliography is still growing: a paper presented at *Automata and Formal Languages* conference, held in Debrecen, Hungary, in September 2017 (*On h-lexicalized restarting automata*, by Martin Platek, Praga, The Czech Republic, and Friedrich Otto, Kassel, Germany), cites and uses the Marcus contextual grammars.

11.6   Applications of formal language theory

In the second class of computer science papers by Solomon Marcus we have included the papers which are dealing with applications of grammars and automata. The application domains are very diverse: natural and programming languages, the semiotics of folklore fairy tales, the modelling of economic processes, diplomatic negotiations, the medical diagnosis, the semiotics of theatre, action theory, learning theory — with a special emphasis deserving the series of papers written in collaboration with acad. Alexandru Balaban and the student at that time Mariana Barasch, of applications in chemistry. Various isoprenoid structures are modelled by means of picture grammars, the research ending with Fortran programs of a direct applicability.

These applications should be placed in a more general framework, under the slogan *linguistics as a pilot-science*, a slogan originated by Claude Levi-Strauss, taken over, extended and transformed by Solomon Marcus in a real research program for the Romanian school of mathematical linguistics and formal language theory led by him. The initial formulation was specified and up-dated to *the formal linguistics as a pilot-science*. In his chapter *Formal languages: foundations, prehistory, sources, and applications* from the volume *Formal Languages and Applications* (Springer-Verlag, 2004, C. Martín-Vide, V. Mitrana, Gh. Păun, eds.), Solomon Marcus explains: "The pattern called formal language has all features of a universal paradigm: it expresses a biological reality, the sequential structure of processes under the privilege of the left hemisphere of the brain; equally sequential are the basic life processes related to DNA, RNA and proteins; moreover, as it was proved in a lot of papers by various authors, strings on a given alphabet occur in the mathematical modelling of some basic operations in logic, combinatorics, quantum physics, organic chemistry, cellular biology, computer programming languages, linguistics (mainly computational linguistics), anthropology of kinship relations, medical diagnosis, tennis game, international relations, musical composition, painting, architecture, poetics, theatrical plays, narrativity, etc." Actually, many other areas of application of formal language theory are discussed in professor Marcus papers, with the starting point placed in a more general approach, of Maria Nowakowska, the author of the book *Languages of Action, Languages of Motivations*, Mouton, Hague-Paris, 1973.

11.7 Bio-informatics

The paper from 1974, *Linguistic structures and generative devices in molecular genetics*, remained for a while isolated, although it is obvious that Solomon Marcus was continuously interested in the possibility to use linguistical instruments in the cellular biology area, in genomics and life sciences. A proof of this interest is the fact that, after the apparition of DNA computing, in 1994, and especially after the initiation of membrane computing, in 1998, he had a series of contributions to these areas, for instance, participating in several international meetings with these subjects, in Romania and abroad.

The inter-disciplinary approach is typical to Marcus — explicit already from the title of many papers. Only two are mentioned here, *Membranes versus DNA* and *Bridging P systems and genomics*, presented at the first meetings devoted to membrane computing (Curtea de Argeş, Romania, 2001, 2002), with the mention that, to a certain extent, the name itself of the domain, *Membrane Computing*, was influenced by professor Marcus, through his plea for the role of membranes in the life of the cell, with details coming from bio-semiotics. A slogan proposed by Marcus in 2002, "Life = DNA software + membrane software", sometimes reformulated in the form "Life = DNA software + membrane hardware", became folklore in this research area.

Grounded on his skills and habit of formulating open problems and research topics, also in bio-informatics there still exist several questions raised by Solomon Marcus which were not answered yet. Here are two significant examples from the membrane computing area: to consider membranes with a topology different from the usually used topology (vesicle-like membranes), where the separation between *inside* and *outside* is crisp (for instance, to consider membranes similar to the *Klein bottle*), and, respectively, to consider multisets of objects described by rough sets in the sense of Pawlak.

11.8 Recursive functions

The last category of computer science papers by Solomon Marcus considered here is that of papers dealing with recursive functions. There are four papers of this type, dedicated to a priority of the Romanian mathematics, clarified by professor Solomon Marcus in collaboration with Cristian Calude and Ionel Ţevy: the first example of a recursive function which is not primitive recursive was provided by Gabriel Sudan, not by Wilhelm Ackermann as believed before (both of them were students of David Hilbert, and, after the intervention of Marcus-Calude-Ţevi, both of them are considered to have simultaneously discovered such a function).

It is important to remind the fact that professor Solomon Marcus was constantly concerned with adequately evaluating the history of the Romanian mathematics. Pointing out the priorities in this area was already one of the main goals of his well known book *Din gândirea matematică românească — From the Romanian Mathematical Thinking*, The Scientific and Encyclopaedic Publishing House, Bucharest, 1975. Furthermore, he has edited the mathematical papers of several Romanian classic mathematicians: Dimitrie Pompeiu, Miron Nicolescu, Gr. C. Moisil, Alexandru Froda, Traian Lalescu.

11.9 Final remarks

While a clearly cut classification of computer science papers of Solomon Marcus is impossible, the same can be said about a time arrangement of his computer science interests and research, including both the theory and the applications. As we have seen, the topics addressed and the tools used in approaching them were systematically interleaved — enriching simultaneously each research direction.

However, what is specific to all papers by Solomon Marcus is the *style*: very careful with all details, accurate and rich references, honesty, constantly having in mind the reader (for instance, by specifying all basic notation and terminology), refined and lucid comments, a model of motivating the issues dealt with, the pleasure and the knowledge of formulating good research topics.

It is also impressive the large number of collaborators, from many countries, a consequence of the richness of ideas, of open problems, but also of his pleasure and skill of communicating, of interacting with the people around.

A high level professor, *contagious*, with many researchers — from Romania to far-away countries, like Japan and Canada — who consider themselves his disciples, Solomon Marcus not only has introduced a special "order of magnitude" in the Romanian mathematics, by means of his productivity and the recognition of his work (citations, followers), but he is also imposing a new order of magnitude in what concerns the durability of his creation. For computer scientists, the two volumes of the book *Solomon Marcus: Selected Papers — Computer Science* published by

Spandugino Publ. House, Bucharest, Romania, 2018, are a proof of this fact and a challenge — to read, reread and continue him.

Solomon Marcus — Computer Science Papers

Formal Language Theory

(1) S. Marcus. Automates finis, progressions arithmétiques et grammaires à un nombre fini d'états. *Comptes rendus de l'Académie des Sciences Paris*, 256, 17 (1963), 3571–3574.

(2) S. Marcus. Sur un modéle de H. B. Curry pour le langage mathématique. *Comptes rendus de l'Académie des Sciences Paris*, 258, 7 (1964), 1954–1956.

(3) S. Marcus. Sur les grammaires à un nombre fini d'états. *Cahiers de Linguistique Théorique et Appliquée*, 2 (1965), 146–164.

(4) S. Marcus. Analytique et génératif dans la linguistique algébrique. In *To Honor Roman Jakobson II*, Mouton, The Hague, 1967, 1252–1261.

(5) S. Marcus. Contextual grammars. *Revue Roumaine de Mathématiques Pures et Appliquées*, 14, 10 (1969), 1525–1534; also, Preprint nr. 48, Intern. Conf. Comput. Ling., Stockholm, 1968.

(6) S. Marcus. Deux types nouveaux de grammaires génératives. *Cahiers de Linguistique Théorique et Appliquées*, 6 (1969), 67–74.

(7) S. Marcus. Darboux property and formal languages. *Revue Roumaine de Mathématiques Pures et Appliquées*, 22, 10 (1977), 1449–1451.

(8) S. Marcus. Problems. *Bulletin of the European Association for Theoretical Computer Science*, 27 (1985), 245.

(9) S. Marcus. Formal languages before Axel Thue? *Bulletin of the European Association for Theoretical Computer Science*, 34 (1988), 62.

(10) S. Marcus. From the history of formal languages (in Romanian). *The Second National Colloquium on Languages, Logic and Mathematical Linguistics*, Braşov, June 1888, 1–9.

(11) S. Marcus, Gh. Păun. Langford strings, formal languages and contextual ambiguity, *Intern. J. Computer Math.*, 26, 3 + 4 (1989), 179–191.

(12) L. Kari, S. Marcus, Gh. Păun, A. Salomaa. In the prehistory of formal languages: Gauss languages. *Bulletin EATCS*, 46 (1992), 124–139.

(13) S. Marcus. Fivefold symmetry: a generative approach. In *Caiet de Semiotică*. Univ. Timişoara, 9 (1992), 1–23.

(14) S. Marcus. Thirty-six years ago. The beginning of the formal language theory. In *Salodays in Theoretical Computer Science*, May 1992 (A. Atanasiu, C.S. Calude, eds.), Univ. Hyperion, Bucharest, 1993.

(15) S. Marcus. Symbols in a multidimensional space. In *SEMIOTICS 1990* (K. Haworth, J. Deely, T. Prewitt, eds.) with *SYMBOLICITY* (J. Bernard, J. Deely, V. Voigt, G. Withalm, eds.), The Semiotic Soc. of America, 1993, 115–126.

(16) J. Dassow, S. Marcus, Gh. Păun. Iterated reading of numbers and "black-holes". *Periodica Mathematica Hungarica*, 27, 2 (1993), 137–152.

(17) J. Dassow, S. Marcus, Gh. Păun. Iterative reading of numbers; Parikh mappings, parallel rewriting, infinite sequences. *Preprint of. Tech. Univ. Otto von Guericke Univ., Magdeburg*, July 1993, 18 pp.

(18) J. Dassow, S. Marcus, Gh. Păun. Iterative reading of numbers: the ordered case. In *Developments in Language Theory. At the Crossroad of Mathematics, Computer Science and Biology* (G. Rozenberg, A. Salomaa, eds.), World Sci. Publ., Singapore, 1994, 157–168.

(19) S. Marcus, Gh. Păun. On symmetry in languages. *Intern. J. Computer Math.*, 52, 1/2 (1994), 1–15.

(20) S. Marcus, Gh. Păun. Infinite words and their associated formal languages. In *Salodays in Auckland* (C. Calude, M. J. J. Lennon, H. Maurer, eds.), Auckland Univ. Press, 1994, 95–99.

(21) S. Marcus, Al. Mateescu, Gh. Păun, A. Salomaa. On symmetry in strings, sequences and languages. *Intern. J. Computer Math.*, 54, 1/2 (1994), 1–13.

(22) S. Marcus, Gh. Păun. Infinite (almost periodic) words, formal languages, and dynamical systems. *Bulletin EATCS*, 54 (1994), 224–231.

(23) S. Marcus, C. Martin-Vide, Gh. Păun. On the power of internal contextual grammars with maximal use of selectors. *Conf. Automata and Formal Languages*, Salgotarjan, 1996, *Publicationes Mathematicae, Debrecen*, 54 (1999), 933–947.

(24) M. Kudlek, S. Marcus, A. Mateescu. Contextual grammars with distributed catenation and shuffle. *Found. of Computation Theory,*

FCT, LNCS 1279 (B.S. Chlebus, L. Czeja, eds.), Springer, Berlin, 1997, 269–280.

(25) J. Dassow, S. Marcus, Gh. Păun. Convex and anti-convex languages. *Intern. J. Computer Math.*, 69, 1-2 (1998), 1–16.

(26) S. Marcus. On the length of words. In *Jewels are Forever. Contributions on Theoretical Computer Science in Honor of Arto Salomaa* (J. Karhumaki, H. Maurer, Gh. Păun, G. Rozenberg, eds.), Springer, Berlin, 1999, 194–203.

(27) S. Marcus. From real analysis to discrete mathematics and back: symmetry, convexity, almost periodicity and strange attractors. *Real Analysis Exchange*, 25, 1 (1999-2000), 125–128.

(28) S. Marcus. Pseudo-slender languages and their infinite hierarchy. *Ninth Intern. Conf. Automata and Formal Languages*, Vasscecseny, Hungary, August 1999, 1-2.

(29) S. Marcus, C. Martin-Vide, V. Mitrana, Gh. Păun. A new–old class of linguistically motivated regulated grammars. *Computational Linguistics in the Netherlands, 2000*, Rodopi, New York, 2001, 111–125.

(30) S. Marcus. Bridging two hierarchies of infinite words. *Journal of Universal Computer Sci.*, 8, 2 (2002), 292–296.

(31) S. Marcus. Quasiperiodic infinite words. *Bulletin EATCS*, 82 (2004), 170–174.

(32) L. Ilie, S. Marcus, I. Petre. Periodic and Sturmian languages. *Information Processing Letters*, 98, 6 (2006), 242–246.

(33) S. Marcus. Mild context-sensitivity, after twenty years. *Fundamenta Informaticae*, 73, 1/2 (2006), 203–204.

(34) T. Monteil, S. Marcus. Quasiperiodic words: multi-scale case and dynamical properties. https://arxiv.org/abs/math/0603354, March 2006.

(35) P. Dömösi, M. Ito, S. Marcus. Marcus contextual languages consisting of primitive words. *Discrete Mathematics*, 308 (2008), 4877–4881.

Applications of Formal Languages

(1) S. Marcus. Linguistique générative, modèles analytiques et linguistique générale. *Revue Roumaine de Linguistique*, 14, 4 (1969), 313–326.

(2) S. Fotino, S. Marcus. The Grammar of Fairy Tales (in Romanian) (I). *Revista de Etnografie şi Folclor*, 18, 4 (1973), 255–277.

(3) S. Fotino, S. Marcus. The Grammar of Fairy Tales (in Romanian) (II). *Revista de Etnografie şi Folclor*, 18, 5 (1973), 349–363.

(4) E. Celan, S. Marcus. Le diagnostique comme langage (I). *Cahiers de Linguistique Théorique et Appliquée*, 10, 2 (1973), 163–173.

(5) S. Marcus. Linguistics as a pilot science. In *Current Trends in Linguistics* (Th. Sebeok, ed.), Mouton, The Hague, 1974, 2871–2887, also in *Studii şi cercetări lingvistice*, 20, 3 (1969), 235–245.

(6) S. Marcus. Applications de la théorie des langages formels en économie et organisation, *Cahiers de Linguistique Théorique et Appliquée*, 13, 2 (1976), 583–594. Also published in *Annales de la Faculté des sciences de l'Université Nationale de Zaïre*, Kinshasa, vol. 3, 1977, nr. 1, p. 125–147

(7) S. Marcus. Languages, grammars and negotiations. Some suggestions. In *Mathematical Approaches to International Relations* (M. Bunge, J. Galtung, M. Maliţa, eds.), vol. 2, Romanian Acad. of Social and Political Sci., Bucharest, 1977, 378–385.

(8) S. Marcus. A new generative approach to fairy-tales. *Ethnologica*, annexe à la publication *Recherches sur l'histoire comparative des constitutions et du droit*, Bucharest, 1978, 14–17.

(9) S. Marcus. Linguistics for programming languages. *Revue Roumaine de Linguistique. Cahiers de Linguistique Théorique et Appliquée*, 16, 1 (1970), 29–39.

(10) S. Marcus. Linguistics and logic (in Romanian). *Studii şi cercetări lingvistice*, 30, 3 (1979), 247–249.

(11) Al. Balaban, M. Barasch, S. Marcus. Computer programs for the recognition of acyclic regular isoprenoid structures. *MATCH - Mathematical Chemistry*, 5 (1979), 239–261.

(12) S. Marcus. Learning, as a generative process. *Revue Roumaine de Linguistique*, 24 (1979), *Cahiers de Linguistique Théorique et Appliquée*, 16, 2 (1979), 117–130.

(13) S. Marcus. Semiotics of theatre: a mathematical linguistic approach, *Revue roumaine de linguistique*, 25, 3 (1980), 161–189.

(14) Al. Balaban, M. Barasch, S. Marcus. Picture grammars in Chemistry. Generation of acyclic isoprenoid structures. *MATCH - Mathematical Chemistry*, 8 (1980), 193–213.

(15) Al. Balaban, M. Barasch, S. Marcus. Computer program for the recognition of standard isoprenoid structures. *MATCH - Mathematical Chemistry*, 8 (1980), 215–268.

(16) Al. Balaban, M. Barasch, S. Marcus. Codification of acyclic isoprenoid structures using context-free grammars and pushdown automata. *MATCH – Mathematical Chemistry*, 12 (1981), 25–64.

(17) S. Marcus. La lecture générative. *Degrés*, 28 (1981), 61–66.

(18) S. Marcus. Natural languages and artificial languages (in Romanian). *The First National Colloquium on Languages, Logic and
Mathematical Linguistics*, Braşov, June 1986, 1–18.

(19) S. Marcus. Interplay of innate and acquired in some mathematical
models of language learning. *Revue Roumaine de Linguistique*, 34,
2 (1989), 101–116.

(20) S. Marcus. Semiotics and formal artificial languages. In *En-
cyclopaedia of Computer Science and Technology* (A. Kent, J.G.
Williams, eds.), vol. 29, Marcel Dekker Inc., New York, 1994, 393–
405.

(21) S. Marcus, C. Martin-Vide, Gh. Păun. Contextual grammars versus natural languages. *Speech and Computers Conf., SPECOM 96*,
St. Petersburg, 1996, 28–33.

(22) S. Marcus. Contextual grammars and natural languages. In *Handbook of Formal Languages* (G. Rozenberg, A. Salomaa, eds.), vol.
II, Springer, Berlin, 1997, 215–235.

(23) S. Marcus, C. Martin-Vide, Gh. Păun. Contextual grammars as
generative models of natural languages. *Fourth Meeting on Mathematics of Language, MOL 4*, Philadelphia, 1995, *Computational
Linguistics*, 24, 2 (1998), 245–274.

(24) S. Marcus. Linguistic and semiotic preliminaries of contextual lan-
guages. *Math. and Comput. Analysis of Natural Languages. Proc.
Second Intern. Conf. on Math. Linguistics* (C. Martin-Vide, ed.),
Tarragona, 1996, John Benjamins, Amsterdam, 1998, 47–57.

(25) S. Marcus. Contextual grammars, learning processes and the
Kolmogorov-Chaitin metaphor. *Math. Found. Computer
Sci. Workshop on Mathematical Linguistics*, Brno, August 1998,
Bericht 213, Univ. Hamburg, July 1998, 1–12.

(26) S. Marcus. Reading numbers as a metaphor of the universe.
In *BRIDGES - Math. Connections in Art, Music and Science*,
Southwestern College, Winfield, Kansas, 1999 (R. Sarhangi, ed.),
Gilliland Printing, Maryland, 1999, 302.

(27) S. Marcus. History as text: Xenopol's series between structuralism
and generative formal grammars. *Romanian J. Information Sci.
and Technology*, 5, 1-2 (2002), 5–8.

(28) S. Marcus. Formal languages: Foundations, prehistory, sources, and applications. In *Formal Languages and Applications* (C. Martín-Vide, V. Mitrana, Gh. Păun, eds.), Springer, Berlin, 2004, 11–53.

Bio-informatics

(1) S. Marcus. Linguistic structures and generative devices in molecular genetics. *Cahiers de Linguistique Théorique et Appliquée*, 11, 1 (1974), 77–104.

(2) C. Calude, S. Marcus, Gh. Păun. The universal grammar as a hypothetical brain. *Revue Roumaine de Linguistique*, 24, 5 (1979), 479–489.

(3) S. Marcus. Hidden grammars. In *Developments in Language Theory* (G. Rozenberg, A. Salomaa, eds.), World Sci. Publ., Singapore, 1994, 453–460.

(4) S. Marcus. Language, at the crossroad of computation and biology. In *Computing with Biomolecules. Theory and Experiments* (Gh. Păun, ed.), Springer, Singapore, 1998, 1–34.

(5) S. Marcus. Bags and beyond them. *Pre-Proceedings. Workshop on Multiset Processing*, Curtea de Argeş, Romania, 21-25 August 2000, Report CDMTCS-140, C. S. Calude, M. J. Dinneen, Gh. Păun, eds., 191–192.

(6) S. Marcus. Tolerance multisets. In *Multiset Processing. Mathematical, Computer Science and Molecular Computing Points of View* (C. S. Calude, Gh. Păun, G. Rozenberg, A. Salomaa, eds.), LNCS 2235, Springer, Berlin, 2001, 217–223.

(7) S. Marcus. Membranes versus DNA. *Pre-Proceedings. Workshop on Membrane Computing* (WMC-CdA 2001) (C. Martin-Vide, Gh. Păun, eds.), Rovira i Virgili Univ., Tarragona, Spain, 2001, 193–198, and *Fundamenta Informaticae*, 49, 1-3 (2002), 223–227.

(8) S. Marcus. Bridging P systems and genomics. In *Membrane Computing. International Workshop, WMC-CdeA 2002, Curtea de Argeş, Romania, August 2002, Revised Papers* (Gh. Păun, G. Rozenberg, A. Salomaa, C. Zandron, eds.), LNCS 2597, Springer, Berlin, 2003, 371–376.

(9) S. Marcus. Symmetry phenomena in infinite words, with biological, philosophical and aesthetic relevance. *Symmetry: Culture and Science*, 14/15 (2003-2004), 477–487.

(10) S. Marcus. The duality of patterning in molecular genetics. In *Aspects of Molecular Computing. Essays Dedicated to Tom Head on the Occasion of His 70th Birthday* (N. Jonoska, Gh. Păun, eds.), LNCS 2950, Springer, Berlin, 2004, 318–321.

(11) S. Marcus. Z. Pawlak, a precursor of DNA computing and of picture grammars. *Fundamenta Informaticae*, 75, 1/4 (2007), 331–334.

(12) G. Ciobanu, S. Marcus, Gh. Păun. New strategies of using the rules of a P system in a maximal way. Power and complexity. *Romanian J. Information Sci. and Technology*, 12, 2 (2009), 157–173.

(13) S. Marcus. The biological cell in spectacle. In *Membrane Computing. 10th Intern. Workshop, WMC 2009, Curtea de Argeş, Romania, August 2009, Revised Selected and Invited Papers* (Gh. Păun, M. J. Pérez-Jiménez, A. Riscos-Núñez, G. Rozenberg, A. Salomaa, eds.), LNCS 5957, Springer, Berlin, 2010, 95–103.

(14) S. Istrail, S. Marcus. Alan Turing and John von Neumann – Their Brains and Their Computers. *Membrane Computing, 13th Intern. Conf., Budapest, August 2012, Revised Selected Papers* (E. Csuhaj-Varjú, M. Gheorghe, G. Rozenberg, A. Salomaa, G. Vaszil, eds.), LNCS 7762, Springer, Berlin, 2013, 26–35.

Recursive Functions

(1) C. Calude, S. Marcus, I. Ţevy. Sur les fonctions récursives qui ne sont pas récursives primitives. *Revue Roumaine des Sciences Sociales*, Série de Philosophie et Logique, 19, 3 (1975), 185–188.

(2) C. Calude, S. Marcus, I. Ţevy. The first example of a recursive function which is not primitive recursive. *Historia Mathematica*, 6 (1979), 380–384.

(3) C. Calude, S. Marcus, I. Ţevy. Recursive properties of Sudan function, *Revue Roum. Math. Pures Appl.*, 25, 4 (1980), 503–507.

(4) C. Calude, S. Marcus. Sudan's recursive but not primitive recursive function: a retrospective look. *Analele Universităţii din Bucureşti, Matematică-Informatică*, 38, 2 (1989), 25–30.

Chapter 12

Entanglement through Path Identification

Karl Svozil

Institute for Theoretical Physics, Vienna University of Technology
Wiedner Hauptstraße 8-10/136, A-1040 Vienna, Austria

svozil@tuwien.ac.at

Abstract. Entanglement in multipartite systems can be achieved by the coherent superposition of product states, generated through a universal unitary transformation, followed by spontaneous parametric down-conversions and path identification. Pure entangled multipartite states are always a unitary transformation away from non-entangled states with complete value definiteness of the individual parts; and *vice versa*.

From a formal point of view, an arbitrary pure (we shall not consider mixed states as we consider them epistemic) state of N particles with dichotomic properties 0, 1 can be written as the coherent superposition

$$|\Psi\rangle = \sum_{i_1,\ldots,i_N=0}^{1} \alpha_{i_1,\ldots,i_N} |i_1,\ldots,i_N\rangle \text{ with}$$

$$\sum_{i_1,\ldots,i_N=0}^{1} |\alpha_{i_1,\ldots,i_N}|^2 = 1 \tag{12.1}$$

of all product states $|i_1,\ldots,i_N\rangle = |i_1\rangle \cdots |i_N\rangle$ of single-particle basis states $|i_j\rangle$, with $i_j \in \{0,1\}$ and $1 \le j \le N$. One possible direct physical implementation of this formula requires (i) a universal (with respect to the unitary group) transformation rendering the coefficients $\alpha_{i_1,\ldots,i_N}$; followed by (ii) spontaneous parametric down-conversions producing the product states whose outputs are properly integrated and identified in a third phase (iii).

In what follows we shall use Fock states (notwithstanding issues such as localization [6, p. 931]) having definite occupation numbers of the quantized field modes. For such states the unitary quantum evolution on elementary quantum optical components can be represented by elementary transition rules, reflecting unitary transformations [2,20]: a symmetrical beam splitter is represented by $|in\rangle \xrightarrow{50:50 \text{ BS}} \frac{1}{\sqrt{2}} (|transit\rangle + i|reflect\rangle)$; and an asymmetrical beam splitter by $|in\rangle \xrightarrow{BS} T|transit\rangle + iR|reflect\rangle$, with $|T|^2 + |R|^2 = 1$. Phase shift(er)s are represented by $|in\rangle \xrightarrow{\varphi \text{ ps}} e^{i\varphi}|in\rangle$, and spontaneous parametric down-conversions by $|in\rangle \xrightarrow{NL} \eta|out1\rangle|out2\rangle = \eta|out1\,out2\rangle$ for supposedly small η.

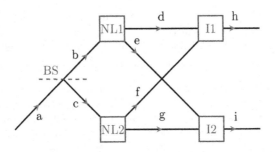

Fig. 12.1 An interferometric experiment involving an incident beam, a beam splitter, and two spontaneous parametric down-conversion crystals.

For the sake of a demonstration, consider an arrangement depicted in Fig. 12.1. It consists of a single particle source producing a state $|a\rangle$ impinging on a symmetrical beam splitter BS whose output ports are identified with the states $|b\rangle$ for transiting $|a\rangle$, and $|c\rangle$ for reflected $|a\rangle$, respectively. Those states are then subjected to two spontaneous parametric down-conversion crystals NL1 and NL2, producing product pairs $|de\rangle$ and $|fg\rangle$, respectively. "Adjacent" beam pairs d–f as well as e–g are then integrated and identified a states $|h\rangle$ and $|i\rangle$, respectively. The aforementioned substitution rules yield

$$|a\rangle \xrightarrow{50:50 \text{ BS}} \frac{1}{\sqrt{2}} (|b\rangle + i|c\rangle) \xrightarrow{NL1, NL2} \frac{\eta}{\sqrt{2}} (|de\rangle + i|fg\rangle). \qquad (12.2)$$

Note that an additional phase shift of $\varphi = \frac{\pi}{2}$ applied to $|c\rangle$, with the identification $d = g = 0$ and $e = f = 1$, would have resulted in the traditional singlet state $|\Psi^-\rangle = \frac{1}{\sqrt{2}} (|01\rangle - |10\rangle)$ of the Bell basis.

The final phase of this experiment is depicted in Fig. 12.1 by the addition of "integrators" I1 and I2 which combine or collimate ingoing ports into a single port. All that is needed is a parametric down-conversion crystal which outputs with certainty the respective states $|01\rangle$ on NL1 and $|10\rangle$ on NL2.

In order to fully realize Eq. (12.1), universal unitary transformations in finite-dimensional Hilbert space need to be operationalized. One conceivable way of doing this is through generalized beam splitters [11], which is based upon the parameterization of the unitary group [9]. Figure 12.2 depicts this configuration for two dichotomic (two possible states per quantum) quanta. A generalization to an arbitrary number of quanta, as well as an arbitrary number of states per quanta can be given along very similar lines.

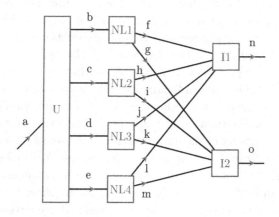

Fig. 12.2   General two-particle state generation.

Let me finally address the question why, even if granted that this might be a novel way of looking at and producing multipartite states (I am quite confident that similar schemes might have been proposed in one way or another before, but I am unaware and thus less than sure about these), one should need yet another scheme. After all, higher-dimensional two-particle entanglements can be realized in principle solely via multiport beam splitters [24]; without some additional final steps involving spontaneous parametric down-conversion and integration. (This conforms to the interpretation of the Clauser-Horne-Shimony-Holt expression as a single operator which can be subjected to min-max considerations [1].) It should also be mentioned that a recent proposal [4], based on an intriguing experiment [18, 23] upon a suggestion of Ou [10], uses path identification as a resource to produce multipartite states.

One good motivation for the aforementioned contemplations might be that the "production" of entanglement in these configurations might yield fresh ways to perceive or "understand" this quantum feature. As expressed by Bennett [3] in quantum physics the possibility exists *"that you have a complete knowledge of the whole without knowing the state of any one part. That a thing can be in a definite state, even though its parts were not. ... It's not a complicated idea but it's an idea that nobody would ever think of."* Bennett, if I interpret him correctly, is referring to Schrödinger's 1935 & 1936 series of papers; both in German [12, 17] and English [13, 14]. Therein Schrödinger has pointed out that the quantum state of multiple particles may evolve in such ways that, say, the initial definiteness of the states of the individual independent constituents without any relational properties among themselves gets re-encoded into purely relational properties among the particles [7, 19, 21, 22], thereby "erasing" the definiteness of the individual particle properties. One may also say that the multipartite state is "breathing in and out of" individuality and entanglement [16].

The formal expression for this is a sort of zero-sum game with respect to knowledge or information encoded by the quantum state: due to the permutative character of the unitary (one-to-one isometry) state evolution, no information is ever lost or gained; that is, any loss of individual definiteness "on" the individual constituents has to be compensated by a gain through "sampling" of their independence; to the effect that they are no longer independent but possess definite relational properties. Conversely, any "scrambling" of these relational properties needs to be (due to the impossibility to "loose" information) compensated by a gain of individual definitiveness.

For the sake of a concrete demonstration discussed by Mermin [8, Section 1.5], consider a general state in 4-dimensional Hilbert space. It can be written as a vector in C^4 which can be parameterized by (T means transposition) $(\alpha_1, \alpha_2, \alpha_3, \alpha_4)^T$, with $\alpha_1, \alpha_3, \alpha_3, \alpha_4 \in C,$. Suppose (wrongly) that all such states can be written in terms of a tensor product $(a_1, a_2)^T \otimes (b_1, b_2)^T \equiv (a_1 b_1, a_1 b_2, a_2 b_1, a_2 b_2)^T$ of two individual particle states corresponding to vectors in C^2, with $a_1, a_2, b_1, b_2 \in C$. A comparison of the coordinates yields $\alpha_1 = a_1 b_1$, $\alpha_2 = a_1 b_2$, $\alpha_3 = a_2 b_1$, and $\alpha_4 = a_2 b_2$. By taking the quotient of the two first and the two last equations, and by equating these quotients, one obtains $\frac{\alpha_1}{\alpha_2} = \frac{b_1}{b_2} = \frac{\alpha_3}{\alpha_4}$, and thus $\alpha_1\alpha_4 = \alpha_2\alpha_3$.

How can this be interpreted? As in many cases, states in the Bell basis, and, in particular, the Bell state, serve as a sort of *Rosetta Stone* for an understanding of this quantum feature. The Bell state $|\Psi^-\rangle$ is a typical example of an entangled state; or, more generally, states in the *Bell basis* can be defined and, with $|0\rangle = (1,0)^T$ and $|1\rangle = (0,1)^T$ encoded by

$$|\Psi^{\mp}\rangle = \frac{1}{\sqrt{2}}(|01\rangle \mp |10\rangle) = (0,1,\mp 1,0)^T,$$
$$|\Phi^{\mp}\rangle = \frac{1}{\sqrt{2}}(|00\rangle \mp |11\rangle) = (1,0,0,\mp 1)^T. \tag{12.3}$$

For instance, in the case of $|\Psi^-\rangle$ a comparison of coefficient yields

$$\alpha_1 = a_1b_1 = 0, \quad \alpha_2 = a_1b_2 = \frac{1}{\sqrt{2}},$$
$$\alpha_3 = a_2b_1 - \frac{1}{\sqrt{2}}, \quad \alpha_4 = a_2b_2 = 0; \tag{12.4}$$

and thus entanglement, since

$$\alpha_1\alpha_4 = 0 \neq \alpha_2\alpha_3 = \frac{1}{2}. \tag{12.5}$$

This shows that $|\Psi^-\rangle$ cannot be considered as a two particle product state. Indeed, the state can only be characterized by considering the *relative properties* of the two particles – in the case of $|\Psi^-\rangle$ they are associated with the statements [22]: "the quantum numbers (in this case "0" and "1") of the two particles are different in (at least) two (orthogonal) directions."

The Bell basis symbolizing entanglement and non-individuality can, in an *ad hoc* manner, be generated from a non-entangled, individual state: suppose such a state is represented by elements of the Cartesian standard basis in 4-dimensional real space R^4, representable as column vectors whose components are $(|\mathbf{e}_i\rangle)_j = \delta_{ij}$, with $1 \leq i,j \leq 4$. Suppose further that the coordinates of the Bell basis (12.3) are arranged as row or column vectors, thereby forming the respective unitary transformation

$$\mathbf{U} = |\Psi^-\rangle\langle \mathbf{e}_1| + |\Psi^+\rangle\langle \mathbf{e}_2| + |\Phi^-\rangle\langle \mathbf{e}_3| + |\Phi^+\rangle\langle \mathbf{e}_4| =$$

$$= (|\Psi^-\rangle, |\Psi^+\rangle, |\Phi^-\rangle, |\Phi^+\rangle) = \frac{1}{\sqrt{2}}\begin{pmatrix} 0 & 0 & 1 & 1 \\ 1 & 1 & 0 & 0 \\ -1 & 1 & 0 & 0 \\ 0 & 0 & -1 & 1 \end{pmatrix}. \tag{12.6}$$

Then successive application of $\mathbf{U}$ and its inverse $\mathbf{U}^T$ transforms an individual, non-entangled state from the Cartesian basis back and forth into an entangled, non-individual state from the Bell basis. For the sake of another demonstration, consider the following perfectly cyclic evolution which permutes all (non-) entangled states corresponding to the Cartesian & Bell bases:

$$|e_1\rangle \overset{\mathsf{U}}{\mapsto} |\Psi^-\rangle \overset{\mathsf{V}}{\mapsto} |e_2\rangle \overset{\mathsf{U}}{\mapsto} |\Psi^+\rangle$$
$$\overset{\mathsf{V}}{\mapsto} |e_3\rangle \overset{\mathsf{U}}{\mapsto} |\Phi^-\rangle \overset{\mathsf{V}}{\mapsto} |e_4\rangle \overset{\mathsf{U}}{\mapsto} |\Phi^+\rangle \overset{\mathsf{V}}{\mapsto} |e_1\rangle. \tag{12.7}$$

This evolution is facilitated by $\mathbf{U}$ of Eq. (12.6), as well as by the following additional unitary transformation [15]:

$$\mathbf{V} = |e_2\rangle\langle\Psi^-| + |e_3\rangle\langle\Psi^+| + |e_4\rangle\langle\Phi^-| + |e_1\rangle\langle\Phi^+|$$

$$= \begin{pmatrix} \langle\Phi^+| \\ \langle\Psi^-| \\ \langle\Psi^+| \\ \langle\Phi^-| \end{pmatrix} = \frac{1}{\sqrt{2}} \begin{pmatrix} 1 & 0 & 0 & 1 \\ 0 & 1 & -1 & 0 \\ 0 & 1 & 1 & 0 \\ 1 & 0 & 0 & -1 \end{pmatrix}. \tag{12.8}$$

One of the ways thinking of this kind of breathing in and out of individuality & entanglement is in terms of sampling & scrambling of information, as quoted from Chiao [2, p. 27] (reprinted in [5]): *"Nothing has really been erased here, only scrambled!"* Indeed, as noted earlier, mere re-coding or "scrambling," and not erasure or creation of information, is tantamount to, and an expression and direct consequence of, the unitary evolution of the quantum state.

Let us now reconsider the configuration depicted in Fig. 12.1: it is quite obvious where the relational properties in the resulting entangled (with a proper identification) state (12.2) come from: they reside in the common origin of either the states $|d\rangle\&|e\rangle$, (exclusive) or $|f\rangle\&|g\rangle$, respectively; and in their coherent superposition rendered by the beam splitter BS. This latter beam splitter BS element "scrambles" all individuality (with respect to "which way" information about the output ports); whereas the pair production at the two spontaneous parametric down-conversion crystals is responsible for the relational — that is, joint — occurrence among the constituents.

Acknowledgments. This work was supported in part by the John Templeton Foundation's *Randomness and Providence: an Abrahamic Inquiry Project.* I thank Johann Summhammer for useful comments and suggestions.

References

[1] Filipp, S., Svozil, K.: Generalizing Tsirelson's bound on Bell in-equalities using a min-max principle. Physical Review Letters **93**, 130,407 (2004). doi:10.1103/PhysRevLett.93.130407. URL http://doi.org/10.1103/PhysRevLett.93.130407

[2] Greenberger, D.M., Horne, M.A., Zeilinger, A.: Multiparticle interferometry and the superposition principle. Physics Today **46**, 22–29 (1993). doi:10.1063/1.881360. URL http://doi.org/10.1063/1.881360

[3] IBM: Charles Bennett – a founder of quantum information theory (2016). URL https://www.youtube.com/watch?v=9q-qoeqVVD0. May 3rd, 2016, accessed July 16th, 2016

[4] Krenn, M., Hochrainer, A., Lahiri, M., Zeilinger, A.: Entanglement by path identity. Physical Review Letter **118**, 080,401 (2017). doi:10.1103/PhysRevLett.118.080401. URL http://doi.org/10.1103/PhysRevLett.118.080401

[5] Macchiavello, C., Palma, G.M., Zeilinger, A.: Quantum Computation and Quantum Information Theory. World Scientific, Singapore (2001). doi:10.1142/9789810248185. URL http://doi.org/10.1142/9789810248185

[6] Mandel, L.: Photon interference and correlation effects produced by independent quantum sources. Physical Review A **28**, 929–943 (1983). doi:10.1103/PhysRevA.28.929. URL http://doi.org/10.1103/PhysRevA.28.929

[7] Mermin, D.N.: What is quantum mechanics trying to tell us? American Journal of Physics **66**(9), 753–767 (1998). doi:10.1119/1.18955. URL http://doi.org/10.1119/1.18955

[8] Mermin, D.N.: Quantum Computer Science. Cambridge University Press, Cambridge (2007). URL http://people.ccmr.cornell.edu/~mermin/qcomp/CS483.html

[9] Murnaghan, F.D.: The Unitary and Rotation Groups, *Lectures on Applied Mathematics*, vol. 3. Spartan Books, Washington, D.C. (1962)

[10] Ou, Z.Y.J.: Multi-Photon Quantum Interference. Springer, New York, NY (2007). doi:10.1007/978-0-387-25554-5. URL http://doi.org/10.1007/978-0-387-25554-5

[11] Reck, M., Zeilinger, A., Bernstein, H.J., Bertani, P.: Experimental realization of any discrete unitary operator. Physical Review Letters **73**, 58–61 (1994). doi:10.1103/PhysRevLett.73.58. URL http://doi.org/10.1103/PhysRevLett.73.58

[12] Schrödinger, E.: Die gegenwärtige Situation in der Quantenmechanik. Naturwissenschaften **23**, 807–812, 823–828, 844–849 (1935). doi:10.1007/BF01491891,10.1007/BF01491914,10.1007/BF01491987. URL http://doi.org/10.1007/BF01491891,http://doi.org/10.1007/BF01491914,http://doi.org/10.1007/BF01491987

[13] Schrödinger, E.: Discussion of probability relations between separated systems. Mathematical Proceedings of the Cambridge Philosophical Society **31**(04), 555–563 (1935). doi:10.1017/S0305004100013554. URL http://doi.org/10.1017/S0305004100013554

[14] Schrödinger, E.: Probability relations between separated systems. Mathematical Proceedings of the Cambridge Philosophical Society **32**(03), 446–452 (1936). doi:10.1017/S0305004100019137. URL http://doi.org/10.1017/S0305004100019137

[15] Schwinger, J.: Unitary operators bases. Proceedings of the National Academy of Sciences (PNAS) **46**, 570–579 (1960). doi:10.1073/pnas.46.4.570. URL http://doi.org/10.1073/pnas.46.4.570

[16] Svozil, K.: Physical [A]Causality. Determinism, Randomness and Uncaused Events. Springer, Berlin, Heidelberg, New York (2017). In print

[17] Trimmer, J.D.: The present situation in quantum mechanics: A translation of Schrödinger's "cat paradox" paper. Proceedings of the American Philosophical Society **124**(5), 323–338 (1980). URL http://www.jstor.org/stable/986572

[18] Wang, L.J., Zou, X.Y., Mandel, L.: Induced coherence without induced emission. Physical Review A **44**, 4614–4622 (1991). doi:10.1103/PhysRevA.44.4614. URL http://doi.org/10.1103/PhysRevA.44.4614

[19] Wootters, W.K.: Local accessibility of quantum states. In: W.H. Zurek (ed.) Complexity, Entropy, and the Physics of Information, SFI Studies in the Sciences of Complexity, Vol. VIII, pp. 39–46. Addison-Wesley, Boston (1990)

[20] Zeilinger, A.: General properties of lossless beam splitters in interferometry. American Journal of Physics **49**(9), 882–883 (1981). doi:10.1119/1.12387. URL http://doi.org/10.1119/1.12387

[21] Zeilinger, A.: Quantum teleportation and the non-locality of information. Philosophical Transactions of the Royal Society of London A **355**, 2401–2404 (1997). doi:10.1098/rsta.1997.0138. URL http://doi.org/10.1098/rsta.1997.0138

[22] Zeilinger, A.: A foundational principle for quantum mechanics. Foundations of Physics **29**(4), 631–643 (1999). doi:10.1023/A:1018820410908. URL http://doi.org/10.1023/A:1018820410908

[23] Zou, X.Y., Wang, L.J., Mandel, L.: Induced coherence and indistinguishability in optical interference. Physical Review Letters **67**, 318–321 (1991). doi:10.1103/PhysRevLett.67.318. URL http://doi.org/10.1103/PhysRevLett.67.318

[24] Zukowski, M., Zeilinger, A., Horne, M.A.: Realizable higher-dimensional two-particle entanglements via multiport beam splitters. Physical Review A **55**, 2564–2579 (1997). doi:10.1103/PhysRevA.55.2564. URL http://doi.org/10.1103/PhysRevA.55.2564

PART 4

Solomon Marcus in Context

Chapter 13

Memories about Solomon Marcus[1]

Andrew Bruckner
University of California, Santa Barbara
USA
andrew.m.bruckner@gmail.com

Much of the early part of my career was influenced by Solomon Marcus, both through his work and through correspondence. Almost fifty five years ago I was working on a project involving generalisations of convex functions of a real variable. I realised that in order to complete this project I need to understand the fine structure of ordinary derivatives of real functions defined on the line. In searching the literature, I discovered a number of useful papers, many of which were written by Solomon Marcus. I wrote him, and he responded with a long letter containing useful insights, many suggestions, and a number of important references. Over the next few years, our correspondence continued and I appreciated the encouragement I received from him. The result was that I spent most of my career working in the area of functions of a real variable, his area of interest at the time. (I never returned to the original convexity project.)

Over the years I noticed that Solomon Marcus had many imaginative ideas that he developed and he posed interesting problems for others to attack. His writings were always well written, well motivated and pleasant to read. Even his short papers prompted others to continue his work. For example, he introduced the notions of stationary sets and determining sets for a class of functions. He wrote several papers on the subject in which he

---

[1]This article is adapted from a text published in L. Spandonide, G. Păun (eds.). *Meetings with Solomon Marcus*, Ed. Spandugino, Bucharest, 2010, 401–404.

characterised such sets for a number of classes of functions related to differentiation theory. A number of authors continued his work by characterising such sets for other classes of functions. His correspondence also contained a number of problems that became of interest to other mathematicians. In a letter to me many years ago, he noted that the class of derivatives is not closed under multiplication. He made a number of insightful comments which led to the problem of characterising the algebra generated by the derivatives. This problem led to many papers, some of which were quite deep, by many authors. The problem was finally solved by David Preiss who obtained the remarkable result that the algebra in question is just the algebra of functions in the first class of Baire.

C. S. Calude, A Bruckner and S. Marcus, Bucharest, 1978

I recall three occasions on which we met. In 1978 Solomon Marcus invited my wife and me to visit a few days in Bucharest and for each of us to present a lecture. He was a most gracious and generous host. He showed us much of Bucharest, invited us to many excellent restaurants and even gave us some Romanian money "to introduce us to Romanian currency". We met again a few years later at a *Real Analysis Symposium* in Santa Barbara, where he presented a lecture that was very well received by the audience. Finally, in 1999, we met at a conference in Lodz. He presented a highly imaginative lecture relating concepts from real analysis to discrete mathematical systems. Some of the theorems from Real Analysis had complete analogues in certain discrete systems. At the time I wondered how he came up with such imaginative ideas!

When I retired in 1994 I had a collection of over 1,000 reprints of papers written by many authors. Many of these I gave to a young scholar who would make good use of them. I saved only two binders of reprints (other than my own), each holding about fifty papers. One of these consisted of the papers I have that were written by Solomon Marcus. I learned a great deal from Solomon Marcus' work and correspondences and I am grateful for that.

Chapter 14

Memories With and About My Uncle

Monica Marcus

120 North Cedar Street, Apt. 3403, Charlotte, North Carolina 28202, USA

monicamarcus12@gmail.com

14.1   Meeting Solomon Marcus for the First Time

I remember with great pleasure and amusement my first meeting with Professor Solomon Marcus. I was only five or six years old at that time (and not going to school yet). I came to Bucharest for several days, together with my parents and my elder sister.

Wait a moment! I wrote "*Professor* Solomon Marcus"! Actually, I could have written "*my uncle*", because Solomon Marcus is one of the younger siblings of my father. In fact, this was a big dilemma during my childhood and adolescence: how should I address such an important and special person? This is how I saw him as a child, and this is how I still consider him now, far from that age.

Then, I decided to avoid any direct way of addressing, during any conversation with my uncle.

Now, let me come back to my first meeting with the great mathematician. The meeting was held – of course – in the Faculty of Mathematics of the University of Bucharest, the chair of Mathematical Analysis. I was at the same time impressed, full of emotion, and proud to meet such a busy man like my uncle. Even though I was not yet a school girl, I knew to hand-write (using upper case letters) and it seems that I knew to do arithmetic (using not very big numbers). Solomon Marcus even asked me some elementary arithmetic questions and my answers were correct! At the end of the meeting I was really proud of myself (but not showing it) because

I was able to answer all the questions correctly and I also spoke with my uncle without addressing him directly. I believe that I already decided then that I needed to come back to the Faculty of Mathematics.

This actually happened many years later, when I became a student in Computer Science at the Faculty of Mathematics in Bucharest. Meantime, there were, of course, additional meetings with Solomon Marcus, as well as with his wife, Professor Paula Diaconescu. Paula was a Professor at the Faculty of Languages and Literature at the University of Bucharest. I was always glad and happy to meet such important people; however, I continued to be rather timid and quiet when I was meeting them. Being a university professor meant a lot to me, even as a child, and I continued to think like this many years later, even today.

Besides, Solomon Marcus is one of the professors I remember with great pleasure. He taught me Mathematical Analysis (on real numbers) during my first two semesters as a Computer Science student. His lectures were different than other professors' lectures due to the way the material was approached and presented. Each lesson used to contain interesting examples which made Mathematical Analysis extremely enjoyable. I can almost hear right now his clear voice full of enthusiasm, his intonation, and the stories used to introduce and to motivate new mathematical ideas, notions, definitions. Quite often, the lectures made also historical references. Sometimes he used to reminisce about the way Mathematical Analysis was taught to him by his Professor, Miron Nicolescu.

One of the stories was related to the authors of the book associated to his course on Mathematical Analysis. These authors were known to be Nicolae Dinculeanu, Solomon Marcus, and Miron Nicolescu. The surprise was due to the fact that the names were not written on the book cover! Why was there such a book without authors? Simply because Nicolae Dinculeanu had left the country (communist Romania) without "official approval", hence illegally.

Another interesting meeting with Solomon Marcus took place while I was a third year high-school student. I happened to have with me my school backpack full of notebooks and handbooks. The backpack was very heavy and this fact was noticed with great astonishment by my uncle. The textbook for Mathematical Analysis for the third year high-school was then in the backpack. My uncle wanted to see the books inside my backpack. While browsing through them, he noticed that they contained a lot of information. This fact caused him to become even more astonished and somehow shocked. He was resentful that a high-school student had to memorise so much information. In particular, he found the Mathematical Analysis textbook to be too demanding for the high-school level.

The sequence of encounters with Solomon Marcus continued over the years. Each time he showed interest for my professional activity. This was expected from somebody fully dedicated to his profession, which my uncle had chosen entirely by himself. At some point I was able to report that I completed my PhD in Computer Science, under the supervision of the late Professor Amir Pnueli, at the Weizmann Institute of Science in Israel. I specialised in Temporal Logic applied to Formal Verification of reactive computer systems. He then asked me about the mathematics that was related to Formal Verification. I am convinced that he continued to love Mathematics and was still thrilled to discover it again and again, as much as he used to do in the beginning.

After a while, due to a huge geographical distance which interposed between us, we started exchanging e-mail messages. In these messages I used to address him by his first name, still unsure whether it was appropriate or not.

Monica and Solomon Marcus in Bucharest, 2006

I admire my uncle more and more, as I also grow older. In his old age he continues to stay active in his profession and scientific career, showing no signs of getting tired. He goes on to work enthusiastically every day, starting new projects and continuing to work on old ones. As for myself, whenever

I seem to feel tired, I think of my uncle, Professor Solomon Marcus, and I tell myself that I am not allowed to feel tired: I am younger.

14.2 After His Death

Actually, what you have read so far had been written almost three years before. Meantime, in March of 2016, Solomon Marcus passed away. Sadly enough, he was just 91 years and a few days old, full of energy until almost the latest days of his life.

It is very difficult for me to imagine my next visit to Bucharest, without being able to meet my uncle. His presence was always contagiously optimistic. He was an example of living the life to the fullest, as a human being and as a mathematician in search of questions and their answers. I wish I could follow in his steps, at least in part.

As I already mentioned, he was my professor of Mathematical Analysis (Real Functions) during my first year as a Computer Science student in the Faculty of Mathematics, University of Bucharest. I started falling in love with calculus and mathematical analysis already during my high-school years, but the lessons taught by Professor Solomon Marcus helped me discover not only new aspects and subjects of Mathematical Analysis; they also showed what it meant to listen to someone who loves his subject matter dearly. Besides, he was passionate about the teaching process and education. He was passionate about and dedicated to each of his projects, scientific or less scientific ones. His scientific interest went besides mathematics teaching and research. He was interested in several other fields, including language and literature.

This is why I want to cite here a fragment from one of Solomon Marcus's own poems. The original poem, written in Romanian, is not published yet (to the best of my knowledge). I thank Professor Sorin Istrail from Brown University for making it possible for me to read the poem. The title of the poem can be translated as "Just an Imagination" (in Romanian: "Decât o-nchipuire".) Here are the last five lines of the poem, in Romanian:

ȘI TOATĂ MATEMATICA
ESTE UN ZBOR SPRE ALTCEVA
NU E DECÂT O ÎNCHIPUIRE
DE CARE, VAI, SUFLETUL MEU
NICICÂND NU S-AR PUTEA LIPSI.

Here is a possible English translation:

"The whole Mathematics is a flight towards something else, it is just an imagination. Alas, my soul could never live without it."

I wrote the original verse in uppercase, just like the Professor wrote it on a piece of paper, with his own hand. Thinking about it, the poem's title might have been "The Flight of the Mathematician".

Now, I imagine that after he left Earth for ever, Professor Solomon Marcus started his flight towards that *"something else"* to which his soul has always been attached to.

Index